taste of home appetizers

taste of home
BOOKS

REIMAN MEDIA GROUP, INC. • GREENDALE, WISCONSIN

taste of home. Reader's Digest

A TASTE OF HOME/READER'S DIGEST BOOK

Editor-in-Chief:	Catherine Cassidy
Vice President, Executive Editor/Books:	Heidi Reuter Lloyd
Creative Director:	Ardyth Cope
North America Chief Marketing Officer:	Lisa Karpinski
Food Director:	Diane Werner RD
Senior Editor/Books:	Mark Hagen
Project Editor:	Beth Kong
Art Director:	Edwin Robles, Jr.
Content Production Supervisor:	Julie Wagner
Design Layout Artist:	Emma Acevedo
Proofreader:	Linne Bruskewitz
Recipe Asset System Manager:	Coleen Martin
Recipe Testing & Editing:	Taste of Home Test Kitchen
Food Photography:	Taste of Home Photo Studio
Administrative Assistant:	Barb Czysz

The Reader's Digest Association, Inc.

President and Chief Executive Officer:	Tom Williams
Executive Vice President, RDA, and President, Lifestyle Communities:	Suzanne M. Grimes
President/Publisher Trade Publishing:	Harold Clarke
Associate Publisher:	Rosanne McManus
Vice President, Sales and Marketing:	Stacey Ashton

Cover Photography

Art Direction:	Edwin Robles, Jr., Gretchen Trautman
Photographers:	Rob Hagen, Lori Foy
Food Stylists:	Sarah Thompson, Alynna Malson
Set Stylist:	Dee Dee Jacq

Pictured on front cover:
Pepper-Crusted Tenderloin Crostini (p. 141); Stuffed Butterflied Shrimp (p. 157); Antipasto Kabobs (p. 59); Espresso Panna Cotta (p. 203); Wonton Kisses (p. 185); Zippy Cranberry Appetizer (p. 243); Veggie Shrimp Egg Rolls (p. 69); and Veggie Wonton Quiches (p. 75).

Pictured on the back cover:
Stuffed Cherries Dipped in Chocolate (p. 197); Sangria (p. 220); and Chicken Bacon Bites (p. 165).

For other Taste of Home books and products, visit us at **tasteofhome.com**.

For more Reader's Digest products and information, visit **rd.com** (in the United States) or see **rd.ca** (in Canada).

International Standard Book Number (10): 0-89821-909-4
International Standard Book Number (13): 978-0-89821-909-8
Library of Congress Control Number: 2009942807

Printed in China
1 3 5 7 9 10 8 6 4 2

table of contents

p. 170   p. 134   p. 217

With the **410 satisfying dips,** *spreads, wraps,* *rolls,* **beverages,** *nibblers,* **munchies,** *sweets* *and more in this* *fabulous collection* *of bite-size* *goodies, you'll be the hostess that serves the most* **sensational assortment** *of appetizers in town!*

EVERYONE LOVES THE OPPORTUNITY TO SAMPLE DIFFERENT AND DELICIOUS FOODS AT PARTIES AND GATHERINGS.

p. 124

And appetizers are the tastiest way to tempt your guests and introduce them to fun, new flavors. Now you can serve up 410 of the most delectable dips and spreads, juicy chicken wings, dainty canapes, unique beverages, mouthwatering finger foods and scrumptious mini desserts—all easy to make and a delight to serve!

The recipes in this collection come from family cooks like you and have been tested by the experienced home economists in the Taste of Home Test Kitchen. So you can rest assured that these tasty tidbits will be a savory success.

In this book, you'll also discover make-ahead preparation tips, practical pointers for keeping party foods hot or cold, helpful hints for serving appetizers, time-saving tips and much more.

So turn to *Taste of Home* **Appetizers** for an abundance of appealing hors d'oeuvres...and make your next party a celebration of flavor!

Serving Up Appetizers

Whenever you offer friends and family appetizers or snacks, you invite them to get comfortable and share time with you and other guests.

Appetizers can be as simple as dip with chips for a casual night of TV watching, include heartier fare like sandwiches and pizza for Sunday football, serve as a first course to a festive meal, entertain a large group at an open house or even be the main meal for a special occasion.

Party Planning

Whether simple or fancy, savory or sweet, hot or cold, appetizers offer versatility and variety when entertaining. And as an added benefit, many appetizers can be made ahead of time—some even weeks in advance and then frozen—so you can be ready for guests at a moment's notice or relaxed when party time arrives.

When planning what appetizers to serve, don't overdo it. It's better to prepare a few good choices than to stress over making a lot of items. Start with one spectacular appetizer and then complete your menu with additional easy but delicious foods and beverages.

Choose from an assortment of hot, cold and room temperature foods. Select recipes that offer a variety of colors, textures (soft and crunchy) and flavors (sour, salty, savory, sweet, spicy or subtle). Mix in one or two lighter options to cater to guests concerned about calories or fat. And, look for appetizers that make a nice presentation and require no last-minute fussing.

p. 42

How Much to Serve

The number of appetizers per person varies on the length of the party, the number of guests and the other items on your menu.

For a social hour before dinner, plan on serving three or four different appetizers and allow four to five pieces per person.

For an open-house affair, plan on serving four to five different appetizers and allow four to six pieces per person per hour.

For an appetizer buffet that is offered in place of a meal, plan on serving six to eight different appetizers and allow 10 to 14 pieces per person.

For larger groups, offer more types of appetizers. For eight guests, three types may be sufficient, 16 guests about four to five types and for 25 guests, serve six to eight types. The more variety you serve, the fewer servings of each type you'll need.

Food Quantities for Appetizers

When serving appetizers, no one wants to run out of food. But the challenge is to know how much will be enough.

Here are some guidelines to estimate how much you'll need per person. The larger the variety of appetizers you serve, the less of each type you will need.

appetizers	beverages (per hour)	miscellaneous
3 tablespoons dips	In warm weather, you may wish to have additional chilled beverages.	1 to 2 ounces chips
2 ounces cheese		4 crackers
3 to 4 cocktail wieners		4 fruit or vegetable dippers
1 to 2 ounces deli meat	1 to 2 cups soda, water or iced tea	1/2 ounce mixed nuts
3 tablespoons spreads	6 ounces juice	3 to 4 pickle slices or 1 pickle spear
2 to 4 small egg rolls	1 to 2 bottles beer	
3 to 4 meatballs	1/2 (750-ml) bottle wine	3 to 4 olives
1 to 2 slices pizza	3/4 cup hot coffee or tea	1 to 2 small rolls
2 to 4 miniature quiches	1/2 cup punch	3 to 4 ounces ice for beverages

Points about Food Safety

The general guideline when serving food is that cooked foods and uncooked foods that require refrigeration should not sit out at room temperature for more than 2 hours or 1 hour on hot days (90° or above). Hot foods should be kept hot (140°) and cold foods should be kept cold (40°). Here are some pointers for safely serving food:

> Divide the food among several serving dishes. Serve one dish, while the others are being chilled or kept warm. Replace the original serving dish as needed or every 2 hours (whichever comes first).

> To keep foods hot when serving, use insulated containers, warming trays, slow cookers or chafing dishes.

> To keep the back-up food hot, arrange on baking sheets and place in a 200° oven.

> To keep food cold, place on ice. You can easily improvise an ice bowl by placing dips, shrimp, cut-up fruits and salads in a bowl. Then set the bowl in a larger one filled with ice cubes or crushed ice. Replenish the ice as it melts throughout the party.

Hosting an Appetizer Party

Although hosting an appetizer party will require some planning, it's a fun way to entertain a group of people for any occasion.

To make it easy on you, include several make-ahead recipes on the menu.

A few weeks before the party:
Cook and freeze meatballs, savory cheesecakes and puffs or mini quiches, such as Crabmeat Appetizer Cheesecake (p. 140) or Cheddar Artichoke Quiche Cups (p. 23). For meatballs, just thaw and reheat in the sauce on your party day. For savory cheesecakes, thaw in the refrigerator 2 to 3 days before the party and bring to room temperature about 20 minutes before serving. Puffs and quiches can be reheated in a 300° oven until warm.

A few days before the party:
Make cheese balls and logs, flavored nut mixes and snack mixes. Store the mixes in airtight containers.

A day before the party:
Make tortilla-type roll-up sandwiches, dips and salsas. Cut up any fruit and vegetables that will be used for dippers. Prep any fillings for hot appetizers or any other food that can be made ahead.

The morning of your party:
Make hero-type sandwiches and assemble canapes. If possible, assemble and arrange any warm appetizers on baking sheets.

Before your guests arrive:
Place any long-cooking items, such as a baked dip in a bread shell, in the oven so that it will be ready to serve within half an hour after the party starts.

As the guests arrive:
Place some of the quickly baked items in the oven.

Arranging the Food

The way you arrange your food will encourage people to mingle with each other and move around your home. Food can be set up as a buffet, served from trays by waitstaff or family or casually placed throughout the house on tables. To keep people moving, set up the food and beverages in separate locations—even in separate rooms.

BUFFETS

For added visual interest to a buffet service, arrange various items such as phone books, sturdy boxes, inverted metal buckets, cake pans and cans as risers on your table (see Figure 1). Drape them with a tablecloth and gently form it around the risers so that the cloth won't pull when platters of food are set on top (see Figure 2).

When arranging the buffet, allow room on one end for the plates, and set the napkins and any utensils on the other end. This way your guests won't need to juggle the napkin and utensils while they serve themselves. Set the food back from the edge of the table to allow room for guests to set their plates down to serve themselves. For foods that need to be skewered, have a container of skewers or toothpicks alongside the serving dish.

If using candles, set them on the table so no one will need to reach over the flames to get the food. Small arrangements of flowers can be placed between serving dishes (see Figure 3). Large arrangements should be placed out of reach, either in the middle of the buffet if service wraps around the table, or in the back if your table is against a wall.

If you're using a table for the buffet, remove the chairs from the table and arrange them in other areas in sitting groups. By removing the chairs, you make it easier for guests to move around the table and reach the food.

TRAYS

Trays can be used to circulate the food among the guests. This can be especially nice for hot finger foods, such as stuffed mushrooms or canapes. Offering food directly to people encourages them to sample the food. The trays will be emptied in a short period of time, eliminating concerns about food standing at room temperature too long. Plus, the trays can easily be replenished with fresh tidbits.

Figure 1

Figure 2

Figure 3

For the best visual presentation, place only one or two types of food on a tray. Leave space around the food to prevent other pieces on the tray from being touched when one piece is picked up. Small tongs can aid in serving the appetizers from the tray. Or, if appropriate, use individual party picks with foods such as cubed cheese. Since the trays are being carried around, avoid making them too heavy. If you don't have enough trays for the occasion, consider renting them.

PLACING FOOD AROUND THE HOUSE

Placing appetizers in various locations throughout the party area invites people to walk around to see what other tasty bites are being served and, most importantly, to meet other guests. Scattered placement around the party area can work well with room temperature foods, chilled items and platters of hot appetizers. For items that need a slow cooker or chafing dish, a central location may be more convenient.

Tips to Make Your Guests Comfortable

Simple touches can enhance the comfort of your guests. Here are a few ideas to make your party even more enjoyable:

> Have music in the background to set the mood and still allow conversations to take place at a normal tone.

> Have chairs for people to sit (not everyone can stand for hours).

> Place the chairs in seating arrangements to encourage conversation.

> If you want your guests to use coasters, have plenty of them available and place them in noticeable locations.

> Have small tables and open surfaces on other furniture, where a guest may set down their glass or plate.

> Have an open floor plan so guests can easily walk from one room to the next. Consider stowing away pieces of furniture that are in the way.

> Have trash containers strategically placed around the area to prevent clutter from building up.

toastytreats

artichoke bread

SHERRY CAMPBELL, ST. AMANT, LOUISIANA
A creamy, rich artichoke spread tops these warm crusty bites that everyone loves. You won't find a much quicker and more delicious appetizer!

1 tube (11 ounces) refrigerated crusty French loaf

1 can (14 ounces) water-packed artichoke hearts, rinsed, drained and chopped

1/2 cup seasoned bread crumbs

1/3 cup grated Parmesan cheese

1/3 cup reduced-fat mayonnaise

2 garlic cloves, minced

1 cup (4 ounces) shredded part-skim mozzarella cheese

> Bake loaf according to package directions; cool. Cut bread in half lengthwise; place on an ungreased baking sheet.

> In a small bowl, combine the artichokes, bread crumbs, Parmesan cheese, mayonnaise and garlic; spread evenly over cut sides of bread. Sprinkle with mozzarella cheese.

> Bake at 350° for 15-20 minutes or until cheese is melted. Slice and serve warm.

YIELD: 1 LOAF (12 SLICES)

 tip When planning for an appetizer buffet that serves as the meal, offer five or six different appetizers (including two or three substantial selections) and plan on eight to nine pieces per guest. If you serve a meal, two to three pieces per person should be sufficient.

feta artichoke bites

LOUISE LEACH, CHINO, CALIFORNIA
You can prepare the flavorful topping for this appetizer ahead of time. Then spread it onto slices of bread and broil for a fast, festive snack.

1 jar (7-1/2 ounces) marinated artichoke hearts

1 cup diced seeded tomatoes

1 cup (4 ounces) crumbled feta cheese

1/3 cup grated Parmesan cheese

2 green onions, thinly sliced

1 loaf sourdough baguette (about 20 inches long)

> Drain artichokes, reserving 2 tablespoons marinade. Chop artichokes and place in a large bowl. Stir in the tomatoes, cheeses, onions and reserved marinade. Cover and refrigerate for 1 hour.

> Cut baguette into 1/2-in. slices. Spread with artichoke mixture. Place on an ungreased baking sheet. Broil 4-6 in. from the heat for 4-5 minutes or until edges of bread are browned. Serve immediately.

YIELD: ABOUT 12 SERVINGS

DOUGLAS WASDYKE, EFFORT, PENNSYLVANIA

Our friends enjoy this special appetizer as part of all our Christmas celebrations. An apricot filling and a raspberry topping make it special.

fruit 'n' almond-stuffed brie

2/3 cup sliced almonds

1/3 cup chopped dried apricots

1/4 cup brandy

1 sheet frozen puff pastry, thawed

1 round (8 ounces) Brie cheese, rind removed

1 egg, lightly beaten

RASPBERRY SAUCE:
1/2 cup sugar

1 tablespoon cornstarch

1/2 cup cold water

2 cups fresh or frozen raspberries

Assorted crackers

> In a small saucepan with high sides, combine the almonds, apricots and brandy. Cook and stir over medium-low heat until liquid is almost evaporated. Remove from the heat; set aside.

> On a lightly floured surface, roll puff pastry into an 11-in. x 9-in. rectangle. Cut cheese in half horizontally; place bottom half in the center of pastry. Spread with half of the almond mixture. Top with remaining cheese and almond mixture.

> Fold pastry around cheese; trim excess dough. Pinch edges to seal. Place seam side down on ungreased baking sheet. Brush with egg.

> Bake at 375° for 30-35 minutes or until puffed and golden brown.

> In a small saucepan, combine the sugar, cornstarch and water until smooth; add raspberries. Bring to a boil over medium heat, stirring constantly. Cook and stir for 1 minute or until slightly thickened. Strain and discard seeds. Transfer sauce to a small pitcher or bowl; serve with stuffed Brie and crackers.

YIELD: 8 SERVINGS

cheddar shrimp nachos

LISA FELD, GRAFTON, WISCONSIN
These fun finger foods in tortilla chip scoops are just the tasty thing for cold weather get-togethers.

3/4 pound deveined peeled cooked shrimp, chopped

1-1/2 cups (6 ounces) shredded cheddar cheese

1 can (4 ounces) chopped green chilies, drained

1/3 cup chopped green onions

1/4 cup sliced ripe olives, drained

1/2 cup mayonnaise

1/4 teaspoon ground cumin

48 tortilla chip scoops

> In a large bowl, combine the shrimp, cheese, chilies, onions and olives. Combine the mayonnaise and cumin; add to shrimp mixture and toss to coat.

> Drop by tablespoonfuls into tortilla scoops. Place on ungreased baking sheets. Bake at 350° for 5-10 minutes or until cheese is melted. Serve warm.

YIELD: 4 DOZEN

tangy cheese bites

PATRICIA WARD, FULLERTON, CALIFORNIA
These hot cheese bites were brought to an election-night party I attended years ago. Sharp cheddar and blue cheese give them a slightly tangy favor.

1 loaf (1 pound) unsliced Italian bread

3/4 cup butter, cubed

4 ounces cream cheese, cubed

1-1/2 cups (6 ounces) shredded cheddar cheese

1-1/2 cups (6 ounces) crumbled blue cheese

3 egg whites

1 teaspoon paprika

> Cut crust off all sides of bread. Cut into 1-1/2-in. cubes; set aside. In a large saucepan, melt butter. Stir in cream cheese until melted. Remove from the heat; stir in cheddar cheese and blue cheese until melted.

> In a small bowl, beat egg whites until stiff peaks form. Fold into cheese mixture. Dip bread cubes into cheese mixture, turning to coat.

> Place on greased baking sheets; sprinkle with paprika. Bake at 375° for 12-15 minutes or until bottoms are golden brown. Serve warm.

YIELD: ABOUT 4-1/2 DOZEN

baked potato skins

TRISH PERRIN, KEIZER, OREGON
Both crisp and hearty, this snack's one that is often requested by my gang.

4 large baking potatoes, baked

3 tablespoons vegetable oil

1 tablespoon grated Parmesan cheese

1/2 teaspoon salt

1/4 teaspoon garlic powder

1/4 teaspoon paprika

1/8 teaspoon pepper

8 bacon strips, cooked and crumbled

1-1/2 cups (6 ounces) shredded cheddar cheese

1/2 cup sour cream

4 green onions, sliced

> Cut potatoes in half lengthwise; scoop out pulp, leaving a 1/4-in. shell (save pulp for another use). Place potato skins on a greased baking sheet. Combine the oil, Parmesan cheese, salt, garlic powder, paprika and pepper; brush over both sides of skins.

> Bake at 475° for 7 minutes; turn. Bake until crisp, about 7 minutes longer. Sprinkle bacon and cheddar cheese inside skins. Bake for 2 minutes or until the cheese is melted. Top with sour cream and onions. Serve immediately.

YIELD: 8 SERVINGS

potato nachos

TONY HORTON, VAN BUREN, ARKANSAS
Cheese, jalapeno pepper, sour cream and green onions top these pretty potato slices, seasoned with dry ranch dressing mix. I love to serve them to guests, and they love to eat them. You can use the nachos as an appetizer or even as a fun side dish.

8 medium red potatoes

1 envelope ranch salad dressing mix

1 jar (12 ounces) pickled jalapeno pepper slices, drained

2 cups (8 ounces) shredded cheddar cheese

2 cups (8 ounces) shredded Monterey Jack cheese

2 cups (16 ounces) sour cream

6 to 8 green onions, chopped

> Place potatoes in a saucepan and cover with water. Bring to a boil. Reduce heat; cover and cook for 15-20 minutes or just until tender. Drain; cool slightly.

> Cut potatoes into 1/4-in.-thick slices. Place in a single layer in three greased 15-in. x 10-in. x 1-in. baking pans. Top each with salad dressing mix, a jalapeno slice, cheddar cheese and Monterey Jack cheese.

> Bake, uncovered, at 350° for 10-12 minutes or until cheese is melted. Top with sour cream and green onions.

YIELD: 12 SERVINGS

tip Wondering what to do with the pulp left over from Baked Potato Skins? Try mashing them with some milk and butter and serve a simple "mashed potato bar." Guests can prepare their own portions in a martini glass and top them with a selection of shredded cheeses, bacon bits, chopped vegetables…or whatever toppings you prefer.

mini hot browns

ANNETTE GRAHL, MIDWAY, KENTUCKY

My Mini Hot Browns are a smaller version of the famous Hot Brown sandwich. Guests quickly saddle up for juicy turkey slices and crispy bacon, piled on toasted rye bread and then topped with a rich cheese sauce.

1 teaspoon chicken bouillon granules

1/4 cup boiling water

3 tablespoons butter

2 tablespoons all-purpose flour

3/4 cup half-and-half cream

1 cup (4 ounces) shredded Swiss cheese

18 slices snack rye bread

6 ounces sliced deli turkey

1 small onion, thinly sliced and separated into rings

5 bacon strips, cooked and crumbled

2 tablespoons minced fresh parsley

> In a small bowl, dissolve bouillon in water; set aside. In a small saucepan, melt butter over medium heat. Stir in flour until smooth; stir in cream and bouillon. Bring to a boil; cook and stir for 1-2 minutes or until thickened. Stir in cheese until melted. Remove from the heat.

> Place bread slices on two baking sheets. Layer each with turkey, onion and cheese sauce. Sprinkle with bacon. Bake at 350° for 10-12 minutes or until heated through. Sprinkle with parsley.

YIELD: 1-1/2 DOZEN

crab-stuffed mushrooms

KELLY ENGLISH, COGAN STATION, PENNSYLVANIA

When my brother arrives at family gatherings, the first thing he asks is whether or not I brought my crabby mushrooms!

3 tablespoons butter, divided

1 tablespoon all-purpose flour

1/2 cup milk

2 slices bread, crusts removed and cubed

1-1/2 teaspoons Worcestershire sauce

1 teaspoon dried minced onion

1/2 cup mayonnaise

1 tablespoon lemon juice

1/2 teaspoon salt

1/8 teaspoon pepper

48 whole medium mushrooms

3 cans (6 ounces each) crabmeat, drained, flaked and cartilage removed

Paprika

> In a large saucepan, melt 1 tablespoon butter. Stir in flour until smooth. Gradually stir in milk. Bring to a boil over medium heat; cook and stir for 2 minutes or until thickened. Reduce heat; stir in the bread cubes, Worcestershire sauce and onion.

> Remove from the heat; cool to room temperature. Stir in mayonnaise, lemon juice, salt and pepper; set aside.

> Remove and chop the mushroom stems; set caps aside. In a skillet, saute chopped mushrooms and crab in the remaining butter. Using a slotted spoon, transfer to the sauce. Stuff 1 tablespoonful into each mushroom cap.

> Place on a greased baking sheet; sprinkle with paprika. Bake at 400° for 25-30 minutes or until mushrooms are tender.

YIELD: 4 DOZEN

beef turnovers

DOROTHY RADICHEL, MANKATO, MINNESOTA
The recipe for these Russian turnovers, called Piroshkis, was given to me by a cousin. Serve some barbecue or sweet-and-sour sauce alongside for extra flavor.

1/2 pound ground beef

1 tablespoon finely chopped onion

2 tablespoons sour cream

1 teaspoon dill weed

1/4 teaspoon salt

1/4 teaspoon prepared mustard

1/8 teaspoon curry powder

1/8 teaspoon pepper

3 sheets refrigerated pie pastry (9 inches)

Barbecue or sweet-and-sour sauce, optional

> In a large skillet, cook the beef and onion over medium heat until meat is no longer pink; drain. Stir in the sour cream, dill, salt, mustard, curry and pepper; remove from the heat.

> Unfold pastry sheets onto a lightly floured surface; cut into 3-in. circles. Place 1-1/2 teaspoons of beef mixture in the center of each circle. Brush edge of pastry with water; fold circles in half.

> Place on greased baking sheets. With a fork, press edges to seal and poke holes in top. Bake at 400° for 10-12 minutes or until golden brown. Serve warm with barbecue or sweet-and-sour sauce if desired.

YIELD: 2-1/2 DOZEN

baked jalapenos

TASTE OF HOME TEST KITCHEN
This baked version of jalapeno poppers pairs a crunchy topping with a creamy filling.

1 package (3 ounces) cream cheese, softened

1/4 teaspoon ground cumin

2/3 cup shredded Monterey Jack cheese

1 teaspoon minced fresh cilantro

8 jalapeno peppers, halved lengthwise and seeded

1 egg, beaten

3/4 cup cornflake crumbs

> In a small mixing bowl, beat cream cheese and cumin until smooth. Beat in Monterey Jack cheese and cilantro. Spoon into jalapeno halves.

> Place egg and cornflake crumbs in separate shallow bowls. Dip filling side of jalapenos in egg, then coat with crumbs. Place crumb side up on a greased baking sheet. Bake at 350° for 25-30 minutes or until top is golden brown. Serve immediately.

YIELD: 16 APPETIZERS

Editor's Note: When cutting hot peppers, disposable gloves are recommended. Avoid touching your face.

CHRIS SENDELBACH, HENRY, ILLINOIS

Whenever I serve ham, I can't wait for the leftovers so I can make these ham buns. They make delicious bite-size treats on an appetizer tray. My husband even likes them for breakfast.

ham bundles

1 package (1/4 ounce) active dry yeast

1/4 cup warm water (110° to 115°)

3/4 cup warm milk (110° to 115°)

1/2 cup shortening

3 eggs, lightly beaten

1/2 cup sugar

1-1/2 teaspoons salt

4-1/2 to 4-3/4 cups all-purpose flour

FILLING:

1 large onion, finely chopped

5 tablespoons butter, divided

4 cups cubed fully cooked ham, coarsely ground

4 bacon strips, cooked and crumbled, optional

1/4 to 1/3 cup sliced pimiento-stuffed olives, optional

1/2 to 3/4 cup shredded cheddar cheese, optional

> In a large bowl, dissolve yeast in warm water. Add the milk, shortening, eggs, sugar, salt and 2 cups flour; beat until smooth. Add enough remaining flour to form a soft dough.

> Turn onto a lightly floured surface; knead until smooth and elastic, about 8 minutes. Place in a greased bowl, turning once to grease top. Cover and let rise in a warm place until doubled, about 1 hour.

> Meanwhile, in a large skillet, saute onion in 2 tablespoons butter until tender. Add ham and mix well; set aside.

> Punch dough down. Turn onto a lightly floured surface; divide into thirds. Roll each portion into a 16-in. x 8-in. rectangle. Cut each rectangle into eight squares. Place a tablespoonful of ham mixture in the center of each square. Add bacon, olives and/or cheese if desired. Fold up corners to center of dough; seal edges.

> Place 2 in. apart on greased baking sheets. Cover and let rise in a warm place until doubled, about 45 minutes.

> Melt remaining butter; brush over dough. Bake at 350° for 16-20 minutes or until golden brown and filling is heated through. Refrigerate leftovers.

YIELD: 2 DOZEN

crab-stuffed cherry tomatoes

MARCIA KECKHAVER, BURLINGTON, WISCONSIN
For a little something special, I include these delicious, petite pleasers on the menu of our holiday parties.

1 pint cherry tomatoes

1 can (6 ounces) crabmeat, drained, flaked and cartilage removed

1/2 cup diced green pepper

2 green onions, diced

2 tablespoons Italian-seasoned bread crumbs

1 teaspoon white wine vinegar

1/2 teaspoon dried parsley flakes

1/4 teaspoon dill weed

1/8 teaspoon salt, optional

> Cut a thin slice off tops of tomatoes and carefully scoop out insides; invert on paper towels to drain. In a small bowl, combine remaining ingredients; mix well.

> Stuff tomatoes; place in an ungreased 13-in. x 9-in. baking dish. Bake, uncovered, at 350° for 8-10 minutes or until heated through. Serve warm.

YIELD: ABOUT 1-1/2 DOZEN

stuffed turkey spirals

RENEE AUPPERLE, LITITZ, PENNSYLVANIA
These impressive appetizers are great for a buffet because you can make them earlier and bake them right before serving.

2 boneless skinless turkey breast halves (1 pound each)

1/4 cup olive oil, divided

4 teaspoons dried basil, divided

1 pound thinly sliced deli ham

1 pound thinly sliced Swiss cheese

1 teaspoon salt

1 teaspoon pepper

BASIL SAUCE:
2 cups mayonnaise

1/2 cup milk

1 to 2 tablespoons dried basil

1 teaspoon sugar

> Cut each turkey breast horizontally from the long side to within 1/2 in. of opposite side. Open flat; cover with plastic wrap. Flatten into 12-in. x 10-in. rectangles.

> Remove plastic; top each with 1 teaspoon oil and 1 teaspoon basil. Layer with ham and cheese to within 1 in. of edges. Roll up jelly-roll style, starting with a long side; tie with kitchen string. Place on a rack in a roasting pan.

> In a small bowl, combine the salt, pepper and remaining oil and basil; spoon some over turkey.

> Bake at 325° for 75-90 minutes or until a meat thermometer reads 170°; basting occasionally with remaining oil mixture.

> In a blender, combine the sauce ingredients; cover and process until blended. Cool turkey for 5 minutes before slicing; serve with basil sauce.

YIELD: ABOUT 30 SERVINGS

onion almond rounds

EDNA COBURN, TUCSON, ARIZONA
Onion lovers will rejoice when they taste this nutty hors d'oeuvre! Along with a robust flavor, these little rounds can be prepared ahead of time and then popped in the oven shortly before guests arrive.

2 medium onions, thinly sliced

1 tablespoon butter

1 loaf (24 ounces) sliced sandwich bread

1 package (8 ounces) cream cheese, softened

1/2 cup chopped almonds

2 teaspoons Worcestershire sauce

1/4 to 1/2 teaspoon lemon-herb seasoning

3 tablespoons mayonnaise

1/2 teaspoon paprika

28 roasted salted almonds

> In a large skillet, saute onions in butter for 7-10 minutes or until golden brown; set aside. With a 2-in. round biscuit cutter, cut 28 circles from bread slices; place on two baking sheets. Bake at 350° for 5-8 minutes or until lightly toasted.

> In a small bowl, combine the cream cheese, chopped almonds, Worcestershire sauce and lemon-herb seasoning. Spread 1 rounded teaspoonful over each bread round.

> Top each with onions and about 1/4 teaspoon mayonnaise. Sprinkle with paprika; top each with an almond.

> Bake at 350° for 5-8 minutes or until heated through.

YIELD: 28 APPETIZERS

eggplant snack sticks

MARY MURPHY, ATWATER, CALIFORNIA
Coated with Italian seasoning, Parmesan cheese and garlic salt, my veggie sticks are broiled so there's no guilt when you crunch into them.

1 medium eggplant (1-1/4 pounds)

1/2 cup toasted wheat germ

1/2 cup grated Parmesan cheese

1 teaspoon Italian seasoning

3/4 teaspoon garlic salt

1/2 cup egg substitute

1 cup meatless spaghetti sauce, warmed

> Cut eggplant lengthwise into 1/2-in.-thick slices, then cut each slice lengthwise into 1/2-in. strips. In a shallow dish, combine the wheat germ, cheese, Italian seasoning and garlic salt. Dip eggplant sticks in egg substitute, then coat with wheat germ mixture. Arrange in a single layer on a baking sheet coated with cooking spray.

> Spritz eggplant with cooking spray. Broil 4 in. from the heat for 3 minutes. Remove from the oven. Turn sticks and spritz with cooking spray. Broil 2 minutes longer or until golden brown. Serve immediately with spaghetti sauce.

YIELD: 8 SERVINGS

tip Take a shortcut when preparing Onion Almond Rounds by chopping the almonds in a food processor. Add only a few at a time to the processor. If you have extra chopped almonds, use them as a topping for your favorite breakfast cereal or yogurt.

DEBORAH FORBES, FORT WORTH, TEXAS

Just add a salad to these appetizers and you have a quick weeknight dinner in under 30 minutes. Folks of all ages just love them.

mini bbq chicken pizzas

1 medium onion, chopped

2 teaspoons olive oil

1-1/2 cups shredded cooked chicken

2/3 cup barbecue sauce

1 can (4 ounces) chopped green chilies

1-1/2 teaspoons garlic powder

1/4 teaspoon pepper

1 package (13 ounces) whole wheat English muffins, split

1-1/2 cups (6 ounces) shredded part-skim mozzarella cheese

> In a large nonstick skillet, saute onion in oil until tender. Stir in the chicken, barbecue sauce, chilies, garlic powder and pepper. Spread over cut sides of muffins; sprinkle with cheese.

> Place on baking sheets; broil 4-6 in. from the heat for 2-3 minutes or until cheese is melted.

YIELD: 12 SERVINGS

> Using a melon baller, scoop out the center of each biscuit, leaving a 3/8-in. shell (discard biscuit center). In a bowl, combine the remaining ingredients. Spoon about 1 tablespoonful into the center of each biscuit.

> Place on an ungreased baking sheet. Bake at 400° for 8-10 minutes or until heated through. Serve warm.

YIELD: 20 APPETIZERS

hot mushroom tidbits

BEVERLY ZDURNE, EAST LANSING, MICHIGAN
You can't miss with tried-and-true appetizers like this. In fact, I've been relying on these yummy bites for more than 20 years!

1 package (3 ounces) cream cheese, softened

1 can (4 ounces) mushroom stems and pieces, drained and chopped

2 tablespoons diced pimientos

1 tablespoon chopped onion

2 drops hot pepper sauce

1 tube (12 ounces) refrigerated flaky buttermilk biscuits

1/3 cup salad croutons, crushed

> In a small bowl, combine the cream cheese, mushrooms, pimientos, onion and hot pepper sauce. Separate dough into 10 biscuits; roll each into a 4-in. circle. Spread each with a heaping teaspoonful of mushroom mixture. Roll up and seal edges. Cut each into four slices; roll in crouton crumbs.

> Place on ungreased baking sheets. Bake at 375° for 12-14 minutes or until golden brown. Serve warm. Refrigerate leftovers.

YIELD: 40 APPETIZERS

cajun canapes

JERRI PEACHEE, GENTRY, ARKANSAS
I came across these filled biscuits at a party—and now they're a family favorite.

2 tubes (12 ounces each) refrigerated buttermilk biscuits

1/2 pound bulk pork sausage, cooked and drained

1-1/2 cups (6 ounces) shredded cheddar cheese

1/4 cup chopped green pepper

1/4 cup mayonnaise

2 green onions, chopped

2 teaspoons lemon juice

1/2 teaspoon salt

1/2 teaspoon paprika

1/4 teaspoon garlic powder

1/4 teaspoon dried thyme

1/8 to 1/4 teaspoon cayenne pepper

> Bake biscuits according to package directions, except turn biscuits over halfway through baking. Remove from pans to wire racks to cool completely.

southwest spanakopita bites

MARIANNE SHIRA, OSCEOLA, WISCONSIN
I'm a big fan of the Southwest-style egg rolls served at restaurants and wanted to re-create them without the fat of deep frying. Phyllo dough was the solution!

2 tablespoons finely chopped sweet red pepper

1 green onion, finely chopped

1 teaspoon canola oil

1 package (10 ounces) frozen chopped spinach, thawed and squeezed dry

3/4 cup shredded reduced-fat Monterey Jack cheese or Mexican cheese blend

1/2 cup frozen corn, thawed

1/2 cup canned black beans, rinsed and drained

1 tablespoon chopped seeded jalapeno pepper

1/2 teaspoon ground cumin

1/2 teaspoon chili powder

1/4 teaspoon salt

8 sheets phyllo dough (14 inches x 9 inches)

Butter-flavored cooking spray

SAUCE:

1/3 cup cubed avocado

1/4 cup reduced-fat mayonnaise

1/4 cup reduced-fat sour cream

1-1/2 teaspoons white vinegar

> In a small skillet, saute red pepper and onion in oil until tender. Transfer to a small bowl; stir in 1/2 cup spinach (save the rest for another use). Stir in the cheese, corn, beans, jalapeno, cumin, chili powder and salt.

> Place one sheet of phyllo dough on a work surface with a short end facing you. (Keep remaining phyllo covered with plastic wrap to prevent it from drying out.) Spray sheet with butter-flavored spray; cut into three 14-in. x 3-in. strips.

> Place a scant tablespoon of filling on lower corner of each strip. Fold dough over filling, forming a triangle. Fold triangle up, then over, forming another triangle. Continue folding, like a flag, until you come to the end of the strip.

> Spritz end of dough with cooking spray and press onto triangle to seal. Turn triangle and spritz top with spray. Repeat with remaining phyllo and filling.

> Place triangles on baking sheets coated with cooking spray. Bake at 375° for 10-12 minutes or until golden brown. For sauce, mash avocado with the mayonnaise, sour cream and vinegar. Serve with warm appetizers.

YIELD: 2 DOZEN (1/2 CUP SAUCE)

Editor's Note: When cutting hot peppers, disposable gloves are recommended. Avoid touching your face.

 tip Can't get enough from just a bite-size portion of Southwest Spanakopita Bites? You can easily turn this recipe into a main dish. Simply fill small flour tortillas with the filling and bake as directed in the recipe.

cheddar artichoke quiche cups

FRAN DELL, LAS VEGAS, NEVADA

No one can resist sampling these savory bites filled with artichokes, onions and cheese. They're at the top of my family's list for every holiday gathering. And whether I serve them hot or cold, there are never any left!

2 jars (7-1/2 ounces each) marinated artichoke hearts

1 small onion, finely chopped

1 garlic clove, minced

4 eggs, beaten

1/4 cup dry bread crumbs

1/4 teaspoon ground mustard

1/8 teaspoon dried oregano

1/8 teaspoon pepper

1/8 teaspoon hot pepper sauce

2 cups (8 ounces) shredded cheddar cheese

2 tablespoons minced fresh parsley

> Drain artichokes, reserving half of the marinade. Chop artichokes; set aside. In a skillet, saute onion and garlic in reserved marinade until tender; set aside.

> In a large bowl, combine the eggs, bread crumbs, mustard, oregano, pepper and hot pepper sauce. Stir in the cheese, parsley, reserved artichokes and onion mixture.

> Fill miniature muffin cups three-fourths full. Bake at 325° for 15-17 minutes or until set. Cool for 5 minutes before removing from pan to wire racks. Serve warm. Refrigerate leftovers.

YIELD: 4 DOZEN

mini phyllo tacos

ROSEANN WESTON, PHILIPSBURG, PENNSYLVANIA

For a winning appetizer, serve crispy phyllo cups filled with taco-seasoned ground beef and a little zesty shredded cheese.

1 pound lean ground beef (90% lean)

1/2 cup finely chopped onion

1 envelope taco seasoning

3/4 cup water

1-1/4 cups shredded Mexican cheese blend, divided

2 packages (1.9 ounces each) frozen miniature phyllo tart shells

> In a small skillet, cook beef and onion over medium heat until meat is no longer pink; drain. Stir in taco seasoning and water. Bring to a boil. Reduce heat; simmer, uncovered for 5 minutes. Remove from the heat; stir in 1/2 cup of the cheese blend.

> Place tart shells in an ungreased 15-in. x 10-in. x 1-in. baking pan. Fill with taco mixture.

> Bake at 350° for 6 minutes. Sprinkle with remaining cheese blend; bake 2-3 minutes longer or until cheese is melted.

YIELD: *2-1/2 DOZEN*

MARIA REGAKIS, SOMERVILLE, MASSACHUSETTS
Seafood lovers will savor these tasty bites. Mushroom caps are stuffed with a simple yet pleasing combination of minced clams, cheese and seasonings.

clam-stuffed mushrooms

24 large fresh mushrooms

2 cans (6-1/2 ounces each) minced clams, drained

3/4 cup dry bread crumbs

1/2 cup grated Parmesan cheese

1/2 cup finely chopped green pepper

1 small onion, finely chopped

2 garlic cloves, minced

2 tablespoons Italian seasoning

2 tablespoons dried parsley flakes

1/8 teaspoon pepper

1-1/2 cups butter, melted, divided

1/2 cup shredded part-skim mozzarella cheese

> Remove mushroom stems (discard or save for another use); set caps aside. In a large bowl, combine the clams, bread crumbs, Parmesan cheese, green pepper, onion, garlic, Italian seasoning, parsley and pepper. Stir in 3/4 cup butter. Fill each mushroom cap with about 1 tablespoon clam mixture.

> Place in an ungreased 15-in. x 10-in. x 1-in. baking pan. Sprinkle with mozzarella cheese; drizzle with the remaining butter. Bake, uncovered, at 350° for 20-25 minutes or until lightly browned. Serve warm.

YIELD: 2 DOZEN

bacon water chestnut wraps

LAURA MAHAFFEY, ANNAPOLIS, MARYLAND
Around our house, the holidays just wouldn't be the same without these classic wraps. Through the years, Christmas Eve guests have proved it's nearly impossible to eat just one.

1 pound sliced bacon

2 cans (8 ounces each) whole water chestnuts, drained

1/2 cup packed brown sugar

1/2 cup mayonnaise

1/4 cup chili sauce

> Cut bacon strips in half. In a skillet over medium heat, cook bacon until almost crisp; drain. Wrap each bacon piece around a water chestnut and secure with a toothpick. Place in an ungreased 13-in. x 9-in. baking dish.

> Combine the brown sugar, mayonnaise and chili sauce; pour over water chestnuts. Bake, uncovered, at 350° for 30 minutes or until hot and bubbly.

YIELD: ABOUT 2-1/2 DOZEN

spinach-cheese mushroom caps

SANDY HERMAN, MARIETTA, GEORGIA
Dainty finger foods like these mushrooms are a nice way to welcome guests into your home. A hearty spinach filling will tide folks over until the meal is ready to be served.

24 large fresh mushrooms

1/4 cup chopped onion

2 garlic cloves, minced

1 tablespoon olive oil

1 package (8 ounces) cream cheese, softened

1 package (10 ounces) frozen chopped spinach, thawed and squeezed dry

1/2 cup plus 2 tablespoons shredded Parmesan cheese, divided

1/2 cup crumbled feta cheese

1 bacon strip, cooked and crumbled

1/2 teaspoon salt

> Remove stems from mushrooms; set caps aside. Finely chop the stems. In a skillet, saute the chopped mushrooms, onion and garlic in oil until tender.

> In a mixing bowl, beat cream cheese until smooth. Add the spinach, 1/2 cup Parmesan cheese, feta cheese, bacon, salt and mushroom mixture. Spoon into mushroom caps. Sprinkle with the remaining Parmesan cheese.

> Place on a baking sheet. Bake at 400° for 15 minutes or until golden brown.

YIELD: 2 DOZEN

tip As you plan your party, remember to appeal to everyone's tastes and diets. You'll want to offer a balance of hearty and low-calorie appetizers as well as hot and cold choices. That way, there will be something for everybody.

veggie nachos

MERRY HOLTHUS, AUBURN, NEBRASKA
My family loves traditional nachos, but I was looking to offer something a little different. Now they gobble up this version with ground beef, vegetables and a creamy cheese sauce.

1 pound ground beef

2-1/2 quarts water, divided

1 envelope taco seasoning

1 medium bunch broccoli, broken into small florets

1 medium head cauliflower, broken into small florets

1 package (15-1/2 ounces) bite-size tortilla chips

1 can (11 ounces) condensed nacho cheese soup, undiluted

1/2 cup milk

1/4 cup chopped sweet red pepper

1 can (2-1/4 ounces) sliced ripe olives, drained

> In a skillet, cook beef over medium heat until no longer pink, drain. Add 3/4 cup water and taco seasoning. Bring to a boil. Reduce heat; simmer, uncovered, for 15 minutes.

> Meanwhile, in a large saucepan, bring remaining water to a boil. Add broccoli and cauliflower. Cook for 2 minutes; drain. Place chips on a large ovenproof serving platter. Top with beef mixture, broccoli and cauliflower.

> In a bowl, combine the soup, milk and red pepper. Drizzle over vegetables. Sprinkle with olives. Bake at 350° for 10 minutes or until heated through. Serve immediately.

YIELD: 12-16 SERVINGS

calico clams casino

PAULA SULLIVAN, BARKER, NEW YORK
A few years ago, I came across this recipe in the back of my files when I was looking for a special appetizer. Everyone raved about it. Now it's one of my most often-requested dishes.

3 cans (6-1/2 ounces each) minced clams

1 cup (4 ounces) shredded part-skim mozzarella cheese

1 cup (4 ounces) shredded cheddar cheese

4 bacon strips, cooked and crumbled

3 tablespoons seasoned bread crumbs

3 tablespoons butter, melted

2 tablespoons each finely chopped onion, celery and sweet red, yellow and green peppers

1 garlic clove, minced

Dash dried parsley flakes

> Drain clams, reserving 2 tablespoons clam juice. In a large bowl, combine the clams and all the remaining ingredients; stir in the reserved clam juice. Spoon into greased 6-oz. custard cups or clamshell dishes; place on baking sheets.

> Bake at 350° for 10-15 minutes or until heated through and lightly browned.

YIELD: 8 SERVINGS

KERRY VAUGHN, KALISPELL, MONTANA

I've made these fluffy puffs for baby showers as well as holiday parties. The savory bites have such a nice mixture of lightness and crunch.

curried chicken cream puffs

1/2 cup water

1/3 cup butter, cubed

Dash salt

1/2 cup all-purpose flour

2 eggs

FILLING:
1 package (8 ounces) cream cheese, softened

1/4 cup milk

1/4 teaspoon salt

1/4 teaspoon curry powder

Dash pepper

1-1/2 cups cubed cooked chicken

1/3 cup slivered almonds, toasted

1 green onion, chopped

> In a large saucepan, bring water, butter and salt to a boil. Add flour all at once and stir until a smooth ball forms. Remove from the heat; let stand for 5 minutes. Add eggs, one at a time, beating well after each addition. Continue beating until mixture is smooth and shiny.

> Drop by rounded teaspoonfuls 2 in. apart onto greased baking sheets. Bake at 425° for 15-20 minutes or until golden brown. Remove to wire racks. Immediately split puffs open; remove tops and set aside. Reduce heat to 375°.

> In a small bowl, beat the cream cheese, milk, salt, curry powder and pepper until smooth. Stir in the chicken, almonds and onion. Spoon into puffs; replace tops. Place on a baking sheet; bake for 5 minutes or until heated through.

YIELD: 2 DOZEN

> In a large bowl, beat the egg yolks, milk and oil. Combine the flour, baking powder, onion powder, salt and pepper; add to yolk mixture and mix well. Stir in the rice, shrimp, parsley and hot pepper sauce.

> In a mixing bowl, beat the egg whites until soft peaks form; fold into shrimp mixture.

> In an electric skillet or deep-fat fryer, heat oil to 350°. Drop batter by tablespoons into hot oil. Fry puffs, a few at a time, for 1-1/2 minutes on each side or until browned and puffy. Drain on paper towels. Serve warm.

YIELD: ABOUT 4 DOZEN

shrimp puffs

MAUDRY RAMSEY, SULPHUR, LOUISIANA
Shrimp and rice are two foods that are abundant in our area. These shrimp puffs are my family's favorite.

2 eggs, separated

3/4 cup milk

1 tablespoon vegetable oil

1 cup all-purpose flour

1-1/2 teaspoons baking powder

1-1/2 teaspoons onion powder

1 teaspoon salt

1/2 teaspoon pepper

3 cups cooked rice

1 pound uncooked shrimp, peeled, deveined and chopped or 2 cans (4-1/2 ounces each) small shrimp, drained

1/4 cup minced fresh parsley

1/2 teaspoon hot pepper sauce

Oil for deep-fat frying

blue cheese crostini

KATE HILTS, GRAND RAPIDS, MICHIGAN
My sister-in-law gave me this great recipe, which includes two of my favorite ingredients—blue cheese and pears. Yum!

4 ounces cream cheese, softened

3 tablespoons butter, softened

1 cup (4 ounces) crumbled blue cheese

1/4 cup finely chopped walnuts, toasted

15 slices French bread (1/2 inch thick), lightly toasted

1 medium ripe pear

> In a small mixing bowl, beat cream cheese and butter until smooth. Stir in the blue cheese and walnuts. Spread evenly over toasted bread.

> Place on a baking sheet. Broil 3-4 in. from the heat for 3-4 minutes or until cheese is bubbly. Core pear and cut into 30 thin slices. Place two pear slices on each crostini. Serve warm.

YIELD: 15 APPETIZERS

italian garlic breadsticks

TASTE OF HOME TEST KITCHEN

A seasoned Parmesan cheese coating gives refrigerated breadsticks a terrific taste twist. The wonderful aroma of these breadsticks baking is so irresistible, you just may need to make another batch!

1/2 cup grated Parmesan cheese

2 teaspoons Italian seasoning

1 teaspoon garlic powder

1/4 cup butter, melted

1 tube (11 ounces) refrigerated breadsticks

> In a shallow bowl, combine the cheese, Italian seasoning and garlic powder. Place butter in another shallow bowl. Separate dough into individual breadsticks. Dip in butter, then in cheese mixture. Twist 2-3 times and place on an ungreased baking sheet.

> Bake at 375° for 12-14 minutes or until golden brown. Serve immediately.

YIELD: 1 DOZEN

seasoned potato wedges

KAREN TREWIN, DECORAH, IOWA

These wedges, seasoned with Parmesan cheese and served with a sour cream dip, make a nice alternative to french fries or baked potatoes. They go great with grilled steak, but my family enjoys them as snacks, too.

1/3 cup all-purpose flour

1/3 cup grated Parmesan cheese

1 teaspoon paprika

3 large baking potatoes (about 2-3/4 pounds)

1/3 cup milk

1/4 cup butter, divided

SOUR CREAM DIP:

2 cups (16 ounces) sour cream

8 bacon strips, cooked and crumbled

2 tablespoons minced chives

1/2 teaspoon garlic powder

> In a large resealable plastic bag, combine the flour, Parmesan cheese and paprika.

> Cut each potato into eight wedges; dip in milk. Place in the bag, a few at a time, and shake to coat.

> Place potatoes on a greased 15-in. x 10-in. x 1-in. baking pan. Drizzle with 2 tablespoons butter. Bake, uncovered, at 400° for 20 minutes.

> Turn wedges; drizzle with remaining butter. Bake 20-25 minutes longer or until potatoes are tender and golden brown.

> In a large bowl, combine dip ingredients. Serve with warm potato wedges.

YIELD: 6-8 SERVINGS

fried onion rings

CHRISTINE WILSON, SELLERSVILLE, PENNSYLVANIA

Sweet Vidalia onion rings are deep-fried to a crispy golden brown, then served with a cool and zesty lime dipping sauce.

1 large Vidalia or sweet onion

3/4 cup all-purpose flour

1/4 cup cornmeal

1/2 teaspoon baking powder

1/2 teaspoon salt

1/4 teaspoon baking soda

1/4 teaspoon cayenne pepper

1 egg

1 cup buttermilk

Oil for deep-fat frying

LIME DIPPING SAUCE:

2/3 cup mayonnaise

3 tablespoons honey

2 tablespoons lime juice

2 tablespoons spicy brown or horseradish mustard

1 teaspoon prepared horseradish

> Cut onion into 1/2-in. slices; separate into rings. In a bowl, combine the flour, cornmeal, baking powder, salt, baking soda and cayenne. Combine the egg and buttermilk stir into dry ingredients just until moistened.

> In an electric skillet or deep-fat fryer, heat 1 in. of oil to 375°. Dip onion rings into batter. Fry a few at a time for 1 to 1-1/2 minutes on each side or until golden brown. Drain on paper towels (keep warm in a 300° oven).

> In a small bowl, combine sauce ingredients. Serve with onion rings.

YIELD: 4 SERVINGS

tater-dipped veggies

EARLEEN LILLEGARD, PRESCOTT, ARIZONA

Fried vegetables are terrific, but it's not always convenient to prepare them for company. Here's an easy recipe that produces the same deliciously crisp results in the oven. Serve with your favorite ranch-style dressing as a dip.

1 cup instant potato flakes

1/3 cup grated Parmesan cheese

1/2 teaspoon celery salt

1/4 teaspoon garlic powder

1/4 cup butter, melted and cooled

2 eggs

4 to 5 cups raw bite-size vegetables (mushrooms, peppers, broccoli, cauliflower, zucchini and/or parboiled carrots)

Prepared ranch salad dressing or dip, optional

> In a small bowl, combine the potato flakes, Parmesan cheese, celery salt, garlic powder and butter. In another bowl, beat eggs. Dip vegetables, one at a time, into eggs, then into potato mixture; coat well.

> Place on an ungreased baking sheet. Bake at 400° for 20-25 minutes. Serve with dressing or dip if desired.

YIELD: 6-8 SERVINGS

pizza poppers

DENISE SARGENT, PITTSFIELD, NEW HAMPSHIRE
Both my husband and I are big pizza fans, so we created these pizza rolls. They'll go fast at any gathering you host.

4 to 4-1/2 cups all-purpose flour

1/3 cup sugar

1 package (1/4 ounce) active dry yeast

1 teaspoon dried oregano

1/2 teaspoon salt

1 cup water

1 tablespoon shortening

1 egg

3 cups (12 ounces) shredded part-skim mozzarella cheese

1-1/3 cups minced pepperoni (about 5 ounces)

2 cups pizza sauce, warmed

> In a large mixing bowl, combine 2 cups flour, sugar, yeast, oregano and salt. In a saucepan, heat water and shortening to 120°- 130°. Add to dry ingredients; beat until moistened. Add egg; beat on medium speed for 1 minute. Stir in cheese and pepperoni; mix well. Stir in enough remaining flour to form a soft dough.

> Turn onto a floured surface; knead until smooth and elastic, about 6-8 minutes. Place in a greased bowl, turning once to grease top. Cover and let rise in a warm place until doubled, about 1 hour.

> Punch dough down. Turn onto a lightly floured surface; divide into four pieces. Divide each piece into eight balls. Roll each ball into a 12-in. rope. Tie into a loose knot, leaving two long ends. Fold top end under roll; bring bottom end up and press into center of roll. Place on greased baking sheets. Cover and let rise until doubled, about 30 minutes.

> Bake at 375° for 10-12 minutes or until golden brown. Serve warm with pizza sauce.

YIELD: 32 APPETIZERS

prosciutto puffs

NELLA PARKER, HERSEY, MICHIGAN
Your guests will come back for seconds and even thirds of these light and tasty puffs. They're so delectable that they practically melt in your mouth.

1 cup water

6 tablespoons butter

1/8 teaspoon pepper

1 cup all-purpose flour

5 eggs

3/4 cup finely chopped prosciutto or fully cooked ham

1/4 cup minced chives

> In a large saucepan, bring the water, butter and pepper to a boil. Add flour all at once and stir until a smooth ball forms. Remove from the heat; let stand for 5 minutes.

> Add eggs, one at a time, beating well after each addition. Continue beating until mixture is smooth and shiny. Stir in prosciutto and chives.

> Drop by heaping teaspoonfuls onto greased baking sheets. Bake at 425° for 18-22 minutes or until golden brown. Remove to wire racks. Serve warm. Refrigerate leftovers.

YIELD: 4-1/2 DOZEN

JEAN ECOS, HARTLAND, WISCONSIN
This Armenian appetizer has a rich-tasting cheese filling that is baked between buttery layers of phyllo dough.

cheese boereg

1 egg, lightly beaten

1 egg white, lightly beaten

1 cup ricotta cheese

1/4 cup minced fresh parsley

4 cups (16 ounces) shredded part-skim mozzarella or Muenster cheese

10 sheets phyllo dough (18 inches x 14 inches)

1/2 cup butter, melted

> In a bowl, combine the egg, egg white, ricotta and parsley. Stir in mozzarella; set aside.

> Unroll phyllo dough; cut stack of sheets in half widthwise. Place one sheet of phyllo dough in a greased 13-in. x 9-in. baking pan; brush with butter. Repeat nine times. Keep remaining dough covered with plastic wrap and a damp towel to prevent it from drying out.

> Spread cheese mixture evenly over top. Layer with remaining dough, brushing butter on every other sheet.

> Bake at 350° for 25-30 minutes or until golden brown. Cut into triangles or squares.

YIELD: 16-20 APPETIZER SERVINGS

> Remove mushroom stems (discard or save for another use). In a large skillet, heat 2 tablespoons butter and oil over medium-high heat. Saute mushroom caps for 2 minutes on each side; sprinkle with salt. Remove with a slotted spoon to paper towels.

> In the same skillet, saute the onion in remaining butter until tender. Remove from the heat; stir in the remaining ingredients.

> Spoon into mushroom caps. Place on a broiler pan; broil 5 in. from the heat for 2-3 minutes or until filling is browned. Serve warm.

YIELD: 12-14 APPETIZERS

pecan stuffed mushrooms

BEVERLY PIERCE, INDIANOLA, MISSISSIPPI
When I had some kitchen remodeling done a few years ago, this recipe disappeared. But I'd shared it so often that I had no trouble getting a copy.

1 pound large fresh mushrooms

4 tablespoons butter, divided

2 tablespoons vegetable oil

1/4 teaspoon salt

2 tablespoons finely chopped onion

1 cup soft bread crumbs

6 bacon strips, cooked and crumbled

2 tablespoons chopped pecans

2 tablespoons sherry or beef broth

2 tablespoons sour cream

2 tablespoons minced chives

bacon-wrapped scallops

PAMELA MACCUMBEE, BERKELEY SPRINGS, WEST VIRGINIA
When I'm looking for an extra-special appetizer, this is the recipe I reach for. I've also served these savory scallops for dinner.

20 fresh baby spinach leaves

10 uncooked sea scallops, halved

10 bacon strips, halved widthwise

Lemon wedges

> Fold a spinach leaf around each scallop half. Wrap bacon over spinach and secure with a toothpick. Place on baking sheet or broiler pan.

> Broil 3-4 in. from the heat for 6 minutes on each side or until bacon is crisp and scallops are opaque. Squeeze lemon over each. Serve immediately.

YIELD: 20 APPETIZERS

tip To prepare mushrooms for stuffing, hold the mushroom cap in one hand and grab the stem with the other hand. Twist to snap off the stem; prepare caps as directed in the recipe. You can use the discarded mushroom stems from Pecan Stuffed Mushrooms as a topping in a tossed salad.

> Brush bottom and sides of a 13-in. x 9-in. baking dish with 1 tablespoon butter; set aside. In a large mixing bowl, combine the remaining butter and the next nine ingredients. Stir in the spinach, cheeses and onion.

> Spread in pan. Bake, uncovered, at 350° for 30-35 minutes or until a toothpick inserted near the center comes out clean and edges are lightly browned. Cut into squares. Garnish with pimientos if desired.

YIELD: 4 DOZEN

crunchy onion sticks

LEORA MUELLERLEILE, TURTLE LAKE, WISCONSIN
Although I've been collecting recipes for more than 50 years, I never tire of tried-and-true ones like this.

2 eggs, lightly beaten

2 tablespoons butter, melted

1 teaspoon all-purpose flour

1/2 teaspoon garlic salt

1/2 teaspoon dried parsley flakes

1/4 teaspoon onion salt

2 cans (2.8 ounces each) french-fried onions, crushed

1 tube (8 ounces) refrigerated crescent rolls

> In a shallow bowl, combine the first six ingredients. Place the onions in another shallow bowl. Separate crescent dough into four rectangles; seal perforations. Cut each rectangle into eight strips. Dip each strip in egg mixture, then roll in onions.

> Place 2 in. apart on ungreased baking sheets. Bake at 375° for 10-12 minutes or until golden brown. Immediately remove from baking sheets. Serve warm.

YIELD: 32 APPETIZERS

spinach squares

PATRICIA KILE, GREENTOWN, PENNSYLVANIA
Even people who don't care for spinach can't pass up these satisfying squares when they're served.

2 tablespoons butter, divided

1 cup milk

3 eggs

1 cup all-purpose flour

1 teaspoon baking powder

3/4 teaspoon salt

1/2 teaspoon dried oregano

1/4 teaspoon pepper

1/4 teaspoon dried basil

1/4 teaspoon dried thyme

2 packages (10 ounces each) frozen chopped spinach, thawed and squeezed dry

2 cups (8 ounces) shredded cheddar cheese

2 cups (8 ounces) shredded Monterey Jack cheese

1 cup chopped onion

Sliced pimientos, optional

tomato leek tarts

KATHLEEN TRIBBLE, SANTA YNEZ, CALIFORNIA

You'll get two attractive, rustic-looking tarts from this delicious recipe. The crisp pastry crust cuts easily into handheld wedges.

1 package (15 ounces) refrigerated pie pastry

4 ounces provolone cheese, shredded

1 pound leeks (white portion only), sliced

6 medium plum tomatoes, thinly sliced

1/4 cup grated Parmesan cheese

1-1/2 teaspoons garlic powder

1/8 teaspoon pepper

1 cup (8 ounces) shredded part-skim mozzarella cheese

> Place both pastry sheets on greased baking sheets. Sprinkle each with provolone cheese, leaving 1 in. around edges. Arrange leeks and tomato slices over provolone cheese. Sprinkle with Parmesan cheese, garlic powder and pepper. Top with mozzarella cheese. Fold edges over the filling.

> Bake at 425° for 18-22 minutes or until crusts are lightly browned. Cut into wedges. Serve warm.

YIELD: 2 TARTS

deep-fried potato skins

LESLIE CUNNIAN, PETERBOROUGH, ONTARIO

The combination of potatoes, cheese, bacon and garlic dip in this recipe is fantastic. The skins can be served as an appetizer or as a side dish with roast prime rib or any other entree you choose.

4 large baking potatoes

2 cups (16 ounces) sour cream

1 envelope onion soup mix

1 tablespoon finely chopped onion

5 garlic cloves, minced

Dash hot pepper sauce

Oil for deep-fat frying

1/2 cup shredded cheddar cheese

1/2 cup shredded Swiss cheese

6 to 8 bacon strips, cooked and crumbled

4 teaspoons minced chives or green onion

> Bake potatoes at 400° for 1 hour or until tender.

> Meanwhile, for dip, combine the sour cream, soup mix, onion, garlic and hot pepper sauce in a bowl. Cover and refrigerate until serving.

> When potatoes are cool enough to handle, cut in half lengthwise. Scoop out pulp, leaving a 1/4-in. shell (save pulp for another use). With a scissors, cut each potato half into three lengthwise strips.

> In an electric skillet or deep-fat fryer, heat oil to 375°. Fry skins in oil for 2-3 minutes or until golden brown and crisp.

> Place potato skins in a 15-in. x 10-in. x 1-in. baking pan. Combine the cheeses and bacon; sprinkle over potatoes. Broil 4 in. from the heat for 1-2 minutes or until cheese is melted. Sprinkle with chives. Serve with the dip.

YIELD: 2 DOZEN

NADIA MIHEYEV, RICHMOND HILL, NEW YORK

If you're looking for a scrumptious way to get a party started, bring out a tray of these cheesy crab puffs. They bake up golden brown and taste wonderful right out of the oven. Try serving them with soup.

crab puffs

1 cup plus 1 tablespoon water

1/2 cup butter

1 tablespoon ground mustard

1 teaspoon salt

1 teaspoon ground cumin

1/8 teaspoon hot pepper sauce

1 cup all-purpose flour

4 eggs

2 cups (8 ounces) shredded Swiss cheese

1 can (6 ounces) crabmeat, drained, flaked and cartilage removed

> In a large saucepan, bring the water, butter, mustard, salt, cumin and hot pepper sauce to a boil. Add flour all at once and stir until a smooth ball forms. Remove from the heat; let stand for 5 minutes.

> Add eggs, one at a time, beating well after each addition. Continue beating until smooth and shiny. Stir in the cheese and crab.

> Drop by rounded teaspoonfuls 2 in. apart onto greased baking sheets. Bake at 400° for 23-26 minutes or until golden brown. Remove to wire racks. Serve warm.

YIELD: ABOUT 4 DOZEN

crisp caraway twists

DOROTHY SMITH, EL DORADO, ARKANSAS

This appetizer is always a hit when I serve it on holidays or special occasions. The flaky cheese-filled twists—made with convenient puff pastry—are baked to a crisp. When our big family gets together, I always make two batches.

1 egg

1 tablespoon water

1 teaspoon country-style Dijon mustard

3/4 cup shredded Swiss cheese

1/4 cup finely chopped onion

2 teaspoons minced fresh parsley

1-1/2 teaspoons caraway seeds

1/4 teaspoon garlic salt

1 sheet frozen puff pastry, thawed

> In a small bowl, beat the egg, water and mustard; set aside. In another bowl, combine the cheese, onion, parsley, caraway seeds and garlic salt.

> Unfold pastry sheet; brush with egg mixture. Sprinkle cheese mixture lengthwise over half of the pastry. Fold pastry over filling; press edges to seal. Brush top with remaining egg mixture. Cut widthwise into 1/2-in. strips; twist each strip several times.

> Place 1 in. apart on greased baking sheets, pressing ends down. Bake at 350° for 15-20 minutes or until golden brown. Serve warm.

YIELD: ABOUT 1-1/2 DOZEN

chicken nut puffs

JO GROTH, PLAINFIELD, IOWA

Of the 15 to 20 items I set out when hosting holiday parties, these savory puffs are the first to get snapped up. People enjoy the zippy flavor. They're a nice finger food since they're not sticky or drippy.

1-1/2 cups finely chopped cooked chicken

1/3 cup chopped almonds, toasted

1 cup chicken broth

1/2 cup vegetable oil

2 teaspoons Worcestershire sauce

1 tablespoon dried parsley flakes

1 teaspoon seasoned salt

1/2 to 1 teaspoon celery seed

1/8 teaspoon cayenne pepper

1 cup all-purpose flour

4 eggs

> Combine the chicken and almonds; set aside. In a saucepan, combine the next seven ingredients; bring to a boil. Add flour all at once; stir until a smooth ball forms. Remove from the heat; let stand for 5 minutes.

> Add eggs, one at a time, beating well after each. Beat until smooth. Stir in chicken and almonds.

> Drop by heaping teaspoonfuls onto greased baking sheets. Bake at 450° for 12-14 minutes or until golden brown. Serve warm.

YIELD: ABOUT 6 DOZEN

cool
nibbles

marinated cheese

LAURIE CASPER, CORAOPOLIS, PENNSYLVANIA
This appetizer always makes it to our neighborhood parties and is the first to disappear at the buffet table. It's attractive, delicious—and easy!

2 blocks (8 ounces each) white cheddar cheese

2 packages (8 ounces each) cream cheese, softened

3/4 cup chopped roasted sweet red peppers

1/2 cup olive oil

1/4 cup white wine vinegar

1/4 cup balsamic vinegar

3 tablespoons chopped green onions

3 tablespoons minced fresh parsley

2 tablespoons minced fresh basil

1 tablespoon sugar

3 garlic cloves, minced

1/2 teaspoon salt

1/2 teaspoon pepper

Toasted sliced French bread or assorted crackers

> Slice each block of cheddar cheese into twenty 1/4-in. slices. Cut each block of cream cheese into 18 slices; sandwich between cheddar slices, using a knife to spread evenly. Create four 6-in.-long blocks of cheese; place in a 13-in. x 9-in. dish.

> In a small bowl, combine the roasted peppers, oil, vinegars, onions, herbs, sugar, garlic, salt and pepper; pour over cheese.

> Cover and refrigerate overnight, turning once. Drain excess marinade. Serve cheese with bread or crackers.

YIELD: ABOUT 2 POUNDS

smoked salmon cucumber canapes

JUDY GREBETZ, RACINE, WISCONSIN
Here's a contribution that I'm always asked to bring to gatherings. It's simple, comes together quickly and is always a winner.

2 medium cucumbers, peeled

4 ounces smoked salmon, flaked

2 tablespoons lemon juice

1 tablespoon finely chopped onion

1 tablespoon capers, drained

1 tablespoon minced fresh parsley

1/2 teaspoon Dijon mustard

1/8 teaspoon pepper

> Cut cucumbers in half lengthwise; remove and discard seeds. In a small bowl, combine the remaining ingredients. Spoon into cucumber halves. Wrap in plastic wrap. Refrigerate for 3-4 hours or until filling is firm. Cut into 1/2-in. slices.

YIELD: ABOUT 3-1/2 DOZEN

individual cheese balls

MILDRED SHERRER, FORT WORTH, TEXAS
With their creamy, nutty flavor, these small cheese balls work great for any function.

2 packages (8 ounces each) cream cheese, softened

1 cup (4 ounces) shredded cheddar cheese

1 to 2 tablespoons chopped onion

1 to 2 tablespoons minced fresh parsley

1 to 2 teaspoons lemon juice

1 to 2 teaspoons Worcestershire sauce

1-1/2 to 2 cups ground walnuts

> In a large bowl, combine the first six ingredients. Shape into 1-1/2-in. balls. Roll in nuts. Chill thoroughly. Serve with crackers.

YIELD: 20 SERVINGS

crab-stuffed snow peas

AGNES WARD, STRATFORD, ONTARIO
These crunchy appetizers have a wonderful crabmeat flavor and make an attractive addition to any hors d'oeuvre tray. Best of all, they're simple to prepare.

1 can (6 ounces) crabmeat, drained, flaked and cartilage removed

2 tablespoons mayonnaise

1 tablespoon chili sauce or seafood cocktail sauce

1/8 teaspoon salt

3 drops hot pepper sauce

Dash pepper

16 fresh snow peas

> In small bowl, combine the crab, mayonnaise, chili sauce, salt, pepper sauce and pepper.

> Place snow peas in a steamer basket; place in a small saucepan over 1 in. of water. Bring to a boil; cover and steam for 30 seconds for until softened. Drain and immediately place snow peas in ice water. Drain and pat dry.

> With a sharp knife, split pea pods along the curved edges. Spoon 1 tablespoon of crab mixture into each. Refrigerate until serving.

YIELD: 16 APPETIZERS

herbed deviled eggs

SUE SEYMOUR, VALATIE, NEW YORK
Wondering what to do with leftover hard-cooked eggs? This version of deviled eggs has a delightful twist—I add a mix of herbs to the filling.

6 hard-cooked eggs

2 tablespoons minced chives

2 tablespoons plain yogurt

2 tablespoons mayonnaise

1 tablespoon chopped fresh tarragon

1 tablespoon minced fresh parsley

2-1/2 teaspoons prepared mustard

1 teaspoon snipped fresh dill

Salt and pepper to taste

> Cut eggs in half lengthwise; remove yolks and set whites aside. In a small bowl, mash yolks with a fork. Stir in the remaining ingredients. Pipe or stuff into egg whites. Refrigerate until serving.

YIELD: 1 DOZEN

stuffed bread appetizers

TRACY WESTROM, LANSDALE, PENNSYLVANIA
You may want to double the recipe for this hearty cold appetizer because I've found that folks just can't seem to stop eating it!

2 packages (one 8 ounces, one 3 ounces) cream cheese, softened

1 cup chopped celery

1 cup (4 ounces) shredded cheddar cheese

1/2 cup chopped sweet red pepper

1/2 cup chopped water chestnuts

1 teaspoon garlic salt

1 loaf (26 inches) French bread, halved lengthwise

Mayonnaise

Dried parsley flakes

4 dill pickle spears

4 slices deli ham

> In a large bowl, combine the first six ingredients; set aside.

> Hollow out top and bottom of bread, leaving a 1/2-in. shell (discard removed bread or save for another use). Spread thin layer of mayonnaise over bread; sprinkle with parsley.

> Fill each half with cheese mixture. Wrap pickle spears in ham; place lengthwise over cheese mixture on bottom half of loaf. Replace top; press together to seal.

> Wrap in foil; refrigerate overnight. Just before serving, cut into 1-in. slices.

YIELD: ABOUT 2 DOZEN

garlic tomato bruschetta

JEAN FRANZONI, RUTLAND, VERMONT
Bruschetta is a popular snack because it is made with fresh and flavorful ingredients and is so tasty.

1/4 cup olive oil

3 tablespoons chopped fresh basil

3 to 4 garlic cloves, minced

1/2 teaspoon salt

1/4 teaspoon pepper

4 medium tomatoes, diced

2 tablespoons grated Parmesan cheese

1 loaf (1 pound) unsliced French bread

> In a bowl, combine the oil, basil, garlic, salt and pepper. Add tomatoes and toss gently. Sprinkle with cheese. Refrigerate for at least 1 hour.

> Bring to room temperature before serving. Cut bread into 24 slices; toast under broiler until lightly browned. Top with tomato mixture. Serve immediately.

YIELD: 12 SERVINGS

WEDA MOSELLIE, PHILLIPSBURG, NEW JERSEY

This is a real favorite on our buffet tables. The large platter of sardines, anchovy fillets, cheese, olives and vegetables disappears quickly.

classic antipasto platter

1 pound fresh mozzarella cheese, sliced

1 jar (16 ounces) pickled pepper rings, drained

1 jar (10 ounces) colossal Sicilian olives, drained

4 large tomatoes, cut into wedges

6 hard-cooked eggs, sliced

1 medium cucumber, sliced

1 medium sweet red pepper, julienned

1 can (3-3/4 ounces) sardines, drained

1 can (2 ounces) anchovy fillets, drained

1/4 cup olive oil

1 teaspoon grated Parmesan cheese

1 teaspoon minced fresh oregano

1/8 teaspoon salt

1/8 teaspoon pepper

> On a large serving platter, arrange the first nine ingredients. In a small bowl, whisk the oil, cheese, oregano, salt and pepper; drizzle over antipasto.

YIELD: 14-16 SERVINGS

garlic-kissed tomatoes

MARGARET ZICKERT, DEERFIELD, WISCONSIN
Everyone I know loves this recipe—even my husband who normally doesn't like garlic! These tomatoes are a hit at potlucks...folks always ask for the recipe.

6 medium tomatoes

1/4 cup canola oil

3 tablespoons lemon juice

2 garlic cloves, thinly sliced

1/2 teaspoon salt

1/2 teaspoon dried oregano

1/8 teaspoon pepper

> Peel and cut tomatoes in half horizontally. Squeeze tomatoes lightly to release seeds. Discard seeds and juices. Place tomato halves in a container with a tight-fitting lid.

> In a small bowl, combine the oil, lemon juice, garlic, salt, oregano and pepper. Pour over tomatoes. Seal lid and turn to coat. Refrigerate for at least 4 hours or up to 2 days, turning occasionally.

YIELD: 12 SERVINGS

savory cucumber sandwiches

CAROL HENDERSON, CHAGRIN FALLS, OHIO
Italian salad dressing easily flavors my simple spread. Serve it as a dip with crackers and veggies or use it as a sandwich filling.

1 package (8 ounces) cream cheese, softened

1/2 cup mayonnaise

1 envelope Italian salad dressing mix

36 slices snack rye bread

1 medium cucumber, sliced

> In a small bowl, combine the cream cheese, mayonnaise and salad dressing mix until blended. Refrigerate for 1 hour.

> Just before serving, spread over rye bread; top each with a cucumber slice.

YIELD: 3 DOZEN

tip To peel a tomato quickly and easily, cut a shallow X on the bottom of the tomato. Put it into a pot of boiling water for about 1 minute, then rinse under cold water. The skin will peel right off.

red pepper green bean roll-ups

MARIE RIZZIO, INTERLOCHEN, MICHIGAN
Delicious and healthy, this appetizer is a yummy way to eat green beans. The roll-ups can be prepared ahead of time, and guests always comment on how tasty and different they are.

1/2 pound fresh green beans, trimmed

1/2 cup Italian salad dressing

15 slices white bread

1/4 cup mayonnaise

2 tablespoons spicy brown mustard

1 jar (7-1/4 ounces) roasted sweet red peppers, well drained

1/3 cup butter, melted

1/2 cup packed minced fresh parsley

> Place green beans in a large saucepan and cover with water. Bring to a boil; cook, uncovered, for 6-8 minutes or until crisp-tender. Drain and rinse in cold water. Pat dry with paper towels. Place the beans in a large resealable plastic bag; add salad dressing. Seal bag and toss to coat; refrigerate overnight.

> Trim crusts from bread. With a rolling pin, flatten each slice slightly. Combine mayonnaise and mustard; spread about 1 teaspoon on each slice of bread.

> Cut roasted peppers into 1/2-in. slices. Drain and discard marinade. Place three green beans and two pepper slices on each slice of bread. Roll up from a long side and secure with a toothpick. Brush with butter; roll in parsley. Cover and refrigerate until serving. Just before serving, discard toothpicks and cut each roll into three pieces.

YIELD: 45 APPETIZERS

easy refrigerator pickles

ANGELA LIENHARD, BLOSSBURG, PENNSYLVANIA
My husband grows cucumbers, garlic and dill in the garden and eagerly waits for me to make these pickles.

14 pickling cucumbers

40 fresh dill sprigs

4 garlic cloves, sliced

2 quarts water

1 cup cider vinegar

1/2 cup sugar

1/3 cup salt

1 teaspoon mixed pickling spices

> Cut each cucumber lengthwise into six spears. In a large bowl, combine the cucumbers, dill and garlic; set aside.

> In a Dutch oven, combine all of the remaining ingredients. Bring to a boil; cook and stir just until the sugar is dissolved. Pour over the cucumber mixture; cool.

> Cover tightly and refrigerate for at least 24 hours.

YIELD: 4-1/2 QUARTS

marinated mushrooms

MARK CURRY, BUENA VISTA, COLORADO
Add these flavorful mushrooms to an antipasto platter, toss in a salad or just serve by themselves.

1 pound small fresh mushrooms

1 small onion, thinly sliced

1/3 cup white wine vinegar

1/3 cup vegetable oil

1 teaspoon salt

1 teaspoon ground mustard

> In a large saucepan, combine all the ingredients. Bring to a boil over medium-high heat. Cook, uncovered, for 6 minutes, stirring once. Cool to room temperature. Transfer to a bowl; cover and refrigerate overnight.

YIELD: 3 CUPS

smoked salmon pinwheels

CRISTINA MATHERS, SAN MIGUEL, CALIFORNIA
Inexpensive and impressive, this recipe is a must-have any time you want to wow friends and family without spending all day in the kitchen.

1 package (8 ounces) cream cheese, softened

1 tablespoon snipped fresh dill

1 tablespoon capers, drained

1/2 teaspoon garlic powder

1/2 teaspoon lemon juice

4 spinach tortillas (8 inches), room temperature

1/2 pound fully cooked smoked salmon fillets, flaked

> In a small bowl, combine the cream cheese, dill, capers, garlic powder and lemon juice. Spread over tortillas; top with salmon. Roll up tightly.

> Cut into 1-in. pieces; secure with toothpicks. Chill until serving. Discard toothpicks before serving. Refrigerate leftovers.

YIELD: 32 APPETIZERS

guacamole-stuffed eggs

PHY BRESSE, LUMBERTON, NORTH CAROLINA
Looking for a quick and easy way to please your guests? Try my flavorful south-of-the-border variation on deviled eggs. Guests say they're heavenly.

6 hard-cooked eggs

1/4 cup guacamole dip

1 teaspoon lime juice

1 tablespoon minced fresh cilantro

1/4 teaspoon salt, optional

Paprika, optional

> Cut eggs in half lengthwise; remove yolks and set whites aside. In a small bowl, mash yolks with a fork. Stir in the guacamole, lime juice, cilantro and salt if desired. Pipe or stuff into egg whites. Refrigerate until serving. Sprinkle with paprika if desired. Refrigerate until serving.

YIELD: 1 DOZEN

smoked salmon
new potatoes

TASTE OF HOME TEST KITCHEN
*This recipe proves that delicious party food and
healthy eating are compatible. Plus, you're bound to
get rave reviews when guests uncover these baby stuffed
potatoes. If you're in a hurry, you can serve the cream
cheese mixture as a spread with whole wheat crackers.*

36 small red potatoes (about 1-1/2 pounds)

1 package (8 ounces) reduced-fat cream cheese, cubed

2 packages (3 ounces each) smoked cooked salmon

2 tablespoons chopped green onion

2 teaspoons dill weed

2 teaspoons lemon juice

1/8 teaspoon salt

1/8 teaspoon pepper

Fresh dill sprigs

> Place the potatoes in a large saucepan and cover
  with water. Bring to a boil. Reduce heat; simmer,
  uncovered, for 20-22 minutes or until tender.

> Meanwhile, in a food processor or blender,
  combine the cream cheese, salmon, onion, dill,
  lemon juice, salt and pepper. Cover and process
  until smooth; set aside.

> Drain potatoes and immediately place in ice
  water. Drain and pat dry with paper towels. Cut a
  thin slice off the bottom of each potato to allow
  it to sit flat. With a melon baller, scoop out a
  small amount of potato (discard or save for
  another use). Pipe or spoon salmon mixture into
  potatoes. Garnish with dill sprigs.

YIELD: 3 DOZEN

tangy mozzarella bites

JULIE WASEM, AURORA, NEBRASKA
*I adapted this recipe from one I found years ago,
substituting ingredients most people have on hand. I
like to serve it with crackers or small bread slices.*

1/4 cup olive oil

1 to 2 teaspoons balsamic vinegar

1 garlic clove, minced

1 teaspoon dried basil

1 teaspoon coarsely ground pepper

1 pound part-skim mozzarella cheese, cut into
1/2-inch cubes

> In a bowl, combine the oil, vinegar, garlic, basil
  and pepper. Add cheese; toss to coat. Cover and
  refrigerate for at least 1 hour.

YIELD: ABOUT 3 CUPS

MARGARET WILSON, SUN CITY, CALIFORNIA

This classic Italian combination of mozzarella, tomatoes and basil is dressed up with marinated artichokes. It looks so lovely on an appetizer buffet. Using fresh mozzarella is the key to its great taste.

artichoke caprese platter

2 jars (7-1/2 ounces each) marinated artichoke hearts

2 tablespoons red wine vinegar

2 tablespoons olive oil

6 plum tomatoes, sliced

2 balls (8 ounces each) fresh mozzarella cheese, halved and sliced

2 cups loosely packed fresh basil leaves

> Drain artichokes, reserving 1/2 cup marinade; cut artichokes in half. In a small bowl, whisk vinegar, oil and reserved marinade.

> On a large serving platter, arrange artichokes, tomatoes, mozzarella cheese and basil. Drizzle with vinaigrette. Serve immediately.

YIELD: 10-12 SERVINGS

> To serve, pour 1/4 cup of soup into 12 cordial glasses. Top each with a raspberry and 1/2 teaspoon sour cream.

YIELD: 12 SERVINGS

oriental pork tenderloin

DIANA BEYER, GRAHAM, WASHINGTON
I first made this appetizer on Christmas Eve a few years ago, and it has since become a tradition. Serve the pork slices alone or on small dinner rolls with hot mustard sauce, ketchup or horseradish.

1 cup soy sauce

1/2 cup packed brown sugar

2 tablespoons red wine vinegar

2 teaspoons red food coloring, optional

1 garlic clove, minced

1 teaspoon ground ginger

1 teaspoon salt

1/2 teaspoon pepper

3 pork tenderloins (about 1 pound each)

Sesame seeds, toasted

> In a bowl, combine the first eight ingredients; mix well. Remove 1/2 cup for basting; cover and refrigerate. Pour the remaining marinade into a large resealable plastic bag; add tenderloins. Seal bag and turn to coat; refrigerate overnight.

> Drain and discard marinade from pork. Place pork on a rack in a shallow roasting pan. Bake, uncovered, at 350° for 55-60 minutes or until a meat thermometer reads 160°, brushing with the reserved marinade every 15 minutes.

> Sprinkle with sesame seeds. Cool for 30 minutes. Refrigerate for 2 hours or overnight. Cut into thin slices.

YIELD: 8-10 SERVINGS

chilled raspberry soup

AMY WENGER, SEVERANCE, COLORADO
Family and friends enjoy sipping this lovely, chilled soup. I often use sugar substitute and reduced-fat sour cream to make it a little lighter.

1/3 cup cranberry juice

1/3 cup sugar

5-1/3 cups plus 12 fresh raspberries, divided

1-1/3 cups plus 2 tablespoons sour cream, divided

> In a blender, combine the cranberry juice, sugar and 5-1/3 cups raspberries; cover and process until blended. Strain and discard seeds. Stir in 1-1/3 cups sour cream. Cover and refrigerate for at least 2 hours.

salmon canapes

TRISTIN CRENSHAW, TUCSON, ARIZONA

My boyfriend's mother gave me the idea for this classy appetizer that I serve for Sunday brunch and special occasions like New Year's Eve. The textures and flavors of the dill, cream cheese and smoked salmon are scrumptious together. Spread on cocktail rye bread, it's sure to be the toast of your buffet!

1 package (8 ounces) reduced-fat cream cheese

1 teaspoon snipped fresh dill or 1/4 teaspoon dill weed

36 slices cocktail rye bread

12 ounces sliced smoked salmon

1 medium red onion, thinly sliced and separated into rings

Fresh dill sprigs, optional

> In a small mixing bowl, combine cream cheese and dill. Spread on rye bread. Top with salmon and red onion. Garnish with dill sprigs if desired.

YIELD: 12 SERVINGS

stuffed banana peppers

CATHY KIDD, MEDORA, INDIANA

I received this recipe from a customer while working at my sister's produce market. The peppers can be made a day in advance, making them great for get-togethers.

2 packages (8 ounces each) cream cheese, softened

1 envelope ranch salad dressing mix

1 cup (4 ounces) finely shredded cheddar cheese

5 bacon strips, cooked and crumbled

8 mild banana peppers (about 6 inches long), halved lengthwise and seeded

> In a small mixing bowl, combine the cream cheese, salad dressing mix, cheese and bacon until blended. Pipe or stuff into pepper halves. Cover and refrigerate until serving. Cut into 1-1/4-in. pieces.

YIELD: 8-10 SERVINGS

Editor's Note: When cutting or seeding banana peppers, use rubber or plastic gloves to protect your hands. Avoid touching your face.

nutty apple wedges

BEATRICE RICHARD, POSEN, MICHIGAN

A crunchy coating turns apples and peanut butter into a finger-licking snack. Even very young kids will have a blast spreading peanut butter on the apple wedges and rolling them in cornflake crumbs.

1 medium unpeeled tart apple, cored

1/2 cup peanut butter

1 cup crushed cornflakes

> Cut apple into 12 thin wedges. Spread peanut butter on cut sides; roll in the cornflakes.

YIELD: 4-6 SERVINGS

MELISSA CARAFA, BROOMALL, PENNSYLVANIA

Salmon creates an elegant appetizer in this vibrant recipe idea. It's simple to prepare and can even be made ahead of time.

salmon salad-stuffed endive leaves

1 salmon fillet (6 ounces), cooked and flaked

1/4 cup tartar sauce

2 teaspoons capers

1 teaspoon snipped fresh dill

1/4 teaspoon lemon-pepper seasoning

1 head Belgian endive (about 5 ounces), separated into leaves

Additional snipped fresh dill, optional

> In a small bowl, combine the salmon, tartar sauce, capers, dill and lemon-pepper. Spoon about 2 teaspoonfuls onto each endive leaf. Garnish with additional dill if desired. Refrigerate until serving.

YIELD: 14 APPETIZERS

tortellini appetizers

CHERYL LAMA, ROYAL OAK, MICHIGAN
The festive green and red of this treat will make it a welcomed addition to your holiday buffet table. Store-bought pesto keeps the preparation fast. I like to heat the garlic in a skillet and use skewers for a different look.

4 garlic cloves, peeled

2 tablespoons olive oil, divided

1 package (10 ounces) refrigerated spinach tortellini

1 cup mayonnaise

1/4 cup grated Parmesan cheese

1/4 cup milk

1/4 cup prepared pesto

1/8 teaspoon pepper

1 pint grape tomatoes

26 frilled toothpicks

> Place garlic cloves on a double thickness of heavy-duty foil; drizzle with 1 tablespoon oil. Wrap foil around garlic. Bake at 425° for 20-25 minutes or until tender. Cool for 10-15 minutes.

> Meanwhile, cook tortellini according to package directions; drain and rinse in cold water. Toss with remaining oil; set aside. In a small bowl, combine the mayonnaise, Parmesan cheese, milk, pesto and pepper. Mash garlic into pesto mixture; stir until combined.

> Alternately thread tortellini and tomatoes onto toothpicks. Serve with pesto dip. Refrigerate leftovers.

YIELD: ABOUT 2 DOZEN (1-1/2 CUPS DIP)

marinated mushrooms and cheese

KIM MARIE VAN RHEENEN, MENDOTA, ILLINOIS
I like to serve these savory mushrooms alongside sliced baguettes and crackers. They're colorful and so versatile. You might like to vary the cheese or add olives, artichokes or a little basil.

1/2 cup sun-dried tomatoes (not packed in oil), julienned

1 cup boiling water

1/2 cup olive oil

1/2 cup white wine vinegar

2 garlic cloves, minced

1/2 teaspoon salt

1/2 pound sliced fresh mushrooms

8 ounces Monterey Jack cheese, cubed

> In a small bowl, combine the tomatoes and water. Let stand for 5 minutes; drain. In a large resealable plastic bag, combine the oil, vinegar, garlic and salt; add the tomatoes, mushrooms and cheese. Seal bag and toss to coat. Refrigerate for at least 4 hours before serving. Drain and discard marinade.

YIELD: 12-14 SERVINGS

shrimp lover squares

ARDYCE PIEHL, POYNETTE, WISCONSIN

These delicious shrimp squares are part of an appetizer buffet I prepare for my family every Christmas. During the holidays, we enjoy having a variety of finger foods as a meal while playing a board game or watching a movie together.

1 tube (8 ounces) refrigerated crescent rolls

1 package (8 ounces) cream cheese, softened

1/4 cup sour cream

1/2 teaspoon dill weed

1/8 teaspoon salt

1/2 cup seafood sauce

24 cooked medium shrimp, peeled and deveined

1/2 cup chopped green pepper

1/3 cup chopped onion

1 cup (4 ounces) shredded Monterey Jack cheese

> In a greased 13-in. x 9-in. baking dish, unroll crescent dough into one long rectangle; seal seams and perforations. Bake at 375° for 10-12 minutes or until golden brown. Cool completely on a wire rack.

> In a small mixing bowl, beat the cream cheese, sour cream, dill and salt until smooth. Spread over crust. Top with seafood sauce, shrimp, green pepper, onion and cheese. Cover and refrigerate for 1 hour. Cut into squares.

YIELD: 2 DOZEN

crispy cheese twists

MARY MAXEINER, LAKEWOOD, COLORADO

My grown son enjoys these cheese twists so much that I'll often bake an extra batch just for him to eat. They make a great anytime snack.

6 tablespoons butter, softened

1 garlic clove, minced

1/8 teaspoon pepper

1 cup (4 ounces) shredded cheddar cheese

2 tablespoons milk

1 tablespoon minced fresh parsley

1 tablespoon snipped fresh dill or 1 teaspoon dill weed

1 cup all-purpose flour

> In a mixing bowl, combine the butter, garlic and pepper; beat until light and fluffy. Stir in cheese, milk, parsley and dill. Gradually add flour, mixing thoroughly.

> Divide dough into 20 pieces. Roll each piece into a 10-in. log; cut each in half and twist together. Place 1 in. apart on an ungreased baking sheet. Bake at 375° for 10-12 minutes or until golden brown. Remove to wire racks to cool.

YIELD: 20 TWISTS

 tip If you want to try making your own seafood sauce, try mixing together 1/4 cup ketchup, 1/4 cup chili sauce, 1/2 tablespoon lemon juice, 1/2 tablespoon prepared horseradish and 1/4 teaspoon hot pepper sauce.

pork pinwheels

MARY LOU WAYMAN, SALT LAKE CITY, UTAH
A flavorful filling peeks out from the swirled slices of pork. This treat is enhanced with garlic mayonnaise.

GARLIC MAYONNAISE:
1 large whole garlic bulb

2 teaspoons olive oil

1/2 cup mayonnaise

1 to 3 teaspoons milk, optional

STUFFING:
3 medium leeks (white portion only), thinly sliced

4 tablespoons olive oil, divided

1 cup minced fresh parsley

1/4 cup grated Parmesan cheese

1 tablespoon minced fresh thyme or 1 teaspoon dried thyme

1/4 teaspoon salt

1/4 teaspoon pepper

1/4 cup chopped walnuts

2 pork tenderloins (3/4 pound each)

> Remove the papery outer skin from garlic (do not peel or separate cloves). Cut top off garlic bulb. Brush with oil. Wrap bulb in heavy-duty foil. Bake at 425° for 30-35 minutes or until softened. Cool for 10-15 minutes. Squeeze softened garlic into a small bowl; mash until smooth. Stir in mayonnaise and milk if needed to achieve a creamy consistency. Cover and refrigerate for at least 3 hours.

> In a large skillet, saute leeks in 1 tablespoon oil until tender; remove from the heat. In a blender or food processor, combine the parsley, Parmesan cheese, thyme, salt and pepper. While processing, gradually add the remaining oil until creamy. Add walnuts and leek mixture; coarsely chop. Set aside.

> Make a lengthwise slit in each tenderloin to within 1/2 in. of the opposite side. Open tenderloins so they lie flat; cover with plastic wrap. Flatten to 3/4-in. thickness; remove plastic wrap. Spread leek mixture to within 1 in. of edges. Roll up from a long side; tie with kitchen string to secure. Place tenderloins seam down on a rack in a shallow roasting pan. Bake, uncovered, at 325° for 45-55 minutes or until a meat thermometer reads 160°. Let stand for 15 minutes. Cover and refrigerate. Discard string; cut pork into 1/2-in. slices. Serve with garlic mayonnaise.

YIELD: ABOUT 2-1/2 DOZEN

bacon-cheddar deviled eggs

LAURA LEMAY, DEERFIELD BEACH, FLORIDA
I created this recipe a few years ago when I was craving something different. I combined three of my favorite foods—bacon, eggs and cheese—in these deviled eggs. I've shared them at parties and have received many compliments.

12 hard-cooked eggs

1/2 cup mayonnaise

4 bacon strips, cooked and crumbled

2 tablespoons finely shredded cheddar cheese

1 tablespoon honey mustard

1/4 teaspoon pepper

> Slice eggs in half lengthwise; remove yolks and set whites aside. In a small bowl, mash yolks. Stir in the mayonnaise, bacon, cheese, mustard and pepper. Stuff or pipe into egg whites. Refrigerate until serving.

YIELD: 2 DOZEN

> In a blender or food processor, combine the mayonnaise, cream cheese, onion, chives, vinegar, Worcestershire sauce and seasonings. Cover and process until blended. Cover and refrigerate for 24 hours.

> Using a 2-1/2-in. biscuit cutter, cut out circles from bread slices. Spread mayonnaise mixture over bread; top with cucumber slices. Garnish with pimientos and dill.

YIELD: 2 DOZEN

italian olives

JEAN JOHNSON, RENO, NEVADA
A friend shared this recipe with me more than 25 years ago, and I still get raves when I set them out.

2 cans (6 ounces each) pitted ripe olives, drained

1 jar (5-3/4 ounces) pimiento-stuffed olives, drained

2 tablespoons finely chopped celery

2 tablespoons finely chopped onion

2 tablespoons capers, rinsed and drained

1/4 cup olive oil

2 tablespoons red wine vinegar

2 garlic cloves, minced

1 teaspoon dried basil

1 teaspoon dried oregano

1 teaspoon crushed red pepper flakes

1/4 teaspoon salt

> In a large bowl, combine the first five ingredients. In a small bowl, whisk the oil, vinegar, garlic, basil, oregano, pepper flakes and salt; pour over olive mixture; toss to coat.

> Cover and refrigerate for at least 3 hours before serving. Store in the refrigerator for up to 3 days.

YIELD: 4 CUPS

cucumber canapes

NADINE WHITTAKER, SOUTH PLYMOUTH, MASSACHUSETTS
I always get requests for the recipe whenever I serve these delicate finger sandwiches with a creamy herb spread and festive red and green garnishes.

1 cup mayonnaise

1 package (3 ounces) cream cheese, softened

1 tablespoon grated onion

1 tablespoon minced chives

1/2 teaspoon cider vinegar

1/2 teaspoon Worcestershire sauce

1 garlic clove, minced

1/4 teaspoon paprika

1/8 teaspoon curry powder

1/8 teaspoon each dried oregano, thyme, basil, parsley flakes and dill weed

1 loaf (1 pound) white or rye bread

2 medium cucumbers, scored and thinly sliced

Diced pimientos and additional dill weed

LEANN WILLIAMS, BEAVERTON, OREGON
Your tea tray will be beautiful with these lily-shaped sandwiches. The tasty chicken, mayonnaise and herb filling will delight guests at your next luncheon or shower.

calla lily tea sandwiches

1 can (4-1/2 ounces) chunk white chicken, drained

1 celery rib, finely chopped

1/4 cup mayonnaise

1 teaspoon grated onion

1/4 teaspoon dried tarragon

1/8 teaspoon pepper

18 slices white bread, crusts removed

2 tablespoons butter, softened

1 tablespoon minced fresh parsley

18 pieces (1 inch each) julienned carrot

> In a small bowl, combine the first six ingredients; set aside. With a rolling pin, flatten each slice of bread to 1/8-in. thickness; cut into 2-1/2-in. squares. Spread with butter. Roll up into a funnel shape, overlapping the two adjacent sides; secure with a toothpick.

> Spoon about 1 teaspoon chicken filling into each sandwich. Cover with plastic wrap; refrigerate for 1 hour.

> Remove toothpicks. Sprinkle sandwiches with parsley. For the spadix, insert a carrot piece in the center of each lily.

YIELD: 1-1/2 DOZEN

savory cheese cutouts

J.R. SMOSNA, WARREN, PENNSYLVANIA
This recipe is always a success because the dough is easy to work with and cuts well. They can be made year-round using cookie cutter shapes to suit the season.

2 cups all-purpose flour

1 cup (4 ounces) shredded Swiss cheese

1 teaspoon sugar

1 teaspoon salt

1/2 teaspoon ground mustard

1/8 to 1/4 teaspoon cayenne pepper

1/2 cup plus 2 tablespoons cold butter

9 tablespoons dry white wine or chicken broth

1 egg, lightly beaten

Sesame seeds and/or poppy seeds

> In a bowl, combine the first six ingredients; cut in butter until the mixture resembles coarse crumbs. Gradually add wine or broth, tossing with a fork until dough forms a ball.

> On a lightly floured surface, roll out dough to 1/8-in. thickness. Cut with floured 2-in. cookie cutters. Place 1 in. apart on ungreased baking sheets.

> Brush tops with egg; sprinkle with sesame and/or poppy seeds. Bake at 400° for 10-12 minutes or until lightly browned. Remove to wire racks to cool.

YIELD: 6 DOZEN

white bean bruschetta

KRISTIN ARNETT, ELKHORN, WISCONSIN
This fabulous bruschetta has a Tuscan flavor. I've made it many times to serve when entertaining guests because it's quick and easy.

1 cup canned great northern beans, rinsed and drained

3 plum tomatoes, seeded and chopped

1/4 cup chopped pitted Greek olives

6 tablespoons olive oil, divided

1/4 cup fresh basil leaves, cut into strips

1 tablespoon minced garlic

Salt and pepper to taste

1 French bread baguette, cut into 1/3-inch-thick slices

1 package (5.3 ounces) goat cheese

> In a medium bowl, combine the beans, tomatoes, olives, 4 tablespoons oil, basil, garlic, salt and pepper. Place bread slices on an ungreased baking sheet. Brush with remaining oil.

> Broil 3-4 in. from the heat until golden, about 1 minute. Spread with cheese; top with bean mixture. Serve immediately.

YIELD: ABOUT 20 SERVINGS

party puffs

KAREN OWEN, RISING SUN, INDIANA
For a substantial appetizer, you can't go wrong with mini sandwiches. Instead of serving egg or ham salad on ordinary bread, I like to use my simple homemade puff pastry.

1 cup water

1/2 cup butter

1 cup all-purpose flour

4 eggs

EGG SALAD FILLING:
6 hard-cooked eggs, chopped

1/3 cup mayonnaise

3 tablespoons chutney, finely chopped

2 green onions, finely chopped

1 teaspoon salt

1/2 teaspoon curry powder

HAM SALAD FILLING:
1 can (4-1/4 ounces) deviled ham

1 package (3 ounces) cream cheese, softened

2 tablespoons finely chopped green pepper

1-1/2 teaspoons prepared horseradish

1 teaspoon lemon juice

> In a saucepan over medium heat, bring water and butter to a boil. Add flour all at once and stir until a smooth ball forms. Remove from the heat; let stand for 5 minutes.

> Add eggs, one at a time, beating well after each addition. Continue beating until mixture is smooth and shiny. Drop by teaspoonfuls 2 in. apart onto greased baking sheets.

> Bake at 400° for 20-25 minutes or until lightly browned. Remove to wire racks. Immediately cut a slit in each puff to allow steam to escape; cool completely.

> In separate bowls, combine the ingredients for egg salad filling and ham salad filling. Split puffs and remove soft dough from inside. Just before serving, spoon filling into puffs; replace tops. Refrigerate the leftovers.

YIELD: 7-1/2 DOZEN

cream-filled strawberries

KARIN POROSLAY, WESLEY CHAPEL, FLORIDA
These plump berries filled with a creamy pudding mixture are so elegant-looking and luscious-tasting that they're perfect for parties or holiday gatherings.

18 large fresh strawberries

1 cup cold fat-free milk

1 package (1 ounce) sugar-free instant vanilla pudding mix

2 cups reduced-fat whipped topping

1/4 teaspoon almond extract

> Remove stems from strawberries; cut a deep X in the top of each berry. Spread berries apart.

> In a bowl, whisk milk and pudding mix for 2 minutes. Fold in whipped topping and almond extract. Pipe or spoon about 5 teaspoons into each berry. Chill until serving.

YIELD: 18 STRAWBERRIES

MARY JANE GUEST, ALAMOSA, COLORADO

These easy shrimp look impressive on a buffet table and taste even better! The zesty sauce has a wonderful, spicy citrus flavor. I especially like this recipe because I can prepare it ahead of time.

zesty marinated shrimp

1/2 cup vegetable oil

1/2 cup lime juice

1/2 cup thinly sliced red onion

12 lemon slices

1 tablespoon minced fresh parsley

1/2 teaspoon salt

1/2 teaspoon dill weed

1/8 teaspoon hot pepper sauce

2 pounds medium shrimp, cooked, peeled and deveined

> In a large bowl, combine the first eight ingredients. Stir in shrimp. Cover and refrigerate for 4 hours, stirring occasionally. Drain before serving.

YIELD: 12 SERVINGS

artichoke crostini

JANNE ROWE, WICHITA, KANSAS
This appetizer is always wonderful when vine-ripened tomatoes are at their best. I often rely on these no-stress, fresh-tasting slices for parties and other events.

1 sourdough baguette (1 pound)

2 cups chopped seeded tomatoes

1 can (14 ounces) water-packed artichoke hearts, rinsed, drained and chopped

2 tablespoons minced fresh basil

2 tablespoons olive oil

1/2 teaspoon seasoned salt

1/8 teaspoon pepper

> Cut the baguette into 32 slices. Place on an ungreased baking sheet; spritz bread with cooking spray. Bake at 325° for 7-10 minutes or until crisp. Cool on a wire rack.

> In a bowl, combine the tomatoes, artichokes, basil, oil, seasoned salt and pepper. Spoon onto bread slices.

YIELD: 32 APPETIZERS

antipasto kabobs

DENISE HAZEN, CINCINNATI, OHIO
My husband and I met at a cooking class, and we have loved creating menus and entertaining ever since. These do-ahead kabobs are always a hit.

1 package (9 ounces) refrigerated cheese tortellini

40 pimiento-stuffed olives

40 large pitted ripe olives

3/4 cup Italian salad dressing

40 thin slices pepperoni

20 thin slices hard salami, halved

> Cook tortellini according to package directions; drain and rinse in cold water.

> In a resealable plastic bag, combine the tortellini, olives and salad dressing. Seal and refrigerate for 4 hours or overnight.

> Drain and discard dressing. For each appetizer, thread a stuffed olive, folded pepperoni slice, tortellini, folded salami piece and ripe olive on a toothpick or short skewer.

YIELD: 40 APPETIZERS

marinated mozzarella

PEGGY CAIRO, KENOSHA, WISCONSIN

I always come home with an empty container when I bring this dish to a party—and I've used the recipe for years. It can be made ahead to free up time later. I serve it with pretty party picks for a festive look.

1/3 cup olive oil

1 tablespoon chopped oil-packed sun-dried tomatoes

1 tablespoon minced fresh parsley

1 teaspoon crushed red pepper flakes

1 teaspoon dried basil

1 teaspoon minced chives

1/4 teaspoon garlic powder

1 pound cubed part-skim mozzarella cheese

> In a large resealable plastic bag, combine the first seven ingredients; add cheese cubes. Seal bag and turn to coat; refrigerate for at least 30 minutes.

> Transfer to a serving dish; serve with toothpicks.

YIELD: 8-10 SERVINGS

chicken ham pinwheels

LAURA MAHAFFEY, ANNAPOLIS, MARYLAND

These pretty pinwheels have been a part of our appetizer buffet for many years. I love them because they can be made a day in advance and taste great alone or served with crackers.

4 boneless skinless chicken breast halves

1/8 teaspoon plus 1/2 teaspoon dried basil, divided

1/8 teaspoon salt

1/8 teaspoon garlic salt

1/8 teaspoon pepper

4 thin slices deli ham

2 teaspoons lemon juice

Paprika

1/2 cup mayonnaise

1 teaspoon grated orange peel

1 teaspoon orange juice

> Flatten chicken to 1/4-in. thickness. Combine 1/8 teaspoon basil, salt, garlic salt and pepper; sprinkle over chicken. Top each with a ham slice.

> Roll up jelly-roll style; place seam side down in a greased 11-in. x 7-in. baking dish. Drizzle with lemon juice and sprinkle with paprika. Bake, uncovered, at 350° for 30 minutes or until chicken juices run clear. Cover and refrigerate.

> Meanwhile, in a bowl, combine the mayonnaise, orange peel, orange juice and remaining basil. Cover and refrigerate until serving. Cut chicken rolls into 1/2-in. slices. Serve with orange spread.

YIELD: 24 SERVINGS

tip Prepare a few extra batches of Marinated Mozzarella and divide among small glass jars. Tuck each jar into a pretty basket along with a small loaf of bread or some crackers to give away as unique party favors. After eating the cheese, the oil can be used for cooking.

shrimp salad on endive

TASTE OF HOME TEST KITCHEN
This simple-to-prepare shrimp salad is served on endive leaves for a from-the-sea version of lettuce wraps.

1/3 cup mayonnaise

1/2 teaspoon lemon juice

1/4 teaspoon dill weed

1/4 teaspoon seafood seasoning

1/8 teaspoon salt

1/8 teaspoon pepper

1/2 pound cooked shrimp, chopped

1 green onion, sliced

2 tablespoons chopped celery

1 tablespoon diced pimientos

2 heads Belgian endive, separated into leaves

> In a small bowl, combine the first six ingredients. Stir in the shrimp, onion, celery and pimientos. Spoon 1 tablespoonful onto each endive leaf; arrange on a platter. Refrigerate until serving.

YIELD: ABOUT 1-1/2 DOZEN

stuffed pepperoncinis

JEANI ROBINSON, WEIRTON, WEST VIRGINIA
To reduce some of the juice in these spicy appetizers, I drain the pepperoncinis for about 3 hours on paper towels before stuffing. This recipe makes a big batch, which is perfect for parties.

1 cup grated Parmesan cheese

1 medium tomato, cut into wedges

1 can (2-1/4 ounces) sliced ripe olives, drained

1/2 cup chopped pepperoni

1/4 cup chopped salami

1/4 cup cubed fully cooked ham

1/4 cup shredded cheddar cheese

1/4 cup shredded Monterey Jack or pepper Jack cheese

1/4 cup zesty Italian salad dressing

2 jars (24 ounces each) whole pepperoncinis, drained

Additional grated Parmesan cheese

> In a food processor, combine the first nine ingredients; cover and process until finely chopped.

> Cut off the stem end of each pepperoncini; remove seeds. Pipe or stuff pepperoncinis with cheese mixture. Dip exposed end into additional Parmesan cheese. Cover and refrigerate until serving.

YIELD: ABOUT 4 DOZEN

Editor's Note: When cutting hot peppers, disposable gloves are recommended. Avoid touching your face.

tip

To save time when preparing Shrimp Salad on Endive, stop by the deli at your grocery store and pick up some pre-made shrimp salad. Simply fill the endive with the salad and garnish with dill weed or minced parsley.

A homemade cucumber-yogurt sauce complements tender slices of beef in this recipe. Since both the meat and sauce are made in advance, this recipe requires very little last-minute preparation.

beef canapes with cucumber sauce

4 cups (32 ounces) plain yogurt

1 whole beef tenderloin (1-1/2 pounds)

2 tablespoons olive oil, divided

1 teaspoon salt, divided

1/4 teaspoon plus 1/8 teaspoon white pepper, divided

1 medium cucumber, peeled, seeded and diced

1 tablespoon finely chopped onion

1 garlic clove, minced

1 tablespoon white vinegar

1 French bread baguette (1 pound), cut into 36 thin slices

1 cup fresh arugula

> Line a fine mesh strainer with two layers of cheesecloth; place over a bowl. Place yogurt in strainer. Cover and refrigerate for at least 4 hours or overnight.

> Rub tenderloin with 1 tablespoon oil. Sprinkle with 1/2 teaspoon salt and 1/4 teaspoon white pepper. In a large skillet, cook the beef tenderloin over medium-high heat until browned on all sides. Transfer meat to a shallow roasting pan. Bake at 400° for 25-30 minutes or until a meat thermometer reads 145°. Cool on a wire rack for 1 hour. Cover and refrigerate.

> Transfer yogurt from strainer to another bowl (discard yogurt liquid). Add the cucumber, onion, garlic and remaining salt and white pepper. In a small bowl, whisk the vinegar and remaining oil; stir into yogurt mixture.

> Thinly slice tenderloin. Spread yogurt mixture over bread slices; top with beef and arugula. Serve immediately or cover and refrigerate until serving.

YIELD: 3 DOZEN

asian spring rolls

NIRVANA HARRIS, MUNDELEIN, ILLINOIS
*The peanut dipping sauce is slightly spicy but pairs
well with these traditional vegetable-filled spring rolls.*

3 tablespoons lime juice

1 tablespoon hoisin sauce

1 teaspoon sugar

1 teaspoon salt

3 ounces uncooked Asian rice noodles

1 large carrot, grated

1 medium cucumber, peeled, seeded and julienned

1 medium jalapeno pepper, seeded and chopped

1/3 cup chopped dry roasted peanuts

8 spring roll wrappers or rice papers (8 inches)

1/2 cup loosely packed fresh cilantro

PEANUT SAUCE:
2 garlic cloves, minced

1/2 to 1 teaspoon crushed red pepper flakes

2 teaspoons vegetable oil

1/4 cup hoisin sauce

1/4 cup creamy peanut butter

2 tablespoons tomato paste

1/2 cup hot water

> In a small bowl, combine the lime juice, hoisin sauce and sugar; set aside. In a large saucepan, bring 2 qts. water and salt to a boil. Add noodles; cook for 2-3 minutes or until tender. Drain and rinse with cold water. Transfer to a bowl and toss with 2 tablespoons reserved lime juice mixture; set aside. In another bowl, combine carrot, cucumber, jalapeno and peanuts. Toss with remaining lime juice mixture; set aside.

> Soak the spring roll wrappers in cool water for 5 minutes. Carefully separate and place on a flat surface. Top each with several cilantro leaves. Place 1/4 cup carrot mixture and 1/4 cup noodles down the center of each wrapper to within 1-1/2 in. of ends. Fold both ends over filling; fold one long side over the filling, then carefully roll up tightly. Place seam side down on serving plate. Cover with damp paper towels and refrigerate until serving.

> In a small saucepan, cook garlic and pepper flakes in oil for 2 minutes. Add the remaining sauce ingredients; cook and stir until combined and thickened. Serve with spring rolls.

YIELD: 8 SPRING ROLLS (1 CUP SAUCE)

Editor's Note: When cutting hot peppers, disposable gloves are recommended. Avoid touching your face.

fruit 'n' cheese kabobs

TASTE OF HOME TEST KITCHEN
*This simple, nutritious snack is a snap to put together,
much to the delight of busy cooks!*

1 block (1 pound) Colby-Monterey Jack cheese

1 block (1 pound) cheddar cheese

1 block (1 pound) baby Swiss cheese

1 fresh pineapple, peeled, cored and cut into 2-inch chunks

1 to 2 pounds seedless green or red grapes

3 pints strawberries

> Cut cheese into chunks or slices. If desired, cut into shapes with small cutters. Alternately thread cheese and fruit onto wooden skewers. Serve immediately.

YIELD: ABOUT 3 DOZEN

potato salad bites

STEPHANIE SHERIDAN, PLAINFIELD, VERMONT
Potatoes make the perfect platform for this colorful potato salad. They are just two or three bites, so you don't need a fork.

10 small red potatoes

1/4 cup chopped pimiento-stuffed olives

2 teaspoons minced fresh parsley

1 teaspoon finely chopped onion

1/2 cup mayonnaise

1-3/4 teaspoons Dijon mustard

1/8 teaspoon pepper

1/4 teaspoon salt

Paprika

Parsley sprigs, optional

> Place the potatoes in a saucepan and cover with water. Bring to a boil. Reduce heat; cover and cook for 12-15 minutes or until tender. Drain and immediately place potatoes in ice water; drain and pat dry.

> Peel two potatoes; finely dice and place in a small bowl. Cut the remaining potatoes in half. With a melon baller, scoop out pulp, leaving a 3/8-in. shell; set shells aside. Dice pulp and add to the bowl. Stir in the olives, parsley and onion. Combine the mayonnaise, mustard and pepper; gently stir into potato mixture.

> Sprinkle potato shells with salt; stuff with potato salad. Sprinkle with paprika. Refrigerate for at least 1 hour before serving. Garnish with parsley if desired.

YIELD: 16 APPETIZERS

shrimp 'n' snow pea wrap-ups

EARNESTINE JACKSON, BEAUMONT, TEXAS
This variation on marinated shrimp gets a splash of color from the snow peas.

1 cup oil and vinegar salad dressing

1 teaspoon minced fresh gingerroot

1 garlic clove, minced

1 pound cooked medium shrimp, peeled and deveined (about 36)

2 cups water

4 ounces fresh snow peas (about 36)

> In a large bowl, combine the salad dressing, ginger and garlic. Stir in shrimp; cover and refrigerate for 2 hours.

> Meanwhile, in a small saucepan, bring water to a boil. Add snow peas; cover and boil for 1 minute. Drain and immediately place peas in ice water; drain and pat dry.

> Drain and discard marinade from shrimp. Wrap a snow pea around each shrimp; secure with a toothpick. Chill until serving.

YIELD: ABOUT 3 DOZEN

red pepper bruschetta

TASTE OF HOME TEST KITCHEN
Roasted red peppers take the place of tomatoes in this twist on traditional bruschetta. If your bakery doesn't offer baguettes, buy regular French bread instead and cut the slices in half to create these crunchy snacks.

1 whole garlic bulb

1 teaspoon plus 2 tablespoons olive oil, divided

2 medium sweet red peppers, halved and seeded

3 tablespoons minced fresh parsley

2 tablespoons minced fresh basil or 2 teaspoons dried basil

1 tablespoon lemon juice

1/2 teaspoon salt

1/4 teaspoon pepper

1 French bread baguette (about 12 ounces)

> Remove papery outer skin from garlic bulb (do not peel or separate cloves). Brush with 1 teaspoon oil. Wrap in heavy-duty foil. Bake at 425° for 30-35 minutes or until softened. Cool.

> Broil red peppers 4 in. from the heat until skins blister, about 10 minutes. Immediately place peppers in a bowl; cover with plastic wrap and let stand for 15-20 minutes.

> Peel off and discard charred skin from peppers and coarsely chop. Cut top off garlic head, leaving root end intact. Squeeze softened garlic from bulb and finely chop.

> In a bowl, combine the parsley, basil, lemon juice, salt, pepper and remaining oil. Add peppers and garlic; mix well. Cut bread into 16 slices, 1/2 in. thick; broil until lightly toasted. Top with pepper mixture. Serve immediately.

YIELD: 8 SERVINGS

antipasto platter

TERI LINDQUIST, GURNEE, ILLINOIS
Here's a delicious change of pace from items you will usually find on a buffet. We entertain often, and this is one of our favorite party pleasers.

1 jar (32 ounces) pepperoncinis, drained

1 can (15 ounces) garbanzo beans or chickpeas, rinsed and drained

2 cups halved fresh mushrooms

2 cups halved cherry tomatoes

1/2 pound provolone cheese, cubed

1 can (6 ounces) pitted ripe olives, drained

1 package (31/2 ounces) sliced pepperoni

1 bottle (8 ounces) Italian vinaigrette dressing

Lettuce leaves

> In a large bowl, combine the peppers, beans, mushrooms, tomatoes, cheese, olives and pepperoni. Pour vinaigrette over mixture; toss to coat. Refrigerate for at least 30 minutes or overnight. Arrange on a lettuce-lined platter. Serve with toothpicks.

YIELD: 14-16 SERVINGS

all wrapped up

vegetable spiral sticks

TERI ALBRECHT, MT. AIRY, MARYLAND

I love to serve these savory wrapped vegetable sticks for parties or special occasions. They're always a simple but impressive appetizer.

3 medium carrots

12 fresh asparagus spears, trimmed

1 tube (11 ounces) refrigerated breadsticks

1 egg white, beaten

1/4 cup grated Parmesan cheese

1/2 teaspoon dried oregano

> Cut carrots lengthwise into quarters. In a large skillet, bring 2 in. of water to a boil. Add carrots; cook for 3 minutes. Add asparagus; cook 2-3 minutes longer. Drain and rinse with cold water; pat dry.

> Cut each piece of breadstick dough in half. Roll each piece into a 7-in. rope. Wrap one rope in a spiral around each vegetable. Place on a baking sheet coated with cooking spray; tuck ends of dough under vegetables to secure.

> Brush with egg white. Combine Parmesan cheese and oregano; sprinkle over sticks. Bake at 375° for 12-14 minutes or until golden brown. Serve warm.

YIELD: 2 DOZEN

tip

The peak months for buying asparagus are April and May, and you should look for firm, straight, uniform-size spears. It's best to use asparagus within a few days of purchase, but you can refrigerate bundled stalks upright in a bowl filled with 1 inch of water. Or wrap the cut ends in moist paper towels, cover the towels with plastic wrap and refrigerate. To clean, soak asparagus in cold water. Cut or snap off the tough white portion before using.

party pesto pinwheels

KATHLEEN FARRELL, ROCHESTER, NEW YORK

I took a couple of my favorite recipes and combined them into these delicious hors d'oeuvres. My easy-to-make snacks are wonderful.

1 tube (8 ounces) refrigerated crescent rolls

1/3 cup prepared pesto sauce

1/4 cup roasted sweet red peppers, drained and chopped

1/4 cup grated Parmesan cheese

1 cup pizza sauce, warmed

> Unroll crescent dough into two long rectangles; seal seams and perforations. Spread each with pesto; sprinkle with red peppers and Parmesan cheese.

> Roll each up jelly-roll style, starting with a short side. With a sharp knife, cut each roll into 10 slices. Place cut side down 2 in. apart on two ungreased baking sheets.

> Bake at 400° for 8-10 minutes or until golden brown. Serve warm with pizza sauce.

YIELD: 20 SERVINGS

STEPHANIE HOWARD, OAKLAND, CALIFORNIA
This recipe is so good, no one will guess how quickly you put it together. These little bites are delicious and oh-so-easy!

crab crescents

1 tube (8 ounces) refrigerated crescent rolls

3 tablespoons prepared pesto

1/2 cup fresh crabmeat

> Unroll crescent dough; separate into eight triangles. Cut each triangle in half lengthwise, forming two triangles. Spread 1/2 teaspoon pesto over each triangle; place 1 rounded teaspoonful of crab along the wide end of each triangle.

> Roll up triangles from the wide ends and place point side down 1 in. apart on an ungreased baking sheet.

> Bake at 375° for 10-12 minutes or until golden brown. Serve warm.

YIELD: 16 APPETIZERS

veggie shrimp egg rolls

CAROLE RESNICK, CLEVELAND, OHIO

These wonderful appetizers will be the hit of your next party. They're versatile in that you can also use cooked crab, lobster or chicken.

2 teaspoons minced fresh gingerroot

1 garlic clove, minced

3 tablespoons olive oil, divided

1/2 pound uncooked medium shrimp, peeled, deveined and chopped

2 green onions, finely chopped

1 medium carrot, finely chopped

1 medium sweet red pepper, finely chopped

1 cup canned bean sprouts, rinsed and finely chopped

2 tablespoons water

2 tablespoons reduced-sodium soy sauce

38 wonton wrappers

DIPPING SAUCE:

3/4 cup apricot spreadable fruit

1 tablespoon water

1 tablespoon lime juice

1 tablespoon reduced-sodium soy sauce

1-1/2 teaspoons Dijon mustard

1/4 teaspoon minced fresh gingerroot

> In a large skillet, saute ginger and garlic in 1 tablespoon oil over medium heat until tender. Add the shrimp, onions, carrot, red pepper, bean sprouts, water and soy sauce; cook and stir for 2-3 minutes or vegetables are crisp-tender and shrimp turn pink. Reduce heat to low; cook for 4-5 minutes or until most of the liquid has evaporated. Remove from the heat; let stand for 15 minutes.

> Place a tablespoonful of shrimp mixture in the center of a wonton wrapper. (Keep wrappers covered with a damp paper towel until ready to use.) Fold bottom corner over filling. Fold sides toward center over filling. Moisten remaining corner with water; roll up tightly to seal.

> In a large skillet over medium heat, cook egg rolls, a few at a time, in remaining oil for 5-7 minutes on each side or until golden brown. Drain on paper towels.

> In a blender or food processor, combine the sauce ingredients; cover and process until smooth. Serve with egg rolls.

YIELD: 38 EGG ROLLS

 tip Wonton wrappers are delicate and dry out quickly. To avoid having them dry out and crack, place a clean damp towel over the opened package of wontons while using them. Use an additional damp towel over the finished wontons until cooking or serving.

> In a skillet, cook the beef, onion, salt and pepper over medium heat until meat is no longer pink; drain. Add the beans, cheese, salsa and jalapenos. Cook and stir over low heat until the cheese is melted. Remove mixture from the heat; cool for 10 minutes.

> Place a teaspoonful of beef mixture in the center of one wonton wrapper. Moisten edges with water. Fold wontons in half, forming a triangle. Repeat.

> In an electric skillet or deep-fat fryer, heat 1 in. of oil to 375°. Fry wontons, a few at a time, for 2-3 minutes or until golden brown. Drain on paper towels. Serve warm with salsa.

YIELD: ABOUT 7-1/2 DOZEN

Editor's Note: Fill wonton wrappers a few at a time, keeping the others covered with a damp paper towel until ready to use.

southwestern appetizer triangles

SHELIA POPE, PRESTON, IDAHO
A nifty cross between egg rolls and tacos, these triangles are great to serve. My mom created the recipe years ago, much to the delight of my family. Since I began making them, my husband insists we have them on Sundays during football season as well as for special celebrations.

1 pound ground beef

1 medium onion, chopped

Salt and pepper to taste

1 can (16 ounces) refried beans

1-1/2 cups (6 ounces) shredded cheddar cheese

1 cup salsa

1 can (4 ounces) diced jalapeno peppers, drained

2 packages (12 ounces each) wonton wrappers

Oil for deep-fat frying

Additional salsa

olive-cheese nuggets

LAVONNE HARTEL, WILLISTON, NORTH DAKOTA
More than 20 years ago, I tried these olive-stuffed morsels at a holiday party. Friends are still asking me to bring them to get-togethers.

2 cups (8 ounces) shredded cheddar cheese

1-1/4 cups all-purpose flour

1/2 cup butter, melted

1/2 teaspoon paprika

36 pimiento-stuffed olives

> In a small mixing bowl, beat cheese, flour, butter and paprika until blended. Pat olives dry; shape 1 teaspoon of cheese mixture around each.

> Place 2 in. apart on ungreased baking sheets. Bake at 400° for 12-15 minutes or until golden brown.

YIELD: 3 DOZEN

pizza turnovers

JANET CROUCH, THREE HILLS, ALBERTA
These little pizza bundles are a real crowd-pleaser. Plus, they can be made ahead and frozen, so you don't have to worry about last-minute preparation.

3 tablespoons chopped fresh mushrooms

2 tablespoons chopped green pepper

2 tablespoons chopped onion

1 tablespoon butter

5 tablespoons tomato paste

2 tablespoons water

1/2 teaspoon dried oregano

1/8 teaspoon garlic powder

1/2 cup shredded part-skim mozzarella cheese

1 package (15 ounces) refrigerated pie pastry

1 egg, lightly beaten

tip Keeping an appetizer or two in the freezer means you're always ready to entertain. Pizza Turnovers may be frozen, unbaked, for up to 2 months. Before serving, bake at 425° for 16-18 minutes or until golden brown and heated through.

> In a small saucepan, saute the mushrooms, green pepper and onion in butter until tender. Add the tomato paste, water, oregano and garlic powder. Reduce heat to medium-low. Stir in cheese until melted. Remove from the heat.

> Cut 3-1/2-in. circles from pie pastry. Place 1 teaspoon filling in the center of each circle. Brush edges of dough with water. Fold each circle in half; seal edges with a fork. Brush the tops with beaten egg. Place the turnovers on a greased baking sheet.

> Bake at 425° for 12-14 minutes or until turnovers are golden brown.

YIELD: 14 TURNOVERS

corn dog snacks

LINDA KNOPP, CAMAS, WASHINGTON
I dress up frozen corn dogs to make tasty bite-size treats. Just slice 'em and spread 'em with pizza sauce and other toppings for a fun snack for kids or an easy appetizer for adults.

1 package (16 ounces) frozen corn dogs, thawed

1/2 cup pizza sauce

3 tablespoons chopped ripe olives

1 jar (4-1/2 ounces) sliced mushrooms, drained

1/4 cup shredded part-skim mozzarella cheese

> Remove stick from each corn dog; cut into 1-in. slices. Place on an ungreased baking sheet. Spread with pizza sauce. Top with olives, mushrooms and cheese.

> Bake at 350° for 15-20 minutes or until the cheese is melted and corn dogs are heated through.

YIELD: 30 SNACKS

taquitos with salsa

TASTE OF HOME TEST KITCHEN
We jazzed up store-bought quesadilla rolls from the freezer section with a zippy salsa that's always a breeze to stir up.

2 packages (9 ounces each) frozen steak quesadilla rolls

1 jar (16 ounces) lime-garlic salsa

1 can (10 ounces) diced tomatoes and green chilies, drained

2 green onions, thinly sliced

2 tablespoons minced fresh parsley

2 tablespoons minced fresh cilantro

2 teaspoons minced garlic

1/2 teaspoon onion salt

1/2 teaspoon pepper

> Prepare quesadilla rolls according to package directions for microwave cooking. Meanwhile, for salsa, combine the remaining ingredients in a small bowl. Serve with quesadilla rolls.

YIELD: 1 DOZEN (2-1/2 CUPS SALSA)

korean wontons

CHRISTY LEE, HORSHAM, PENNSYLVANIA
Korean wontons (mandoo) are not hot and spicy like many of the traditional Korean dishes. The fried dumplings, filled with vegetables and beef, are easy to prepare, and the ingredients are inexpensive.

2 cups shredded cabbage

1 cup canned bean sprouts

1/2 cup shredded carrots

1-1/2 teaspoons plus 2 tablespoons vegetable oil, divided

1/3 pound ground beef

1/3 cup sliced green onions

1-1/2 teaspoons sesame seeds, toasted

1-1/2 teaspoons minced fresh gingerroot

3 garlic cloves, minced

1-1/2 teaspoons sesame oil

1/2 teaspoon salt

1/2 teaspoon pepper

1 package (12 ounces) wonton wrappers

1 egg, lightly beaten

3 tablespoons water

> In a wok or large skillet, stir-fry cabbage, bean sprouts and carrots in 1-1/2 teaspoons oil until tender; set aside. In a skillet, cook beef over medium heat until no longer pink; drain. Add to vegetable mixture. Stir in onions, sesame seeds, ginger, garlic, sesame oil, salt and pepper.

> Place about 1 tablespoon of filling in the center of each wonton wrapper. Combine egg and water. Moisten wonton edges with egg mixture; fold opposite corners over filling and press to seal. Heat remaining vegetable oil in a large skillet. Cook the wontons in batches for 1-2 minutes on each side or until golden brown, adding additional oil if needed.

YIELD: 5 DOZEN

Editor's Note: Fill wonton wrappers a few at a time, keeping the others covered with a damp paper towel until ready to use.

> Cut each roll into seven pieces. Place cut side down 1 in. apart on greased baking sheets. Combine butter and garlic powder; brush over spirals. Bake at 375° for 10-12 minutes or until golden brown.

YIELD: 28 APPETIZERS

curried chicken triangles

ANNE MARIE CARDILINO, KETTERING, OHIO

Plain refrigerated crescent rolls shape up into these time-saving treats. Serve the savory triangles warm, then stand back and watch them vanish.

2 tubes (8 ounces each) refrigerated crescent rolls

1 can (8 ounces) sliced water chestnuts, drained and chopped

1 cup (4 ounces) shredded Swiss cheese

1/2 cup chopped green onions

1/3 cup mayonnaise

1 teaspoon lemon juice

1/2 teaspoon curry powder

1/2 teaspoon garlic salt

1 can (5 ounces) chunk white chicken, undrained

Paprika, optional

> Separate crescent dough into triangles. Cut each piece into four triangles. Place on greased baking sheets. In a large bowl, combine the water chestnuts, cheese, onions, mayonnaise, lemon juice, curry powder and garlic salt. Crumble chicken over mayonnaise mixture; stir to coat.

> Place rounded teaspoonfuls in the center of each triangle. Sprinkle with paprika if desired. Bake at 350° for 12-15 minutes or until edges are lightly browned. Serve warm.

YIELD: 64 APPETIZERS

asparagus ham spirals

LINDA FISCHER, STUTTGART, ARKANSAS

These appealing appetizers are sure to be a hit at your next party. I'm on the arts council in our small town, so I came up with this snack recipe to serve at some of the events we cater. People will think you really fussed over these yummy bites!

8 fresh asparagus spears, trimmed

1 tube (8 ounces) refrigerated crescent rolls

1 carton (8 ounces) spreadable chive-and-onion cream cheese

4 thin rectangular slices deli ham

2 tablespoons butter, melted

1/4 teaspoon garlic powder

> Place asparagus in a skillet; add 1/2 in. of water. Bring to a boil. Reduced heat; cover and simmer for 3-5 minutes or until crisp-tender. Drain and set aside.

> Separate crescent dough into four rectangles; seal perforations. Spread cream cheese over each rectangle to within 1/4 in. of edges. Top each with ham, leaving 1/4 in. uncovered on one long side. Place two asparagus spears along the long side with the ham; roll up and press seam to seal.

BENNY DIAZ, AZUSA, CALIFORNIA
Tender bits of lobster are nestled in golden puff pastry for an easy, elegant appetizer. Get ready to hand out the recipe to guests.

puffy lobster turnovers

1 cup chopped fresh lobster meat

1/4 cup finely chopped onion

1 teaspoon minced fresh basil

1 teaspoon minced fresh thyme

1 teaspoon paprika

1 garlic clove, minced

1 teaspoon tomato paste

1/8 teaspoon salt

1/8 teaspoon pepper

2 packages (17.3 ounces each) frozen puff pastry, thawed

1 egg, lightly beaten

> In a small skillet, combine the first nine ingredients. Cook and stir over medium heat for 4-5 minutes or until lobster is firm and opaque; set aside.

> Unfold puff pastry. Using a 4-in. round cookie cutter, cut out four circles. Place on a greased baking sheet. Repeat with remaining pastries. Spoon 1 tablespoon lobster mixture in the center of each circle. Brush edges with egg; fold dough over filling. Press edges to seal.

> Bake at 400° for 8-10 minutes or until puffy and golden brown. Serve warm.

YIELD: 16 APPETIZERS

mozzarella puffs

JOAN MOUSLEY DZIUBA, WAUPACA, WISCONSIN
These savory cheesy biscuits go over great at my house. Since they're so quick to make, I can whip up a batch anytime I want.

1 tube (7-1/2 ounces) refrigerated buttermilk biscuits

1 teaspoon dried oregano

1 block (2 to 3 ounces) part-skim mozzarella cheese

2 tablespoons pizza sauce

> Make an indentation in the center of each biscuit; sprinkle with oregano. Cut the mozzarella into 10 cubes, 3/4 in. each; place a cube in the center of each biscuit. Pinch dough tightly around cheese to seal. Place seam side down on an ungreased baking sheet. Spread pizza sauce over tops. Bake at 375° for 10-12 minutes or until golden brown. Serve warm. Refrigerate leftovers.

YIELD: 10 SERVINGS

veggie wonton quiches

TASTE OF HOME TEST KITCHEN
With green broccoli and red pepper, these cute mini quiches are always a fitting finger food for Christmas. Crispy wonton cups make a fun crust.

24 wonton wrappers

1 cup finely chopped fresh broccoli

3/4 cup diced fresh mushrooms

1/2 cup diced sweet red pepper

1/4 cup finely chopped onion

2 teaspoons vegetable oil

3 eggs

1 tablespoon water

2 teaspoons dried parsley flakes

1/4 teaspoon salt

1/4 teaspoon dried thyme

1/4 teaspoon white pepper

Dash cayenne pepper

3/4 cup shredded cheddar cheese

> Gently press wonton wrappers into miniature muffin cups coated with cooking spray. Lightly coat wontons with cooking spray. Bake at 350° for 5 minutes. Remove wontons from cups; place upside down on baking sheets. Lightly coat with cooking spray. Bake 5 minutes longer or until light golden brown.

> Meanwhile, in a nonstick skillet, cook the broccoli, mushrooms, red pepper and onion in oil over medium heat for 4-5 minutes or until crisp-tender. In a bowl, whisk eggs and water; stir in the parsley, salt, thyme, white pepper and cayenne. Add to the vegetable mixture; cook over medium heat for 4-5 minutes or until eggs are completely set.

> Remove from the heat; stir in cheese. Spoon about 1 tablespoonful into each wonton cup. Bake for 5 minutes or until filling is heated through. Serve warm.

YIELD: 2 DOZEN

Editor's Note: Fill wonton wrappers a few at a time, keeping the others covered with a damp paper towel until ready to use.

> In an electric skillet, heat 1 in. of oil to 375°. Fry wontons for 1-2 minutes or until golden brown, turning once. Drain on paper towels. Serve with sweet-and-sour sauce.

YIELD: 16 APPETIZERS

Editor's Note: Fill wonton wrappers a few at a time, keeping the others covered with a damp paper towel until ready to use.

artichoke wonton cups

PAIGE SCOTT, MURFREESBORO, TENNESSEE
I came up with this recipe by combining several dip recipes. Wonton cups add a fancy look that's perfect for special occasions. If you're serving a large crowd, you may want to double the recipe.

1 cup grated Parmesan cheese

1 cup mayonnaise

1/2 teaspoon onion powder

1/2 teaspoon garlic powder

2 cups (8 ounces) shredded part-skim mozzarella cheese

1 can (14 ounces) water-packed artichoke hearts, rinsed, drained and chopped

1 package (12 ounces) wonton wrappers

> In a small mixing bowl, combine the Parmesan cheese, mayonnaise, onion powder and garlic powder; mix well. Stir in the mozzarella cheese and artichokes; set aside.

> Coat one side of each wonton wrapper with cooking spray; press greased side down into miniature muffin cups. Bake at 350° for 5 minutes or until edges are lightly browned.

> Fill each cup with 1 tablespoon artichoke mixture. Bake 5-6 minutes longer or until golden brown. Serve warm.

YIELD: ABOUT 4 DOZEN

crispy crab rangoon

CATHY BLANKMAN, WARROAD, MINNESOTA
My husband loved the appetizers we ordered at a Chinese restaurant so much that I was determined to make them at home. After two more trips to the restaurant to taste them again and about four home trials, I had them perfected. I often make the filling earlier in the day to save time later.

1 package (3 ounces) cream cheese, softened

2 green onions, finely chopped

1/4 cup finely chopped imitation crabmeat

1 teaspoon minced garlic

16 wonton wrappers

Oil for frying

Sweet-and-sour sauce

> In a small mixing bowl, beat the cream cheese until smooth. Add the onions, crab and garlic; mix well.

> Place about 1-1/2 teaspoons in the center of each wonton wrapper. Moisten edges with water; fold opposite corners over filling and press to seal.

ham and cheese tarts

DELORES ROMYN, STRATTON, ONTARIO

*These savory tarts have been a family favorite for years.
Make the ham mixture in advance to save time when
guests arrive.*

2 packages (3 ounces each) cream cheese, softened

1/2 cup French onion dip

1 tablespoon milk

1/4 teaspoon ground mustard

1/4 teaspoon grated orange peel

1/2 cup finely chopped fully cooked ham

1 tube (12 ounces) refrigerated buttermilk biscuits

1/4 teaspoon paprika

> In a small mixing bowl, beat the cream cheese,
>   onion dip, milk, mustard and orange peel until
>   blended. Stir in the ham.

> Split each biscuit into thirds; press into lightly
>   greased miniature muffin cups. Spoon a scant
>   tablespoonful of the ham mixture into each cup;
>   sprinkle with paprika. Bake at 375° for 12-17
>   minutes or until golden brown. Serve warm.

YIELD: 2-1/2 DOZEN

bite-size crab quiches

VIRGINIA RICKS, ROY, UTAH

*These mouthwatering morsels make an appealing
party starter when you invite a few friends to the house
to watch a movie or ball game.*

1 tube (16.3 ounces) large refrigerated buttermilk biscuits

1 can (6 ounces) crabmeat, drained, flaked and cartilage
removed or 1 cup chopped imitation crabmeat

1/2 cup shredded Swiss cheese

1 egg

1/2 cup milk

1/2 teaspoon dill weed

1/4 teaspoon salt

> Separate each biscuit into five equal pieces. Press
>   onto the bottom and up the sides of 24 ungreased
>   miniature muffin cups (discard remaining piece of
>   dough). Fill each cup with 2 teaspoons crab and
>   1 teaspoon Swiss cheese. In a small bowl, combine
>   the egg, milk, dill and salt; spoon about 1-1/2
>   teaspoons into each cup.

> Bake at 375° for 15-20 minutes or until edges are
>   golden brown. Let stand for 5 minutes before
>   removing from pans. Serve warm.

YIELD: 2 DOZEN

LOIS HOLDSON, MILLERSVILLE, MARYLAND
Pineapple and almonds enhance the creamy chicken salad in these cute tartlets made with convenient refrigerated pie pastry.

chicken salad cups

1 package (15 ounces) refrigerated pie pastry

2 cups diced cooked chicken

1 can (8 ounces) unsweetened crushed pineapple, drained

1/2 cup slivered almonds

1/2 cup chopped celery

1/2 cup shredded cheddar cheese

1/2 cup mayonnaise

1/2 teaspoon salt

1/2 teaspoon paprika

TOPPING:

1/2 cup sour cream

1/4 cup mayonnaise

1/2 cup shredded cheddar cheese

> Cut each sheet of pie pastry into 4-1/2-in. rounds; reroll scraps and cut out additional circles. Press pastry onto the bottom and up the sides of 14 ungreased muffin cups. Bake at 450° for 6-7 minutes or until golden brown. Cool cups on a wire rack.

> In a bowl, combine the chicken, pineapple, almonds, celery, cheese, mayonnaise, salt and paprika; refrigerate until chilled.

> Just before serving, spoon two rounded tablespoonfuls of chicken salad into each pastry cup. Combine sour cream and mayonnaise; spoon over filling. Sprinkle with cheese.

YIELD: 14 SERVINGS

pizza rolls

JULIE GAINES, NORMAL, ILLINOIS

This is my husband's version of store-bought pizza rolls, and our family loves them. Although they take some time to make, they freeze well. So when we're through, we get to enjoy the fruits of our labor for a long time!

4 cups (16 ounces) shredded pizza cheese blend or part-skim mozzarella cheese

1 pound bulk Italian sausage, cooked and drained

2 packages (3 ounces each) sliced pepperoni, chopped

1 medium green pepper, finely chopped

1 medium sweet red pepper, finely chopped

1 medium onion, finely chopped

2 jars (14 ounces each) pizza sauce

32 egg roll wrappers

Oil for frying

Additional pizza sauce for dipping, warmed, optional

> In a large bowl, combine the cheese, sausage, pepperoni, peppers and onion. Stir in pizza sauce until combined. Place about 1/4 cup filling in the center of each egg roll wrapper. (Keep wrappers covered with a damp paper towel until ready to use.) Fold bottom corner over filling; fold sides toward center over filling. Moisten remaining corner with water and roll up tightly to seal.

> In an electric skillet, heat 1 in. of oil to 375°. Fry pizza rolls for 1-2 minutes on each side or until golden brown. Drain on paper towels. Serve with additional pizza sauce if desired.

YIELD: 32 ROLLS

sausage breadsticks

TASTE OF HOME TEST KITCHEN

Bring out the kid in everyone by preparing these snacks. This old-fashioned finger food is a fun addition to any breakfast buffet.

1 tube (11 ounces) refrigerated breadstick dough

8 smoked sausage links or hot dogs

> Separate the dough into eight strips; unroll and wrap one strip around each sausage. Place on an ungreased baking sheet.

> Bake at 350° for 15-17 minutes or until golden brown. Serve warm.

YIELD: 4 SERVINGS

tip

When planning your menu, remember to choose a selection of snacks that can be picked up and eaten without a plate such as cubed sausage and cheese, skewered meatballs, fruit kabobs and vegetables. Avoid foods that require guests to do a lot of slicing. Also, make extra napkins readily available.

mushroom puffs

MARILIN ROSBOROUGH, ALTOONA, PENNSYLVANIA
You can make these attractive appetizers in a jiffy with refrigerated crescent roll dough. The tasty little spirals disappear fast at parties!

4 ounces cream cheese, cubed

1 can (4 ounces) mushroom stems and pieces, drained

1 tablespoon chopped onion

1/8 teaspoon hot pepper sauce

1 tube (8 ounces) crescent roll dough

> In a blender or food processor, combine cream cheese, mushrooms, onion and hot pepper sauce; cover and process until blended. Unroll crescent dough; separate into four rectangles. Press perforations to seal. Spread mushroom mixture over dough.

> Roll up jelly-roll style, starting with a long side. Cut each roll into five slices; place on an ungreased baking sheet. Bake at 425° for 8-10 minutes or until puffed and golden brown.

YIELD: 20 APPETIZERS

gouda bites

PHYLIS BEHRINGER, DEFIANCE, OHIO
I season refrigerated dough with garlic powder to create these golden cheese-filled cups.

1 tube (8 ounces) refrigerated reduced-fat crescent rolls

1/2 teaspoon garlic powder

5 ounces Gouda cheese, cut into 24 pieces

> Unroll crescent dough into one long rectangle; seal the seams and perforations. Sprinkle with garlic powder. Cut into 24 pieces; lightly press onto the bottom and up the sides of ungreased miniature muffin cups.

> Bake at 375° for 3 minutes. Place a piece of the cheese in each cup. Bake 8-10 minutes longer or until golden brown and cheese is melted. Serve warm.

YIELD: 2 DOZEN

mini sausage bundles

TASTE OF HOME TEST KITCHEN
These hors d'oeuvres cut fat as well as cleanup by keeping the deep fryer at bay. The savory bundles are filled with turkey sausage, garlic and onion.

1/2 pound turkey Italian sausage links, casings removed

1 small onion, finely chopped

1/4 cup finely chopped sweet red pepper

1 garlic clove, minced

1/2 cup shredded cheddar cheese

8 sheets phyllo dough (14 inches x 9 inches)

12 whole chives, optional

> Crumble the sausage into a large skillet; add onion, red pepper and garlic. Cook over medium heat until meat is no longer pink; drain. Stir in cheese; cool slightly.

> Place one sheet of phyllo dough on a work surface; coat with cooking spray. Cover with a second sheet of phyllo; coat with cooking spray. (Until ready to use, keep remaining phyllo covered with plastic wrap and a damp towel to prevent drying out.) Cut widthwise into three 4-in. strips, discarding trimmings. Top each with 2 rounded tablespoons of sausage mixture; fold bottom and side edges over the filling and roll up. Repeat with remaining phyllo and filling.

> Place seam side down on an ungreased baking sheet. Bake at 425° for 5-6 minutes or until lightly browned. Tie a chive around each bundle if desired. Serve warm.

YIELD: 1 DOZEN

empanditas

MARY ANN KOSMAS, MINNEAPOLIS, MINNESOTA
Mini chicken pockets are one of my favorite appetizers because they can be made ahead of time and frozen. They're a perfect snack when unexpected company drops by the house.

1/2 pound boneless skinless chicken breast halves, thinly sliced

1 tablespoon vegetable oil

1/8 teaspoon ground cumin

1 can (4 ounces) chopped green chilies, drained

1/2 cup shredded pepper Jack cheese or Monterey Jack cheese

2 tablespoons all-purpose flour

Pastry for 2 double-crust pies

1/4 cup milk

> In a large skillet, saute chicken in oil for 7-8 minutes or until juices run clear. Sprinkle with cumin. Chop into very small pieces and place in a bowl. Add chilies and cheese. Sprinkle with flour; toss to coat.

> Turn pastry dough onto a floured surface; roll to 1/8-in. thickness. Cut with a 2-in. round cutter. Fill each circle with about 1 tablespoon of filling. Wet edges of circle with water. Fold half of pastry over filling; seal with fingers, then press with the tines of a fork. Repeat until all filling is used.

> Place on a greased baking sheet. Brush lightly with milk. Bake at 375° for 20-25 minutes or until golden brown. Serve warm.

YIELD: 3 DOZEN

Editor's Note: Empanditas may be frozen after sealing. Brush with milk and bake for 30-35 minutes.

JENNIFER BUMGARNER, TOPEKA, KANSAS
I love that these handheld bundles are so easy and have so few ingredients. I've made them for potlucks, family gatherings...and I never have any leftovers.

beef-stuffed crescents

1 pound ground beef

1 can (4 ounces) chopped green chilies

1 package (8 ounces) cream cheese, cubed

1/4 teaspoon ground cumin

1/4 teaspoon chili powder

3 tubes (8 ounces each) refrigerated crescent rolls

> In a large skillet, cook beef and chilies over medium heat until meat is no longer pink; drain. Add the cream cheese, cumin and chili powder. Cool slightly.

> Separate crescent dough into 24 triangles. Place 1 tablespoon of beef mixture along the short end of each triangle; carefully roll up.

> Place point side down 2 in. apart on ungreased baking sheets. Bake at 375° for 11-14 minutes or until golden brown. Serve warm.

YIELD: 2 DOZEN

tip If your family enjoys a little more heat, make Beef-Stuffed Crescents with canned jalapeno pieces in place of the green chilies. To quickly chop canned chilies, olives or peppers with less mess, simply drain and move a sharp knife up and down and back and forth in the can to chop.

gorgonzola figs with balsamic glaze

SARAH VASQUES, MILFORD, NEW HAMPSHIRE
For a fancy, eye-catching appetizer, try my delightful stuffed figs wrapped with prosciutto.

1 cup balsamic vinegar

16 dried figs

1/2 cup crumbled Gorgonzola cheese

8 thin slices prosciutto, halved widthwise

2 teaspoons minced fresh rosemary

1/4 teaspoon pepper

> For glaze, in a small saucepan, bring vinegar to a boil over medium heat; cook until reduced to about 1/4 cup.

> Cut a lengthwise slit down the center of each fig; fill with 1-1/2 teaspoons cheese. Wrap each with a piece of prosciutto; place on a baking sheet. Sprinkle with rosemary and pepper.

> Bake at 425° for 10-12 minutes or until prosciutto is crisp. Serve warm with glaze.

YIELD: 16 APPETIZERS

chili chicken strips

TASTE OF HOME TEST KITCHEN
Instead of ordinary bread crumbs, seasoned crushed corn chips coat these slightly crunchy chicken fingers. If your family likes food with zip, use the full amount of chili powder.

3/4 cup crushed corn chips

2 tablespoons dry bread crumbs

1 tablespoon all-purpose flour

1 to 1-1/2 teaspoons chili powder

1/2 teaspoon seasoned salt

1/2 teaspoon poultry seasoning

1/4 teaspoon pepper

1/4 teaspoon paprika

1 egg

1-1/2 pounds boneless skinless chicken breasts, cut into 1/2-inch strips

4 tablespoons butter, divided

> In a shallow bowl, combine the first eight ingredients. In another shallow bowl, beat egg. Dip chicken in egg, then roll in corn chip mixture.

> In a large skillet, cook half of the chicken in 2 tablespoons butter for 8-10 minutes or until the juices run clear. Repeat with remaining chicken and butter.

YIELD: 6 SERVINGS

beef 'n' egg pockets

KATHY VAIL, CANAVOY, PRINCE EDWARD ISLAND
*My mother shared the recipe for these handheld snacks.
that disappear whenever I make them. For added flavor,
I sometimes toss in sliced fresh mushrooms or chopped
green pepper.*

2 cups all-purpose flour

2-1/2 teaspoons baking powder

1 teaspoon salt

2/3 cup shortening

2/3 cup milk

FILLING:

1/2 pound ground beef

1 medium onion, chopped

1 medium tomato, seeded and chopped

1 hard-cooked egg, finely chopped

Salt and pepper to taste

> In a large bowl, combine the flour, baking powder
  and salt; cut in shortening until the mixture
  resembles coarse crumbs. Gradually add milk,
  tossing with a fork until a ball forms. Cover and
  refrigerate.

> Meanwhile, in a large skillet, cook beef and onion
  over medium heat until meat is no longer pink;
  drain. Stir in the tomato, egg, salt and pepper.

> Roll out pastry into an 18-in. x 9-in. rectangle; cut
  into 3-in. squares. Place a rounded tablespoonful
  of filling in the center of each square. Fold in half,
  forming triangles; crimp edges to seal. Place on
  greased baking sheets.

> Bake at 400° for 15-20 minutes or until pockets
  are golden brown.

YIELD: 1-1/2 DOZEN

blue cheese date wraps

SUSAN HINTON, APEX, NORTH CAROLINA
*My friends and I used to make the traditional bacon-
wrapped jalapenos at cookouts. I decided to sweeten
them up a bit with dates and apricots, which are also
more kid-friendly.*

12 bacon strips

36 pitted dates

2/3 cup crumbled blue cheese

> Cut each bacon strip into thirds. In a large skillet,
  cook bacon in batches over medium heat until
  partially cooked but not crisp. Remove to paper
  towels to drain; keep warm.

> Carefully cut a slit in the center of each date; fill
  with blue cheese. Wrap a bacon piece around
  each stuffed date; secure with wooden
  toothpicks.

> Place on ungreased baking sheets. Bake at 375°
  for 10-12 minutes or until bacon is crisp.

YIELD: 3 DOZEN

JACQUELYNNE STINE, LAS VEGAS, NEVADA

Chicken and mushrooms make up the filling in these potstickers, a traditional Chinese dumpling. Greasing the steamer rack makes it easier to remove them once they're steamed.

chicken potstickers

1 pound boneless skinless chicken thighs, cut into chunks

1-1/2 cups sliced fresh mushrooms

1 small onion, cut into wedges

2 tablespoons hoisin sauce

2 tablespoons prepared mustard

2 tablespoons sriracha Asian hot chili sauce or 1 tablespoon hot pepper sauce

1 package (14 ounces) potsticker dumpling wrappers

1 egg, lightly beaten

SAUCE:

1 cup soy sauce

1 green onion, chopped

1 teaspoon ground ginger

> In a food processor, combine the uncooked chicken, mushrooms, onion, hoisin sauce, mustard and chili sauce; cover and process until blended.

> Place 1 tablespoon of chicken mixture in the center of each wrapper. (Until ready to use, keep wrappers covered with a damp towel to prevent them from drying out.) Moisten edges with egg. Bring opposite sides together to form a semicircle; pinch to seal.

> Place potstickers in a single layer on a large greased steamer basket rack; place in a Dutch oven over 1 in. of water. Bring to a boil; cover and steam for 8-10 minutes or until filling juices run clear.

> Meanwhile, in a small bowl, combine sauce ingredients. Serve with potstickers. Refrigerate leftovers.

YIELD: 4 DOZEN

KATHY MARTINEZ, ENID, OKLAHOMA
Here's a change-of-pace crowd-pleaser. If you want to wow your family with Southwestern flavor, try this delightful bread filled with a zesty chicken filling.

chicken taco ring

2 tubes (8 ounces each) refrigerated reduced-fat crescent rolls

2/3 cup finely crushed tortilla chips, divided

2 cups finely chopped rotisserie chicken

3/4 cup shredded reduced-fat Mexican cheese blend

1/2 cup reduced-fat mayonnaise

1 can (4 ounces) chopped green chilies, undrained

1/4 cup chopped pitted ripe olives

1 plum tomato, seeded and chopped

1 tablespoon taco seasoning

1 tablespoon lime juice

GARNISH:
1 cup (8 ounces) reduced-fat sour cream

1 cup salsa

2 plum tomatoes, sliced

1 medium lime, halved and sliced

> Grease a 12-in. pizza pan. Unroll crescent dough. Sprinkle with 1/4 cup tortilla chips; press down gently. Separate into 16 triangles.

> Place wide end of one triangle, chip side down, 3 in. from edge of prepared pan, with point overhanging edge of pan. Repeat with remaining triangles, overlapping the wide ends (dough will look like a sun when complete). Lightly press wide ends together.

> In a small bowl, combine the chicken, cheese, mayonnaise, chilies, olives, tomato, taco seasoning, lime juice and remaining tortilla chips. Spoon over wide ends of dough. Fold points of triangles over filling and tuck under wide ends (filling will be visible).

> Bake at 375° for 20-25 minutes or until golden brown. Garnish with sour cream, salsa, tomatoes and lime.

YIELD: 16 SERVINGS

chorizo-queso egg rolls

KARI WHEATON, BELOIT, WISCONSIN
Little bites deliver big flavor in this combination of tangy sausage and creamy cheese in crisp wontons. The recipe is a yummy take-off on my favorite Mexican entree.

1/2 cup mayonnaise

1/2 cup sour cream

2 ounces cream cheese, softened

2 tablespoons minced fresh cilantro

1 tablespoon chipotle peppers in adobo sauce

6 ounces uncooked chorizo or bulk spicy pork sausage

2 cups crumbled queso fresco

1/4 cup enchilada sauce

1/4 cup chopped green chilies

1 package (12 ounces) wonton wrappers

Oil for frying

> For dipping sauce, in a small bowl, combine the mayonnaise, sour cream, cream cheese, cilantro and chipotle peppers. Cover and refrigerate until serving.

> In a large skillet, cook chorizo over medium heat until no longer pink; drain. Stir in the queso fresco, enchilada sauce and chilies.

> Position a wonton wrapper with one point toward you. Place 2 teaspoons of filling in the center. Fold bottom corner over filling; fold sides toward center over filling. Roll toward the remaining point. Moisten top corner with water; press to seal. Repeat with remaining wrappers and filling.

> In an electric skillet, heat 1 in. of oil to 375°. Fry egg rolls in batches for 1-2 minutes on each side or until golden brown. Drain on paper towels. Serve warm with dipping sauce.

YIELD: 4 DOZEN

Editor's Note: Fill wonton wrappers a few at a time, keeping the others covered with a damp paper towel until ready to use.

mozzarella tomato tartlets

AMY GOLDEN, EAST AURORA, NEW YORK
Convenient frozen phyllo shells add to this impressive appetizer's easy preparation. Although I make them year-round, the tartlets are especially tasty with garden-fresh tomatoes.

1 garlic clove, minced

1 tablespoon olive oil

1-1/2 cups seeded chopped tomatoes

3/4 cup shredded part-skim mozzarella cheese

1/2 teaspoon dried basil

Pepper to taste

24 frozen miniature phyllo tart shells

6 pitted ripe olives, quartered

Grated Parmesan cheese

> In a small skillet, saute garlic in oil for 1 minute. Add the tomatoes; cook until liquid has evaporated. Remove from the heat; stir in the mozzarella cheese, basil and pepper.

> Spoon 1 teaspoonful into each tart shell. Top each with a piece of olive; sprinkle with Parmesan cheese. Place on an ungreased baking sheet. Bake at 450° for 5-8 minutes or until bubbly.

YIELD: 2 DOZEN

apple & blue cheese on endive

KATIE FLEMING, EDMONDS, WASHINGTON
This elegant appetizer features a creamy blue cheese and apple spread inside crunchy endive leaves. You can use pears instead of apples or simply use the no-fuss spread to top crackers.

1 tablespoon lemon juice

1 tablespoon water

1 large red apple, finely chopped

2 celery ribs, finely chopped

3/4 cup crumbled blue cheese

3 tablespoons mayonnaise

4 heads Belgian endive, separated into leaves

1/2 cup chopped hazelnuts, toasted

> In a small bowl, combine lemon juice and water; add apple and toss to coat. Drain and pat dry.

> Combine the apple, celery, blue cheese and mayonnaise; spoon 1 tablespoonful onto each endive leaf. Sprinkle with hazelnuts.

YIELD: 32 APPETIZERS

sesame chicken with honey sauce

DONNA SHULL, PIPERSVILLE, PENNSYLVANIA
Between working and raising three children, we don't have much time on our hands. These crispy chicken bites can be prepared in a hurry for a super snack.

1/2 cup fine dry bread crumbs

1/4 cup sesame seeds

1/2 cup mayonnaise

1 teaspoon dried minced onion

1 teaspoon ground mustard

4 cups cubed cooked chicken breast

SAUCE:
1/2 cup mayonnaise

1/4 cup honey

> In a large resealable plastic bag, combine bread crumbs and sesame seeds; set aside. In a small bowl, combine the mayonnaise, onion and mustard. Coat chicken pieces with mayonnaise mixture, then toss in crumb mixture.

> Place on a greased baking sheet. Bake at 425° for 10-12 minutes or until lightly browned. Combine sauce ingredients; serve with chicken.

YIELD: 6-8 SERVINGS

SUSAN DUGAT, ROCKPORT, TEXAS

These are always a hit when my husband and I bring them to parties. They're especially great for sporting events and always seem to complement the other food being served.

crab-stuffed jalapenos

24 large jalapeno peppers

6 ounces fat-free cream cheese

2 teaspoons Worcestershire sauce

1/4 teaspoon garlic powder

1 package (8 ounces) imitation crabmeat, chopped

1/4 cup shredded reduced-fat cheddar cheese

12 turkey bacon strips, halved widthwise

> Cut stems off jalapenos; remove seeds and membranes; set aside. In a small bowl, beat the cream cheese, Worcestershire sauce and garlic powder until blended. Stir in crab and cheddar cheese.

> Transfer to a resealable plastic bag; cut a small hole in a corner of the bag. Pipe filling into jalapenos. Wrap each with a piece of bacon; secure with toothpicks.

> Place on an ungreased baking sheet. Bake at 350° for 40-50 minutes or until peppers are crisp-tender.

YIELD: 2 DOZEN

Editor's Note: When cutting hot peppers, disposable gloves are recommended. Avoid touching your face.

onion brie appetizers

CAROLE RESNICK, CLEVELAND, OHIO
Guests will think you spent hours preparing these cute morsels, but they're really easy to assemble using purchased puff pastry. And the tasty combination of Brie, caramelized onions and caraway is terrific.

2 medium onions, thinly sliced

3 tablespoons butter

2 tablespoons brown sugar

1/2 teaspoon white wine vinegar

1 sheet frozen puff pastry, thawed

4 ounces Brie or Camembert, rind removed, softened

1 to 2 teaspoons caraway seeds

1 egg

2 teaspoons water

> In a large skillet, cook the onions, butter, brown sugar and vinegar over medium-low heat until onions are golden brown, stirring frequently. Remove with a slotted spoon; cool to room temperature.

> On a lightly floured surface, roll puff pastry into an 11-in. x 8-in. rectangle. Spread Brie over pastry. Cover with the onions; sprinkle with caraway seeds.

> Roll up one long side to the middle of the dough; roll up the other side so the two rolls meet in the center. Using a serrated knife, cut into 1/2-in. slices. Place on parchment paper-lined baking sheets; flatten to 1/4-in. thickness. Refrigerate for 15 minutes.

> In a small bowl, beat egg and water; brush over slices. Bake at 375° for 12-14 minutes or until puffed and golden brown. Serve warm.

YIELD: 1-1/2 DOZEN

appetizer roll-ups

MARCELLA FUNK, SALEM, OREGON
Cream cheese and a variety of herbs and vegetables make even deli cold cuts a fancy and filling party starter. Bite-size pieces look so pretty set on a platter in a circle. But the arrangement never stays complete for long once it's served.

4 ounces cream cheese, softened

1/4 cup minced fresh cilantro

2 to 3 tablespoons minced banana peppers

1 garlic clove, minced

1/2 pound thinly sliced cooked roast beef

HAM AND TURKEY ROLL-UPS:
12 ounces cream cheese, softened

1/2 cup shredded carrot

1/2 cup shredded zucchini

4 teaspoons dill weed

1/2 pound thinly sliced fully cooked ham

1/2 pound thinly sliced cooked turkey

> In a small bowl, combine the cream cheese, cilantro, peppers and garlic. Spread about 2 tablespoons on each slice of beef. Roll up tightly and wrap in plastic wrap.

> For ham and turkey rolls, in another bowl, combine the cream cheese, carrot, zucchini and dill. Spread about 2 tablespoons on each slice of ham and turkey. Roll up tightly; wrap in plastic wrap. Refrigerate overnight. Slice the roll-ups into 1-1/2-in. pieces.

YIELD: 6-7 DOZEN

Editor's Note: When cutting or seeding banana peppers, use rubber or plastic gloves to protect your hands. Avoid touching your face.

> Meanwhile, for filling, in a large bowl, combine the Zwieback crumbs, salt and pepper. Crumble beef and pork over mixture and mix well. Shape rounded tablespoonfuls of meat mixture into 3-in. logs.

> On a floured surface, knead one portion of dough 8-10 times. Roll dough to 1/8-in. thickness; cut with a floured 3-in. round cutter. Place one log in the center of each circle. Brush edges of dough with water; fold dough over filling and pinch edges to seal. Reroll scraps. Repeat with remaining dough and filling.

> Place on greased racks in shallow baking pans. Bake at 350° for 35-40 minutes or until meat is no longer pink. Serve with mustard if desired.

YIELD: ABOUT 4-1/2 DOZEN

pigs in a blanket

CYNDI FYNAARDT, OSKALOOSA, IOWA

This fun take on classic pigs in a blanket wraps up pork-and-beef logs in from-scratch pastry dough. Bet you can't eat just one!

3 cups all-purpose flour

1 tablespoon sugar

2 teaspoons baking powder

1/2 cup shortening

1/2 cup cold butter, cubed

1 cup milk

10 crushed Zwieback or Holland rusks (1-1/4 cups)

1/4 teaspoon salt

1/4 teaspoon pepper

1-3/4 pounds ground beef

1-3/4 pounds bulk pork sausage

Dijon mustard, optional

> In a large bowl, combine the flour, sugar and baking powder. Cut in shortening and butter until mixture resembles coarse crumbs. Gradually add milk, tossing with a fork until dough forms a ball. Divide dough into three portions. Refrigerate until chilled.

cheese and sausage appetizers

DEBBIE HOGAN, TSAILE, ARIZONA

I got this recipe from a home economics instructor when I was a teacher. With its spicy flavor, it can be used as an appetizer before a Mexican meal or served as a snack any time.

16 ounces (4 cups) shredded cheddar cheese

1 cup butter, softened

2 cups all-purpose flour

1/2 teaspoon salt

1/2 teaspoon black or cayenne pepper

8 ounces pork sausage, cooked and drained

> In large bowl, beat the cheese, butter, flour, salt and pepper on medium-low speed. Stir in cooked sausage. Form dough into 1-in. balls; place on ungreased baking sheet.

> Bake at 400° for 15-20 minutes or until light golden brown. Serve warm or cold. Store in refrigerator or freezer.

YIELD: ABOUT 5-1/2 DOZEN

spreads&dips

sun-dried tomato dip

ANDREA REYNOLDS, ROCKY RIVER, OHIO
I love to serve this dip for just about any occasion. It's so fast and easy to pull together and just full of flavor!

1 package (8 ounces) cream cheese, softened

1/2 cup sour cream

1/2 cup mayonnaise

1/4 cup oil-packed sun-dried tomatoes, drained and patted dry

1/2 teaspoon salt

1/4 teaspoon pepper

1/4 teaspoon hot pepper sauce

2 green onions, sliced

Assorted crackers and/or fresh vegetables

> Place the first seven ingredients in a food processor; cover and process until blended. Add green onions; cover and pulse until finely chopped. Serve with crackers and/or vegetables.

YIELD: 2 CUPS

lime cucumber salsa

MARCIA KWIECINSKI, CORREGIDOR, PHILIPPINES
This special salsa is great served with tortilla chips. We also love it topping a baked potato or over fish or chicken.

1 large cucumber, seeded and diced

1 to 2 garlic cloves, minced

1 jalapeno pepper, finely chopped

3 green onions, sliced

2 tablespoons minced fresh cilantro

2 tablespoons lime juice

2 tablespoons olive oil

1 teaspoon grated lime peel

1/2 teaspoon salt, optional

1/4 teaspoon pepper

> In a large bowl, combine all the ingredients. Refrigerate for at least 2 hours before serving.

YIELD: 2-1/2 CUPS

Editor's Note: When cutting hot peppers, disposable gloves are recommended. Avoid touching your face.

caramel peanut butter dip

SANDRA MCKENZIE, BRAHAM, MINNESOTA
When crisp autumn apples are available, I quickly use them up when I serve this delicious dip.

30 caramels

1 to 2 tablespoons water

1/4 cup plus 2 tablespoons creamy peanut butter

1/4 cup finely crushed peanuts, optional

Sliced apples

> In a microwave-safe bowl, microwave the caramels and water on high for 1 minute; stir. Microwave 1 minute longer or until smooth. Add peanut butter and mix well; microwave for 30 seconds or until smooth. Stir in the peanuts if desired. Serve warm with apples.

YIELD: 1 CUP

> Broil red peppers 4 in. from the heat until skins blister, about 5 minutes. With tongs, rotate peppers a quarter turn. Broil and rotate until all sides are blistered and blackened. Immediately place peppers in a bowl; cover and let stand for 15-20 minutes.

> Peel off and discard charred skin. Remove stems and seeds. Place the peppers in a food processor. Add beans, lemon juice, tahini, oil, garlic and seasonings; cover and process until blended. Transfer to a serving bowl. Serve with pita bread and crackers. Garnish with additional beans if desired.

YIELD: 3 CUPS

roasted red pepper hummus

NANCY WATSON-PISTOLE, SHAWNEE, KANSAS

My son taught me how to make hummus, which is a great alternative to calorie-filled dips. This recipe is simply delicious. Fresh roasted red bell peppers make it special.

2 large sweet red peppers

2 cans (15 ounces each) garbanzo beans or chickpeas, rinsed and drained

1/3 cup lemon juice

3 tablespoons tahini

1 tablespoon olive oil

2 garlic cloves, peeled

1-1/4 teaspoons salt

1 teaspoon curry powder

1/2 teaspoon ground coriander

1/2 teaspoon ground cumin

1/2 teaspoon pepper

Pita bread, warmed and cut into wedges, and reduced-fat wheat snack crackers

Additional garbanzo beans or chickpeas, optional

lobster spread

JEFF AND JUDI BURKE, ISLE AU HAUT, MAINE

We like to enjoy this with crispy whole wheat crackers. It's always a hit when we serve it, and it takes only a few minutes to whip up.

1 package (8 ounces) cream cheese, softened

1 tablespoon milk

1-1/2 cups flaked lobster or crabmeat

2 tablespoons chopped onion

1/2 teaspoon horseradish

1/4 teaspoon salt

Dash pepper

Paprika

1/4 cup sliced almonds

Assorted crackers

> In a bowl, combine cream cheese and milk until smooth. Add the lobster, onion, horseradish, salt and pepper. Spread into a greased 8-in. ovenproof dish. Sprinkle with paprika and almonds. Bake at 375° for about 15 minutes until bubbly. Serve warm with assorted crackers.

YIELD: 2-3/4 CUPS

CATHY MYERS, MONROEVILLE, OHIO

Great for summer, this tasty appetizer is a must on our weekend family gatherings. It's well worth the time it takes to grill the corn and cut from the cob.

grilled corn dip

6 medium ears sweet corn, husks removed

1 large onion, chopped

1 jalapeno pepper, finely chopped

2 tablespoons butter

2 garlic cloves, minced

1 cup mayonnaise

1/2 cup sour cream

1/2 teaspoon chili powder

2 cups (8 ounces) shredded Monterey Jack cheese

1 can (2-1/4 ounces) sliced ripe olives, drained

2 tablespoons sliced green onions

Tortilla chips

> Grill corn, covered, over medium heat for 10-12 minutes or until tender, turning occasionally.

> Cut corn from cobs. In a large skillet, saute the onion and jalapeno in butter for 2-3 minutes or until almost tender. Add corn and garlic; saute 1-2 minutes longer or until vegetables are tender. Remove from the heat.

> In a large bowl, combine the mayonnaise, sour cream and chili powder. Stir in cheese and corn mixture. Transfer to a greased 2-qt. baking dish.

> Bake, uncovered, at 400° for 25-30 minutes or until bubbly and golden brown. Sprinkle with olives and green onions; serve with chips.

YIELD: 5 CUPS

Editor's Note: When cutting hot peppers, disposable gloves are recommended. Avoid touching your face.

1/2 cup minced fresh cilantro

3/4 cup jalapeno-stuffed olives, sliced

Tortilla chips

> Crumble beef and chorizo into a large skillet; add onion and taco seasoning. Cook over medium heat until meat is no longer pink; drain.

> Spread the beans into a greased 13-in. x 9-in. baking dish. Layer with the meat mixture, cheese, salsa and ripe olives. Cover and bake at 350° for 20-25 minutes or until heated through.

> Spread guacamole over the top. Combine the green onions, sour cream and cilantro; spread over guacamole. Sprinkle with stuffed olives. Serve immediately with tortilla chips. Refrigerate leftovers.

YIELD: 48 SERVINGS

Editor's Note: When cutting hot peppers, disposable gloves are recommended. Avoid touching your face.

chorizo bean dip

ELAINE SWEET, DALLAS, TEXAS
With its zesty Mexican flavors and tempting toppings, this dish is the first to empty on the appetizer table. I serve it with extra-thick tortilla chips for some serious scooping.

1 pound ground sirloin

1/3 pound uncooked chorizo or bulk spicy pork sausage

1 medium onion, chopped

1 envelope taco seasoning

2 cans (16 ounces each) refried black beans

1 cup (4 ounces) shredded Monterey Jack cheese

1-1/3 cups salsa

2 cans (2-1/4 ounces each) sliced ripe olives, drained

2 cups guacamole

6 green onions, thinly sliced

1 cup (8 ounces) sour cream

salsa guacamole

LAUREN HEYN, OAK CREEK, WISCONSIN
I've never tasted better guacamole than this. If there's time, I make homemade tortilla chips by frying 1-inch strips of flour tortillas in oil and salting them.

6 small ripe avocados, halved, pitted and peeled

1/4 cup lemon juice

1 cup salsa

2 green onions, finely chopped

1/4 teaspoon salt or salt-free seasoning blend

1/4 teaspoon garlic powder

Tortilla chips

> In a bowl, mash avocados with lemon juice. Stir in the salsa, onions, salt and garlic powder. Serve immediately with tortilla chips.

YIELD: 4 CUPS

fruited feta spread

LUCILLE TERRY, FRANKFORT, KENTUCKY
This chunky feta and cream cheese spread offers a wonderfully pleasing sweet-savory flavor.

1 package (8 ounces) cream cheese, softened

1 package (4 ounces) crumbled feta cheese

1 cup seedless red grapes, diced

1 large tart apple, diced

3/4 cup chopped pecans, toasted

1 jar (4 ounces) diced pimientos, drained

1/4 cup mayonnaise

3 tablespoons honey

2 tablespoons minced fresh parsley

Assorted crackers

> In a small bowl, beat cream cheese and feta until smooth. Stir in the grapes, apple, pecans, pimientos, mayonnaise, honey and parsley. Chill until serving. Serve with crackers.

YIELD: 4 CUPS

chutney cheddar spread

REGINA COSTLOW, EAST BRADY, PENNSYLVANIA
This party starter can be whipped together in minutes with ingredients I have on hand in the kitchen.

4 ounces cheddar cheese, cubed

1/4 cup chutney

2 tablespoons butter, softened

1 tablespoon finely chopped onion

1/4 teaspoon Worcestershire sauce

Dash hot pepper sauce

Assorted crackers

> In a food processor, combine the first six ingredients; cover and process until mixture achieves spreading consistency. Refrigerate until serving. Serve with crackers.

YIELD: ABOUT 1 CUP

ham cream cheese balls

JILL KIRBY, CALHOUN, GEORGIA
It seems like I'm always hosting a shower, birthday or other celebration, and this spread is one I rely on.

2 packages (8 ounces each) cream cheese, softened

1 package (2-1/2 ounces) thinly sliced deli ham, finely chopped

3 green onions, finely chopped

2 tablespoons Worcestershire sauce

1 cup finely chopped peanuts

Crackers and raw vegetables

> In a bowl, combine the cream cheese, ham, onions and Worcestershire sauce; mix well. Shape into 3/4-in. balls. Roll in peanuts. Cover and refrigerate until serving. Serve with crackers and vegetables.

YIELD: ABOUT 5 DOZEN

MICHELLE BOUCHER, MILFORD, NEW HAMPSHIRE

This warm and savory treat is sure to be a hit with any hungry crowd! During the holidays, use green spinach tortellini and serve with fancy, frilled party picks.

tortellini with roasted red pepper dip

1 package (19 ounces) frozen cheese tortellini

1 jar (7 ounces) roasted sweet red peppers, drained

3 garlic cloves, minced

1/2 cup fat-free mayonnaise

1/2 teaspoon balsamic vinegar

1/4 teaspoon salt

1/8 teaspoon pepper

1 tablespoon olive oil

1 large zucchini, cut into strips

> Prepare tortellini according to package directions. Meanwhile, place red peppers and garlic in a food processor; cover and process until combined. Add the mayonnaise, vinegar, salt and pepper; cover and process until blended. Transfer to a small bowl.

> Drain tortellini; toss with oil. Serve with zucchini strips and red pepper dip.

YIELD: 10 SERVINGS

sweet cheese ball

MELISSA FRIEND, OAKLAND, MARYLAND
You'll need only a few items for this unique cheese ball. Coconut comes through in the cherry-flecked mixture that's coated in pecans. It looks pretty and tastes delicious served with apple slices, pineapple wedges, berries and other fresh fruit.

2 packages (8 ounces each) cream cheese, softened

1/2 cup confectioners' sugar

2/3 cup flaked coconut

8 maraschino cherries, finely chopped

3/4 cup finely chopped pecans

Assorted fresh fruit

> In a small mixing bowl, beat cream cheese and confectioners' sugar until smooth. Beat in the coconut and cherries. Shape into a ball; roll in pecans. Cover and refrigerate until serving. Serve with fruit.

YIELD: 1 CHEESE BALL (3-1/2 CUPS)

dijon-bacon dip for pretzels

ISABELLE ROONEY, SUMMERVILLE, SOUTH CAROLINA
With just four ingredients that you likely have on hand, this quick appetizer comes together in a snap. If you like the zip of horseradish, start with one or two teaspoons and add more to your taste.

1 cup mayonnaise

1/2 cup Dijon mustard

1/4 cup real bacon bits or crumbled cooked bacon

1 to 3 teaspoons prepared horseradish

Pretzels

> In a small bowl, combine the mayonnaise, mustard, bacon and horseradish. Cover and chill until serving. Serve with pretzels.

YIELD: 1-1/2 CUPS

tip You can cook bacon ahead of time and freeze it to use in recipes like Dijon-Bacon Dip for Pretzels. Put the strips in a single layer on baking pans and pop them in the oven to bake at 350° for 30-45 minutes or until they're crisp. Place the strips on paper towels to drain before storing them in a freezer container.

baked spinach dip in bread

SHAUNA DITTRICK, LEDUC, ALBERTA

This is the only way my kids will eat spinach! The dip can be made ahead and chilled. Place in the bread shell and bake just before company arrives.

2 packages (8 ounces each) cream cheese, softened

1 cup mayonnaise

1 package (10 ounces) frozen chopped spinach, thawed and squeezed dry

1 cup (4 ounces) shredded cheddar cheese

1 pound sliced bacon, cooked and crumbled

1/4 cup chopped onion

1 tablespoon dill weed

1 to 2 garlic cloves, minced

1 round loaf (1 pound) unsliced sourdough bread

Assorted fresh vegetables

> In a large mixing bowl, beat the cream cheese and mayonnaise until blended. Stir in the spinach, cheese, bacon, onion, dill and garlic; set aside.

> Cut a 1-1/2-in. slice off top of bread; set aside. Carefully hollow out bottom, leaving a 1/2-in. shell. Cube removed bread and place on a baking sheet. Broil 3-4 in. from the heat for 1-2 minutes or until golden brown; set aside.

> Fill bread shell with spinach dip; replace top. Place any dip that doesn't fit in shell in a greased baking dish. Wrap in a large piece of heavy-duty foil (about 18 in. square). Place on a baking sheet.

> Bake at 350° for 1 hour or until dip is heated through. Cover and bake additional dip for 40-45 minutes or until heated through. Open foil carefully. Serve dip warm with vegetables and reserved bread cubes.

YIELD: 4 CUPS

Editor's Note: Fat-free cream cheese and mayonnaise are not recommended for this recipe.

texas caviar

KATHY FARIS, LYTLE, TEXAS

My neighbor gave me a container of this zippy, tangy salsa one Christmas, and I had to have the recipe. I fix it regularly for potlucks and get-togethers and never have any left over. I bring copies of the recipe with me whenever I take the salsa.

1 can (15-1/2 ounces) black-eyed peas, rinsed and drained

3/4 cup chopped sweet red pepper

3/4 cup chopped green pepper

1 medium onion, chopped

3 green onions, chopped

1/4 cup minced fresh parsley

1 jar (2 ounces) diced pimientos, drained

1 garlic clove, minced

1 bottle (8 ounces) fat-free Italian salad dressing

Tortilla chips

> In a large bowl, combine the peas, peppers, onions, parsley, pimientos and garlic. Pour salad dressing over pea mixture; stir gently to coat. Cover and refrigerate for 24 hours. Serve with tortilla chips.

YIELD: 4 CUPS

pineapple cheese ball

ANNE HALFHILL, SUNBURY, OHIO
Pineapple lends a fruity flavor to this fun and tasty appetizer. Instead of one large cheese ball, you can make two smaller ones...one to take to a party and one to surprise your family.

2 packages (8 ounces each) cream cheese, softened

1 can (8 ounces) unsweetened crushed pineapple, drained

1/4 cup finely chopped green pepper

2 tablespoons finely chopped onion

2 teaspoons seasoned salt

1-1/2 cups finely chopped walnuts

Assorted crackers

> In a small bowl, beat the cream cheese, pineapple, green pepper, onion and seasoned salt until blended. Cover and refrigerate for 30 minutes. Shape into a ball; roll in walnuts. Cover and refrigerate overnight. Serve with crackers.

YIELD: 1 CHEESE BALL (3 CUPS)

gooey pizza dip

KITTI BOESEL, WOODBRIDGE, VIRGINIA
Pepperoni, tomatoes and olives dress up my cheesy baked dip. I serve it with breadsticks and wedges of a packaged pizza crust. You can even prepare individual servings in ramekins.

1 cup (8 ounces) reduced-fat ricotta cheese

1 cup fat-free mayonnaise

1-1/2 cups (6 ounces) shredded part-skim mozzarella cheese, divided

1/4 cup grated Parmesan cheese

3/4 cup diced seeded plum tomatoes, divided

1 can (2-1/2 ounces) sliced ripe olives, drained, divided

1/4 cup sliced turkey pepperoni

1 teaspoon garlic powder

1 teaspoon Italian seasoning

1/8 teaspoon crushed red pepper flakes

Assorted crackers

> In a large bowl, combine the ricotta, mayonnaise, 1 cup mozzarella, Parmesan cheese, 1/2 cup tomatoes, 6 tablespoons olives, pepperoni, garlic powder, Italian seasoning and pepper flakes.

> Spread into a 9-in. pie plate coated with cooking spray. Sprinkle with remaining mozzarella.

> Bake at 350° for 25-30 minutes or until edges are bubbly and top is golden brown. Sprinkle with remaining tomatoes and olives. Serve with crackers.

YIELD: 3 CUPS

tip Here's a quick tip for seeding tomatoes to use in Gooey Pizza Dip. Slice a tomato down the middle and gently squeeze each tomato half. Seeding a tomato this way not only removes the seeds but also eliminates some of the juice that can make a dish too watery. If you want to retain some of the juice, try using a small spoon to scoop out the seeds.

ten-minute zesty salsa

KIM MORIN, LAKE GEORGE, COLORADO
The view from our mountain home includes Pikes Peak, so we frequently eat on our wraparound porch when the weather is good. During family get-togethers, we often savor this zippy salsa with chips while we feast on the natural beauty all around us.

1 can (10 ounces) diced tomatoes and green chilies, undrained

1 tablespoon seeded chopped jalapeno pepper

1 tablespoon chopped red onion

1 tablespoon minced fresh cilantro

1 garlic clove, minced

1 tablespoon olive oil

Dash salt

Dash pepper

Tortilla chips

> In a small bowl, combine the tomatoes, jalapeno, onion, cilantro, garlic, oil, salt and pepper. Refrigerate until serving. Serve with tortilla chips.

YIELD: 1-1/2 CUPS

Editor's Note: When cutting hot peppers, disposable gloves are recommended. Avoid touching your face.

guacamole dip

VIRGINIA BURWELL, DAYTON, TEXAS
Since guacamole is a favorite in this area with its emphasis on Mexican food, I decided to create my own recipe. I serve it as a dip for chips, with baked chicken or to top off a bed of lettuce.

1 large ripe avocado, peeled

1/4 cup plain yogurt

2 tablespoons picante sauce or salsa

1 tablespoon finely chopped onion

1/8 teaspoon salt

2 to 3 drops hot pepper sauce, optional

Tortilla chips

> In a bowl, mash avocado until smooth. Stir in the yogurt, picante sauce, onion, salt and hot pepper sauce if desired. Cover and refrigerate until serving. Serve with tortilla chips.

YIELD: 3/4 CUP

LORI ADAMS, MOORESVILLE, INDIANA
The buttery Brie-and-onion flavor of this spread just melts in your mouth. Plus, you can even eat the bread bowl, which my husband says is the best part!

baked onion brie spread

1 large onion, chopped

2 tablespoons minced garlic

2 tablespoons butter

1 round (8 ounces) Brie or Camembert cheese, rind removed and cubed

1 package (8 ounces) cream cheese, cubed

3/4 cup sour cream

2 teaspoons brown sugar

2 teaspoons lemon juice

1 teaspoon Worcestershire sauce

1/8 teaspoon salt

1/8 teaspoon pepper

1 round loaf (1 pound) sourdough bread

Paprika

Fresh vegetables

> In a large skillet, cook onion and garlic in butter over medium heat for 8-10 minutes or until onion is golden brown, stirring frequently. Remove from the heat; set aside.

> Place Brie and cream cheese in a microwave-safe dish. Microwave, uncovered, until softened. Whisk in the sour cream, brown sugar, lemon juice, Worcestershire sauce, salt, pepper and onion mixture.

> Cut top off loaf of bread; set aside. Hollow out loaf, leaving a 3/4-in. shell. Cut removed bread into cubes. Fill shell with cheese mixture; replace top. Wrap in a large piece of heavy-duty foil (about 18 in. square). Place on a baking sheet.

> Bake at 400° for 1 hour or until spread is bubbly. Remove top of bread. Sprinkle paprika over spread. Serve with vegetables and bread cubes.

YIELD: 2-3/4 CUPS

crabmeat appetizer cheesecake

ANDREA MACINTIRE, DELAWARE WATER GAP, PENNSYLVANIA
I found a lobster cheesecake recipe and decided to come up with my own version using crabmeat instead. It tastes great, so now I make it often!

1/2 cup seasoned bread crumbs

1/2 cup grated Parmesan cheese

1/4 cup butter, melted

FILLING:
1/4 cup each chopped sweet red, yellow and green pepper

1/4 cup chopped onion

1/4 cup butter

4 packages (three 8 ounces, one 3 ounces) cream cheese, softened

3 eggs, lightly beaten

2 cups heavy whipping cream

2 cups canned crabmeat, drained, flaked and cartilage removed

2 cups (8 ounces) shredded Swiss cheese

1/2 teaspoon salt

> In a bowl, combine bread crumbs, Parmesan cheese and butter. Press onto the bottom of a 10-in. springform pan; set aside. In a skillet, saute peppers and onion in butter until tender; set aside.

> In a mixing bowl, beat cream cheese until smooth. Add eggs; beat on low speed just until combined. Stir in the cream, crab, Swiss cheese, pepper mixture and salt. Pour over crust.

> Place pan on a baking sheet. Bake at 325° for 60-65 minutes or until center is almost set. Cool on a wire rack for 10 minutes. Carefully run a knife around edge of pan to loosen. Cool for 1 hour longer. Refrigerate overnight.

> Remove sides of pan. Let stand at room temperature for 30 minutes before serving. Refrigerate leftovers.

YIELD: 16-18 SERVINGS

zesty berry dip

DOROTHY PRITCHETT, WILLS POINT, TEXAS
This savory dipping sauce has a festive red color and is packed with lots of flavor.

1 can (16 ounces) jellied cranberry sauce

2 to 3 tablespoons prepared horseradish

2 tablespoons honey

1 tablespoon Worcestershire sauce

1 tablespoon lemon juice

1 garlic clove, minced

1/4 to 1/2 teaspoon ground cayenne pepper

Pineapple chunks, orange sections and warmed mini fully cooked sausages

> In a medium saucepan, combine first seven ingredients. Bring to a boil. Reduce heat; cover and simmer for 5 minutes. Serve warm with the pineapple, oranges and sausages.

YIELD: 2 CUPS

honey champagne fondue

SHANNON ARTHUR, PORTSMOUTH, OHIO
This special fondue has wonderful flavor from Swiss cheese and honey. It clings well to the fruit and bread dippers.

1/4 cup finely chopped shallot

1 tablespoon butter

1 garlic clove, minced

1-1/4 cups champagne

4 teaspoons cornstarch

1 teaspoon ground mustard

1/4 teaspoon white pepper

1/3 cup honey

4 cups (16 ounces) shredded Swiss cheese

2 tablespoons lemon juice

Pinch ground nutmeg

French bread cubes, tart apple slices or pear slices

> In a large saucepan, saute shallot in butter until tender. Add garlic; cook 1 minute longer. Combine the champagne, cornstarch, mustard and pepper until smooth; gradually stir into pan. Bring to a boil; cook and stir for 2 minutes or until thickened.

> Stir in honey; heat through. Remove from the heat. Combine cheese and lemon juice; gradually stir into champagne mixture until melted. Keep warm. Sprinkle with nutmeg. Serve with bread cubes, apple or pear slices.

YIELD: 3 CUPS

hot artichoke spread

VICTORIA CASEY, COEUR D'ALENE, IDAHO
Green chilies add a bit of zip to this rich cracker spread. I serve it often at parties because it makes a lot, is quick to prepare and looks so pretty with the red tomatoes and green onions on top.

1 can (14 ounces) water-packed artichoke hearts, rinsed, drained and chopped

1 cup mayonnaise

1 cup grated Parmesan cheese

1 can (4 ounces) chopped green chilies, drained

1 garlic clove, minced

1 cup chopped fresh tomatoes

3 green onions, thinly sliced

Crackers or pita bread

> In a large bowl, combine the first five ingredients. Spread into a 1-qt. baking dish or 9-in. pie plate.

> Bake, uncovered, at 350° for 20-25 minutes or until top is lightly browned. Sprinkle with tomatoes and onions. Serve with crackers or pita bread.

YIELD: 4-1/2 CUPS

Editor's Note: Reduced-fat or fat-free mayonnaise is not recommended for this recipe.

tip Most fondue pots hold up to six fondue forks. Depending on your number of guests, you'll need several pots or sets of forks. Extra pots also are needed if you're cooking different types of fondue. For recipes where the fondue simply needs to be warmed, you could use a small slow cooker instead.

TASTE OF HOME TEST KITCHEN
Folks will think you fussed over this pretty appetizer, but it takes only minutes to top a round of smooth and creamy Brie with warm sweet apricots. This is one easy spread that's certain to make any occasion special.

brie with apricot topping

1/2 cup chopped dried apricots

2 tablespoons brown sugar

2 tablespoons water

1 teaspoon balsamic vinegar

Dash salt

1/2 to 1 teaspoon minced fresh rosemary or 1/4 teaspoon dried rosemary, crushed

1 round Brie cheese (8 ounces)

Assorted crackers

> In a small saucepan, combine the apricots, brown sugar, water, vinegar and salt. Bring to a boil. Reduce heat to medium; cook and stir until slightly thickened. Remove from the heat; stir in rosemary.

> Remove rind from top of cheese. Place in an ungreased ovenproof serving dish. Spread apricot mixture over cheese. Bake, uncovered, at 400° for 10-12 minutes or until cheese is softened. Serve with crackers.

YIELD: 6-8 SERVINGS

> In a small bowl, beat remaining cream cheese and sour cream until smooth. Spread over blue cheese layer to within 1 in. of the edges. Sprinkle with walnuts just before serving. Serve with breads or crackers.

YIELD: 4 CUPS

feta olive dip

DEBBIE BURTON, CALLANDER, ONTARIO
Feta cheese, garlic and ripe olives, along with a hint of hot sauce, give a Greek salad-like flavor to this distinctive dip. Besides pita chips, it's terrific with crackers, tortilla chips, pita bread, pretzels and carrot and celery sticks.

4 ounces reduced-fat cream cheese

1/2 cup crumbled feta cheese

1/2 cup reduced-fat sour cream

1/4 cup sliced ripe olives

2 garlic cloves, minced

2 teaspoons dried oregano

1 teaspoon minced fresh parsley

1/4 teaspoon salt

1/4 to 1/2 teaspoon hot pepper sauce

Baked pita chips

> In a food processor or blender, combine the first nine ingredients; cover and process until blended. Transfer to a bowl. Cover and refrigerate for at least 1 hour before serving. Serve with pita chips.

YIELD: ABOUT 1-1/2 CUPS

layered blue cheese spread

LILLIAN JULOW, GAINESVILLE, FLORIDA
This is an attractive and tasty spread to present guests at parties. Serve it with crackers or even vegetable dippers.

3 packages (8 ounces each) cream cheese, softened, divided

1 cup (4 ounces) crumbled blue cheese

1/4 cup plus 1 tablespoon sour cream, divided

2 tablespoons minced fresh parsley

1 tablespoon minced fresh cilantro

1 tablespoon minced chives

1/2 teaspoon coarsely ground pepper

1/2 cup chopped walnuts

Assorted breads or crackers

> On a serving plate, spread two packages of cream cheese into an 8-in. circle. In a small bowl, combine the blue cheese, 1/4 cup sour cream, parsley, cilantro, chives and pepper until blended. Spread over cream cheese layer to within 1/2 in. of the edges.

> Line a 3-cup bowl with plastic wrap. Spread half of the cheddar cheese mixture in prepared bowl. Layer with the spinach and chutney mixtures. Top with remaining cheddar cheese mixture. Cover and refrigerate overnight.

> Unmold onto a serving plate; garnish with additional spinach. Serve with crackers and vegetables.

YIELD: ABOUT 3 CUPS

warm asparagus-crab spread

CAMILLE WISNIEWSKI, JACKSON, NEW JERSEY
When my children entertain, I like to help them with the cooking. This warm and flavorful dip is a favorite contribution of mine. Cashew nuts give this creamy mixture a nice crunch.

1 medium sweet red pepper, chopped

3 green onions, sliced

2 medium jalapeno peppers, seeded and finely chopped

2 teaspoons vegetable oil

1 can (15 ounces) asparagus spears, drained and chopped

2 cans (6 ounces each) crabmeat, drained, flaked and cartilage removed

1 cup mayonnaise

1/2 cup grated or shredded Parmesan cheese

1/2 cup chopped cashews

Assorted crackers

> In a large skillet, saute the red pepper, onions and jalapenos in oil until tender. Add the asparagus, crab, mayonnaise and Parmesan cheese; mix well.

> Transfer to a greased 1-qt. baking dish. Sprinkle with cashews. Bake, uncovered, at 375° for 20-25 minutes or until bubbly. Serve with crackers.

YIELD: 3 CUPS

Editor's Note: Reduced-fat or fat-free mayonnaise is not recommended for this recipe. When cutting hot peppers, disposable gloves are recommended. Avoid touching your face.

four-layer cheese spread

SHERRY HULSMAN, LOUISVILLE, KENTUCKY
When entertaining, I often count on this streamlined party starter. I like to invert the chilled mold onto a platter lined with baby spinach.

1 package (8 ounces) cream cheese, softened, divided

1/4 cup fresh baby spinach, chopped

4-1/2 teaspoons chutney

2 cups (8 ounces) shredded cheddar cheese

2/3 cup mayonnaise

1/2 cup chopped pecans

1/4 cup finely chopped onion

Dash hot pepper sauce

Additional fresh baby spinach

Assorted crackers and fresh vegetables

> In a small bowl, combine 4 oz. cream cheese and chopped spinach. In another bowl, combine chutney and remaining cream cheese. In a large bowl, combine cheddar cheese, mayonnaise, pecans, onion and hot pepper sauce.

pesto cheese blossom

MARY LOU TIMPSON, COLORADO CITY, ARIZONA
With colorful layers, this pretty spread is a real attention-getter. I like the convenience of making it ahead of time.

9 slices provolone cheese, divided

1/3 cup oil-packed sun-dried tomatoes

CREAM CHEESE LAYER:
2 packages (8 ounces each) cream cheese, cubed

1/2 cup pistachios

2 garlic cloves, peeled

PESTO LAYER:
1/2 cup pine nuts

1/2 cup packed fresh basil leaves

1/2 cup packed fresh parsley sprigs

1/4 teaspoon salt

1/4 teaspoon pepper

1 tablespoon olive oil

Assorted crackers

> Line a 1-qt. bowl with plastic wrap, overlapping the sides of the bowl. Arrange six cheese slices on the bottom and up the sides of the bowl, overlapping each slice; set aside.

> Drain tomatoes, reserving 3 teaspoons oil mixture. In a food processor, combine tomatoes and reserved oil mixture; cover and process until blended. Transfer to a small bowl; set aside.

> Place cream cheese, pistachios and garlic in the food processor; cover and process until blended. Transfer to a small bowl; set aside.

> Add the pine nuts, basil, parsley, salt and pepper to food processor; cover and process until blended. While processing, add oil; process for 15 seconds or until combined. Transfer to a small bowl.

> Spread a third of the cream cheese mixture over provolone cheese in prepared bowl. Layer with pesto mixture, another third of the cream cheese mixture, tomato mixture and remaining cream cheese mixture. Top with remaining provolone slices.

> Bring edges of plastic wrap together over cheese; press down gently to seal. Refrigerate for at least 4 hours or until firm. Open plastic wrap; invert mold onto a serving plate. Serve with crackers.

YIELD: 24 SERVINGS

tip

When hosting an appetizer buffet, provide guests with small, sturdy plates that are easy to handle. Consider making simple-to-carry bundles of cutlery and napkins. People are more inclined to eat something when they know exactly what it is, so consider labeling the appetizers on your buffet table with place cards. Guests will appreciate your attention to detail.

CAROL BARLOW, BERWYN, ILLINOIS

Now that we have kids, my husband and I don't entertain much. But when we do, I serve this savory spread. The combination of goat cheese, garlic and onions always earns rave reviews.

roasted goat cheese with garlic

6 to 8 garlic cloves, peeled

1 tablespoon vegetable oil

1 medium red onion, thinly sliced

2 tablespoons butter

1 tablespoon brown sugar

8 ounces crumbled goat or feta cheese

1 tablespoon white balsamic vinegar

Salt and pepper to taste

1/4 cup thinly sliced fresh basil

Thinly sliced French bread or crackers

> Place garlic and oil in a pie plate. Cover and bake at 350° for 30 minutes.

> Meanwhile, in a skillet, saute onion in butter until tender and lightly browned. Add brown sugar; cook and stir until sugar is dissolved. Remove from the heat.

> Remove garlic from pie plate. Spread onion in pie plate; top with cheese. Place garlic over cheese. Bake, uncovered, for 15-20 minutes or until cheese is melted.

> Mash garlic with a fork. Stir vinegar, salt and pepper into garlic, onion and cheese mixture. Transfer to a serving bowl; sprinkle with basil. Serve warm with French bread or crackers.

YIELD: ABOUT 1-1/4 CUPS

> In a small bowl, whisk the lime juice, mustard, garlic and salt. Stir in cilantro. Pour over corn mixture and stir to coat. Serve with tortilla chips. Refrigerate leftovers.

YIELD: 4 CUPS

calico corn salsa

JENNIFER GARDNER, SANDY, UTAH
A friend gave me the recipe for this colorful salsa, and when I took it to a luncheon, everyone loved it. This recipe makes 4 cups, but it is easily doubled for large gatherings of friends and family.

1-1/2 cups frozen corn, thawed

1 cup frozen peas, thawed

1/2 teaspoon ground cumin

1/8 teaspoon dried oregano

1 tablespoon olive oil

1 can (15 ounces) black beans, rinsed and drained

1 medium tomato, chopped

1/3 cup chopped red onion

1/4 cup lime juice

1 tablespoon Dijon mustard

1 garlic clove, minced

1/2 teaspoon salt

2 tablespoons minced fresh cilantro

Tortilla chips

> In a large bowl, combine the corn and peas. In a nonstick skillet, cook cumin and oregano in oil over medium heat for 2 minutes. Pour over corn mixture; stir to coat evenly. Stir in the beans, tomato and onion.

dijon chicken liver pate

KATHERINE WELLS, BRODHEAD, WISCONSIN
I first served this chicken liver pate at a holiday party quite a few years ago, and it was a real hit. The special flavoring comes from cream cheese, mustard and pork sausage.

1/2 pound bulk pork sausage

1 small onion, chopped

1/2 pound chicken livers, cut in half

1/3 cup milk

2 tablespoons Dijon mustard

1 package (8 ounces) cream cheese, softened

1/2 teaspoon garlic powder

1/4 teaspoon each minced chives, dried parsley flakes, tarragon and marjoram

Assorted crackers

> In a large skillet, cook sausage and onion over medium heat until meat is no longer pink; remove with a slotted spoon and set aside. In the drippings, cook chicken livers over medium heat for 6-8 minutes or until no longer pink. Drain; cool for 10 minutes.

> Place chicken livers, milk and mustard in a blender or food processor; cover and process. Add the sausage mixture, cream cheese and seasonings; cover and process until nearly smooth.

> Pour into a 3-cup serving bowl. Cover and refrigerate for 6 hours or overnight. Serve with crackers.

YIELD: 3 CUPS

pesto cream cheese spread

CYNTHIA EMSHOFF, SARASOTA, FLORIDA

This is a terrific appetizer to serve when hosting an Italian-themed meal. People may be a little hesitant to try it, but once they dip in, they love it!

1 package (8 ounces) cream cheese, softened

1/8 teaspoon garlic powder

1/3 cup grated Parmesan cheese

3 tablespoons butter, softened

1/2 cup minced fresh parsley

1 garlic clove, minced

1 teaspoon dried basil

1/2 teaspoon dried marjoram

1/4 cup finely chopped walnuts

3 tablespoons olive oil

Assorted crackers

> Line a 5-3/4-in. x 3-in. x 2-in. loaf pan with plastic wrap. In a small mixing bowl, combine cream cheese and garlic powder until blended; set aside. In a bowl, combine Parmesan cheese, butter, parsley, garlic, basil and marjoram until blended. Stir in walnuts. Gradually stir in oil.

> Spread about 1/4 cup cream cheese mixture in prepared pan. Carefully spread with a third of the Parmesan mixture. Repeat layers twice. Top with remaining cream cheese mixture. Cover and refrigerate for at least 5 hours. Unmold; serve with crackers.

YIELD: ABOUT 1-1/2 CUPS

blue cheese cheesecake

NIKI TRAPP, CUDAHY, WISCONSIN

Whenever I set out this savory cheese spread, guests can't seem to stop eating it!

1 cup crushed butter-flavored crackers

3 tablespoons butter, melted

12 ounces cream cheese, softened

2 packages (4.4 ounces each) crumbled blue cheese

1 carton (6-1/2 ounces) garlic-herb cheese spread

1 cup (8 ounces) sour cream

3 eggs, lightly beaten

1/3 cup milk

1/4 cup sherry

1/4 teaspoon coarsely ground pepper

Assorted crackers

> In a small bowl, combine cracker crumbs and butter; press onto the bottom of an ungreased 9-in. springform pan. Bake at 350° for 5 minutes or until lightly browned.

> In a blender, combine the cream cheese, blue cheese, cheese spread, sour cream, eggs, milk, sherry and pepper; cover and process until blended. Pour over crust. Place pan in a large baking pan; add 1 in. of hot water to larger pan.

> Bake for 50-55 minutes or until center is almost set. Remove springform pan from water bath. Cool on a wire rack for 10 minutes. Carefully run a knife around edge of pan to loosen. Refrigerate overnight. Serve with crackers.

YIELD: 20 SERVINGS

sauce and garlic. Add cheddar cheese; cover and process until well blended. Transfer to a bowl. Cover and refrigerate overnight.

> Let cheese stand at room temperature for 30 minutes before serving. Serve with crackers.

YIELD: 3 CUPS

roasted eggplant dip

NINA HALL, SPOKANE, WASHINGTON
Here's a fun way to use some of your garden-fresh eggplant crop. This chunky guacamole-like dip—seasoned with lemon juice, onions and chives—goes great with pita wedges or carrots.

1 medium eggplant (about 1 pound)

9 green onions (white portion only)

3 tablespoons reduced-fat plain yogurt

1 tablespoon lemon juice

1 tablespoon olive oil

1/2 teaspoon salt

1/4 teaspoon pepper

3 tablespoons minced chives, divided

Pita breads (6 inches), cut into 6 wedges

Carrot sticks, optional

> Pierce eggplant several times with a fork. Place eggplant and onions in a shallow foil-lined baking pan. Bake at 400° for 25-30 minutes or until tender. Cool. Peel and cube the eggplant.

> In a blender or food processor, combine the yogurt, lemon juice, oil, salt, pepper, eggplant and onions. Cover and process until almost smooth. Add 2 tablespoons chives; cover and process until blended.

> Transfer to a serving bowl; sprinkle with remaining chives. Serve with pita wedges and carrots if desired.

YIELD: 1-1/2 CUPS

beer cheese

PAT WARTMAN, BETHLEHEM, PENNSYLVANIA
I like to serve this zesty cheese spread with crackers and veggie dippers. It's great to take along to picnics.

1/3 cup beer or nonalcoholic beer

4 ounces cream cheese, cubed

3 ounces crumbled blue cheese

1/4 cup Dijon mustard

2 tablespoons grated onion

1/2 to 1 teaspoon hot pepper sauce

1 garlic clove, minced

3 cups (12 ounces) shredded cheddar cheese

Assorted crackers

> In a small saucepan, bring beer to a boil. Remove from the heat and cool to room temperature.

> In a food processor, combine the beer, cream cheese, blue cheese, mustard, onion, hot pepper

> In a mixing bowl, beat the cheese until creamy. Add the beef, sour cream, relish and horseradish; mix well. Spoon into wax shell. Chill.

> Serve with apple slices or crackers.

YIELD: 1-1/2 CUPS

orange chocolate fondue

MARY JEAN DEVRIES, GRANDVILLE, MICHIGAN
Invite your family and friends to dip cubes of cake and pieces of fruit into this rich, luscious fondue for a special treat during the holiday season.

1/2 cup milk chocolate chips

3 squares (1 ounce each) bittersweet chocolate

1/2 cup heavy whipping cream

3 tablespoons orange juice concentrate

1 frozen pound cake (16 ounces), thawed and cut into 1-inch cubes

Sliced bananas and star fruit, orange segments, sweet cherries or strawberries or fruit of your choice

> In a heavy saucepan, cook and stir the chocolate chips, bittersweet chocolate and cream over low heat until smooth. Stir in the orange juice concentrate. Transfer to a fondue pot and keep warm. Serve with cake and fruit.

YIELD: 1-1/3 CUPS

hearty cheese spread

FERNIE NICOLAISEN, CHEROKEE, IOWA
Here's a cheese spread that will please a hungry crowd with its bold taste. Prepare this spread early in the day, spoon it into the wax shell and refrigerate until you are ready to serve.

1 Gouda cheese round in red wax covering (7 ounces), room temperature

1 package (2-1/2 ounces) thinly sliced smoked beef, finely chopped

1/4 cup sour cream

2 tablespoons sweet pickle relish

2 teaspoons prepared horseradish

Apple slices or crackers

> Carefully slice through wax and cheese to within 1 in. of the bottom, forming eight pie-shaped wedges. Carefully fold wax back to expose cheese; remove cheese.

LINDA NORTON, SONORA, CALIFORNIA
Pimientos give great color to this soft-textured cheese log. I make it for many occasions throughout the year.

pimiento-olive cheese log

1 package (8 ounces) cream cheese, softened

1 jar (2 ounces) diced pimientos, drained

2 tablespoons finely chopped ripe olives

1-1/2 teaspoons grated onion

1 teaspoon lemon juice

1 garlic clove, minced

1/4 teaspoon salt

1/8 teaspoon dried thyme

1/8 teaspoon ground mustard

1/8 teaspoon hot pepper sauce

Assorted crackers

> In a small bowl, beat cream cheese until smooth. Stir in the next nine ingredients. Cover and refrigerate for 1 hour or until firm. Shape into a log. Cover and refrigerate for 4 hours or overnight. Serve with crackers.

YIELD: 1-1/4 CUPS

handheld snacks

tuscan kabobs

ELAINE SWEET, DALLAS, TEXAS
With chicken, bacon, tomatoes and bread cubes, this is a hearty appetizer that all guests will clamor for. The sauce provides a fantastic finishing touch.

16 bacon strips, cut in half widthwise

1-1/2 pounds boneless skinless chicken breasts

1 loaf (1/2 pound) French bread

32 fresh basil leaves

32 cherry tomatoes

1/2 cup lemon juice

5 tablespoons olive oil

1 teaspoon salt

1 teaspoon pepper

RED PEPPER AIOLI:
1 cup mayonnaise

1/2 cup roasted sweet red peppers

4 garlic cloves, peeled and halved

1/2 teaspoon crushed red pepper flakes

> In a large skillet, cook bacon over medium heat until partially cooked but not crisp. Remove to paper towels to drain.

> Cut chicken into 32 cubes, about 1 in. each. Wrap a bacon piece around each cube. Cut bread in half lengthwise, then cut into 32 slices.

> On 32 metal or soaked wooden appetizer skewers, thread a wrapped chicken cube, basil leaf, bread slice and cherry tomato. Place on baking sheets.

> In a small bowl, combine the lemon juice, oil, salt and pepper; brush over kabobs. Let stand for 10 minutes.

> Broil 3-4 in. from the heat for 6-8 minutes or grill until chicken juices run clear, turning frequently. Meanwhile, place aioli ingredients in a food processor; cover and process until blended. Serve with kabobs.

YIELD: 32 KABOBS (1-1/4 CUPS SAUCE)

apricot chicken drumsticks

MARY ANN SKLANKA, BLAKELY, PENNSYLVANIA
During the summer months, you can find my family gathered around the grill enjoying delicious bites like these. You can serve the drumsticks hot off the grill or try them chilled.

12 chicken drumsticks (3 pounds)

1 teaspoon salt

1/4 teaspoon pepper

1/4 cup canola oil

1/4 cup apricot jam, warmed

1/4 cup prepared mustard

1 tablespoon brown sugar

> Sprinkle chicken with salt and pepper. For sauce, in a small bowl, combine the remaining ingredients.

> Coat grill rack with cooking spray before starting the grill. Grill, covered, over medium heat for 15-20 minutes or until a meat thermometer reads 180°, turning and basting occasionally with sauce. Cool 5 minutes. Cover; refrigerate until chilled.

YIELD: 6 SERVINGS

mini burgers with the works

LINDA LANE, BENNINGTON, VERMONT
I started preparing these tiny burgers several years ago as a way to use up bread crusts accumulating in my freezer. They're delicious.

1/4 pound ground beef

3 slices process American cheese

4 slices white bread (heels of loaf recommended)

2 tablespoons prepared Thousand Island salad dressing

2 pearl onions, thinly sliced

4 baby dill pickles, thinly sliced

3 cherry tomatoes, thinly sliced

> Shape beef into twelve 1-in. patties. Place on a microwave-safe plate lined with paper towels. Cover with another paper towel; microwave on high for 1 minute or until meat is no longer pink. Cut each slice of cheese into fourths; set aside.

> Using a 1-in. round cookie cutter, cut out six circles from each slice of bread. Spread half of the bread circles with dressing. Layer with the burgers, cheese, onions, pickles and tomatoes. Top with remaining bread circles; secure with toothpicks. Serve immediately.

YIELD: 1 DOZEN

Editor's Note: This recipe was tested in a 1,100-watt microwave.

reuben roll-ups

PATTY KILE, GREENTOWN, PENNSYLVANIA
This recipe turns the popular Reuben sandwich into an interesting and hearty snack. We love these roll-ups at our house.

1 tube (13.8 ounces) refrigerated pizza crust

1 cup sauerkraut, well drained

1 tablespoon Thousand Island salad dressing

4 slices corned beef, halved

4 slices Swiss cheese, halved

> Roll dough into a 12-in. x 9-in. rectangle. Cut into eight 3-in. x 4-1/2-in. rectangles. Combine sauerkraut and salad dressing. Place a slice of beef on each rectangle. Top with about 2 tablespoons sauerkraut mixture and a slice of cheese. Roll up.

> Place with seam side down on a greased baking sheet. Bake at 425° for 12-14 minutes or until golden.

YIELD: 8 ROLL-UPS

KENDRA DOSS, SMITHVILLE, MISSOURI
Filled with chicken, mushrooms, water chestnuts and carrots, these wraps are both healthy and yummy. The gingerroot, rice wine vinegar and teriyaki sauce give them an Asian flair.

chicken lettuce wraps

1-1/2 pounds boneless skinless chicken breasts, cubed

1 tablespoon plus 1-1/2 teaspoons peanut oil, divided

3/4 cup chopped fresh mushrooms

1 can (8 ounces) water chestnuts, drained and diced

1 tablespoon minced fresh gingerroot

2 tablespoons rice vinegar

2 tablespoons reduced-sodium teriyaki sauce

1 tablespoon reduced-sodium soy sauce

1/2 teaspoon garlic powder

1/4 teaspoon crushed red pepper flakes

1-1/2 cups shredded carrots

1/2 cup julienned green onions

12 Bibb or Boston lettuce leaves

1/3 cup sliced almonds, toasted

> In a large nonstick skillet coated with cooking spray, cook chicken in 1 tablespoon oil for 3 minutes; drain. Add the mushrooms, water chestnuts and ginger; cook 4-6 minutes longer or until chicken is no longer pink. Drain and set aside.

> In a small bowl, whisk the vinegar, teriyaki sauce, soy sauce, garlic powder, red pepper flakes and remaining oil. Stir in the carrots, onions and chicken mixture.

> Spoon onto lettuce leaves; sprinkle with almonds. If desired, fold sides of lettuce over filling and roll up.

YIELD: 6 SERVINGS

salt, fennel seed and garlic powder. Spoon over mozzarella cheese. Sprinkle with Parmesan cheese. Bake at 350° for 25-35 minutes or until crust is golden brown.

YIELD: 6 SLICES

appetizer artichoke bread

MAUREEN BUSCHKO, PHOENIX, ARIZONA
This comforting loaf is often requested at many family gatherings. You can serve it as a party starter or even alongside soup for lunch.

1 loaf (1 pound) unsliced French bread

1-1/2 cups (12 ounces) sour cream

1/2 cup butter, melted

2 tablespoons sesame seeds

2 cups (8 ounces) shredded Monterey Jack cheese

1 cup (4 ounces) shredded cheddar cheese

1/4 cup grated Parmesan cheese

1 jar (6-1/2 ounces) marinated artichoke hearts, drained and chopped

4 garlic cloves, minced

2 tablespoons minced fresh parsley

2 teaspoons lemon-pepper seasoning

> Cut bread in half lengthwise; hollow out, leaving 1/2-in. shells. Set aside. Place removed bread in a food processor; cover and process until crumbly.

> In a large bowl, combine the bread crumbs, sour cream, butter and sesame seeds; spread onto a baking sheet. Broil 4 in. from the heat for 8-10 minutes or until lightly browned, stirring once.

> In a large bowl, combine the crumb mixture, cheeses, artichokes, garlic, parsley and lemon-pepper. Spoon into bread shells.

> Place on a baking sheet. Bake at 350° for 25 minutes or until golden. Slice and serve warm.

YIELD: 12-14 SERVINGS

chicago-style pan pizza

NIKKI MACDONALD, SHEBOYGAN, WISCONSIN
I developed a love for Chicago's deep-dish pizzas while attending college in the Windy City. This simple recipe relies on frozen bread dough, so I can indulge in the mouthwatering sensation without leaving home.

1 loaf (1 pound) frozen bread dough, thawed

1 pound bulk Italian sausage

2 cups (8 ounces) shredded part-skim mozzarella cheese

1/2 pound sliced fresh mushrooms

1 small onion, chopped

2 teaspoons olive oil

1 can (28 ounces) diced tomatoes, drained

3/4 teaspoon dried oregano

1/2 teaspoon salt

1/2 teaspoon fennel seed, crushed

1/4 teaspoon garlic powder

1/2 cup grated Parmesan cheese

> Press dough onto the bottom and up the sides of a greased 13-in. x 9-in. baking dish. In a large skillet, cook sausage over medium heat until no longer pink; drain. Sprinkle over dough. Top with mozzarella cheese.

> In a skillet, saute mushrooms and onion in oil until onion is tender. Stir in the tomatoes, oregano,

cheddar-veggie appetizer torte

BARBARA ESTABROOK, RHINELANDER, WISCONSIN
A line forms quickly behind this quiche-like torte at get-togethers. The wedges are easy to eat as finger food, and they are delicious hot or cold.

1-1/3 cups finely crushed multigrain crackers

1/4 cup butter, melted

2 cups (8 ounces) shredded sharp cheddar cheese

1 small zucchini, finely chopped

5 small fresh mushrooms, sliced

1/3 cup finely chopped red onion

1/4 cup finely chopped sweet red pepper

1 tablespoon olive oil

1 carton (8 ounces) spreadable garlic and herb cream cheese

4 eggs, lightly beaten

2 tablespoons crumbled cooked bacon

2 tablespoons grated Parmesan cheese

> In a small bowl, combine cracker crumbs and butter. Press onto the bottom of a greased 9-in. springform pan. Sprinkle with cheddar cheese. In a large skillet, saute the zucchini, mushrooms, onion and red pepper in oil until tender. Spoon over cheese.

> In a large bowl, beat cream cheese until smooth. Add eggs; beat on low speed just until combined. Stir in bacon. Pour over vegetable mixture. Sprinkle with Parmesan cheese.

> Place pan on a baking sheet. Bake at 375° for 30-35 minutes or until center is almost set. Cool on a wire rack for 10 minutes. Carefully run a knife around edge of pan to loosen; remove sides of pan. Serve warm or chilled. Refrigerate leftovers.

YIELD: 16 SERVINGS

salsa strips

JOANN WOLOSZYN, FREDONIA, NEW YORK
Refrigerated crescent rolls make these Southwestern appetizers a breeze to prepare. Choose mild, medium or hot salsa to suit your taste.

1 tube (8 ounces) refrigerated crescent rolls

2 tablespoons Dijon mustard

3/4 cup salsa

1 cup (4 ounces) shredded part-skim mozzarella cheese

Minced fresh cilantro

> Unroll crescent roll dough and separate into four rectangles. Place on greased baking sheets. Spread mustard and salsa on each rectangle.

> Bake at 350° for 10 minutes. Sprinkle with cheese; bake 8-10 minutes longer or until golden brown. Cool for 10 minutes. Cut each into four strips; sprinkle with cilantro.

YIELD: 16 APPETIZERS

ARLIENE HILLINGER, RANCHO PALOS VERDES, CALIFORNIA
I like to serve this quiche at my annual party. Narrow wedges are easy for guests to nibble on as they mingle. The recipe makes two pies, so it's convenient when you're hosting a crowd.

crab and spinach quiche

2 unbaked pastry shells (9 inches each)

5 eggs

1-1/2 cups milk

1/4 teaspoon salt

1/8 teaspoon pepper

1/8 teaspoon ground nutmeg

1-1/2 cups grated Parmesan cheese

1 cup (4 ounces) shredded Swiss Cheese

3 tablespoons all-purpose flour

6 to 8 ounces canned or frozen crabmeat, thawed, drained, flaked and cartilage removed

1 package (10 ounces) frozen chopped spinach, thawed and well-drained

> Line each unpricked pastry shell with a double thickness of heavy-duty foil. Bake at 400° for 5 minutes. Remove foil; bake 5 minutes longer.

> In a large bowl, combine the eggs, milk, salt, pepper and nutmeg; set aside. Combine cheeses and flour; add to egg mixture. Stir in crab and spinach. Pour into pastry shells.

> Bake at 350° for 50-55 minutes or until a knife inserted near the center comes out clean. Let stand for 10 minutes before cutting. Serve warm.

YIELD: 32-36 SERVINGS

italian cheese loaf

MARY ANN MARINO, WEST PITTSBURG, PENNSYLVANIA
Here's a deliciously different sandwich. It's yummy warm from the oven or off the grill at a cookout. The cheesy filling is complemented by a mix of garden-fresh tomatoes and herbs.

1 loaf (1 pound) French bread

2 cups diced fresh tomatoes

1 cup (4 ounces) shredded part-skim mozzarella cheese

1 cup (4 ounces) shredded cheddar cheese

1 medium onion, finely chopped

1/4 cup grated Romano cheese

1/4 cup chopped ripe olives

1/4 cup Italian salad dressing

1 teaspoon chopped fresh basil

1 teaspoon chopped fresh oregano

> Cut top half off loaf of bread; set aside. Carefully hollow out bottom of loaf, leaving a 1/2-in. shell (discard removed bread or save for another use).

> In a bowl, combine the remaining ingredients. Spoon into bread shell; replace top. Wrap in foil. Bake at 350° for 25 minutes or until cheese is melted. Slice and serve warm.

YIELD: 12 SERVINGS

cranberry camembert pizza

HEIDI MELLON, WAUKESHA, WISCONSIN
After I'd tasted this quick, yummy pizza at a party, I just knew I had to have the recipe. I've been serving it for years, and it always disappears in minutes.

1 tube (13.8 ounces) refrigerated pizza crust

8 ounces Camembert or Brie cheese, rind removed and cut into 1/2-inch cubes

3/4 cup whole-berry cranberry sauce

1/2 cup chopped pecans

> Unroll crust onto a lightly greased 12-in. pizza pan; flatten dough and build up edges slightly. Bake at 425° for 10-12 minutes or until light golden brown.

> Sprinkle cheese over crust. Spoon cranberry sauce evenly over crust; sprinkle with pecans. Bake 8-10 minutes longer or until the cheese is melted and crust is golden brown. Cool for 5 minutes before cutting.

YIELD: 12-14 SLICES

tip When you hollow out a loaf of bread in a recipe, you may not use all of that bread. Don't discard it; get creative! For example, the remaining bread from Italian Cheese Loaf can be blended in a food processor into crumbs. You can use those crumbs as a coating for chicken or fish.

> In a small bowl, beat the cream cheese, milk and mayonnaise until smooth. Stir in the pimientos, onion, salt and pepper.

> Unroll crescent dough and separate into triangles; place on an ungreased baking sheet. Spoon 1 teaspoon of cream cheese mixture into the center of each triangle; top with asparagus. Top each with another teaspoonful of cream cheese mixture. Bring three corners of dough together and twist; pinch edges to seal.

> Brush with butter; sprinkle with bread crumbs. Bake at 375° for 15-18 minutes or until golden brown.

YIELD: 8 SERVINGS

asparagus brunch pockets

CYNTHIA LINTHICUM, TOWSON, MARYLAND
These cute bundles are stuffed with a savory asparagus and cream cheese mixture. They're wonderful during a brunch or even as a fun side dish.

1 pound fresh asparagus, trimmed and cut into 1-inch pieces

4 ounces cream cheese, softened

1 tablespoon milk

1 tablespoon mayonnaise

1 tablespoon diced pimientos

1 tablespoon finely chopped onion

1/8 teaspoon salt

Pinch pepper

1 tube (8 ounces) refrigerated crescent rolls

2 teaspoons butter, melted

1 tablespoon seasoned bread crumbs

> In a large saucepan, bring 1/2 in. of water to a boil. Add asparagus; cover and boil for 3 minutes. Drain and set aside.

broiled shrimp toast

TASTE OF HOME TEST KITCHEN
This open-faced sandwich has pretty flecks of pink shrimp, red tomatoes and green parsley. To save time the day of your party, blend the spread the night before and refrigerate.

2 cups frozen cooked salad shrimp, thawed

2 cups (8 ounces) shredded cheddar cheese

1 cup mayonnaise

3/4 cup chopped fresh tomatoes

1/3 cup minced fresh parsley

2 tablespoons grated onion

1/4 teaspoon cayenne pepper

6 slices English muffin bread or bread of your choice, toasted

> In a large bowl, combine the first seven ingredients. Place about 1/4 cup of mixture on top of each slice of bread.

> Broil 3-4 in. from the heat for 6-7 minutes or until top is lightly browned and cheese is melted. Serve immediately.

YIELD: 6 SERVINGS

puff pastry holly leaves

ANGELA KING, WALNUT COVE, NORTH CAROLINA
*These elegant appetizers look like you worked long in
the kitchen, but they can be assembled in a jiffy. They
always earn raves at my office holiday party.*

1 package (17.3 ounces) frozen puff pastry, thawed

1 egg

1 tablespoon water

4 ounces cream cheese, softened

1 cup (4 ounces) crumbled feta cheese

1/2 cup minced fresh parsley

1/2 cup prepared pesto

24 pimiento pieces

> Unfold pastry sheets onto a lightly floured
surface. From each sheet, cut out 12 leaves with a
floured 3-1/2-in. leaf-shaped cookie cutter. Place
on ungreased baking sheets. With a toothpick,
score veins in leaves. In a small bowl, beat egg
and water; brush over pastry.

> Bake at 400° for 12-14 minutes or until golden
brown. Remove to wire racks to cool.

> In a large bowl, combine the cheeses, parsley and
pesto. Split pastry leaves in half. Spread 1
tablespoon cheese mixture over bottom halves;
replace tops. Add a pimiento piece on each for a
holly berry. Refrigerate leftovers.

YIELD: 2 DOZEN

deli vegetable roll-ups

NANCY DIVELBISS, LEO, INDIANA
*I make these loaded tortilla sandwiches for my husband
and son for lunch or for a snack. My son thought I
could peddle them on a street corner—and be sold out
in an hour!*

1/2 cup garden vegetable cream cheese spread

4 flour tortillas (10 inches)

1 medium tomato, seeded and diced

2 sweet banana peppers, seeded and julienned

1 cup sliced ripe olives

4 slices Colby cheese

4 slices part-skim mozzarella cheese

8 thick dill pickle slices

1/4 cup ranch salad dressing

4 lettuce leaves

4 thin slices deli turkey

4 thin slices salami

Additional ranch salad dressing, optional

> Spread about 2 tablespoons of cream cheese
spread over each tortilla. Layer with tomato,
peppers, olives, cheeses and pickle slices. Drizzle
with salad dressing. Top with the lettuce, turkey
and salami. Roll up tightly; wrap in plastic wrap.
Refrigerate until ready to serve. Serve
with additional dressing if desired.

YIELD: 4 SERVINGS

double sausage pizza

EMALEE SATOSKI, UNION MILLS, INDIANA

This recipe has been in the family since I was a kid. It was a Sunday night ritual then, and remains one today in my home. A dressed-up hot roll mix gives us enough dough for two flavorful crusts, so there is plenty of sausage-pepperoni pizza to serve company.

1 package (16 ounces) hot roll mix

2 tablespoons garlic powder

2 tablespoons dried oregano

2 tablespoons Italian seasoning

1-1/4 cups warm water (120° to 130°)

2 tablespoons vegetable oil

1 can (15 ounces) pizza sauce

1/2 cup grated Parmesan cheese

1 pound bulk pork sausage, cooked and crumbled

1/2 pound sliced fresh mushrooms

1 package (8 ounces) sliced pepperoni

4 cups (28 ounces) shredded part-skim mozzarella cheese

> In a large bowl, combine the hot roll mix, contents of yeast packet, garlic powder, oregano and Italian seasoning. Stir in water and oil until dough pulls away from sides of bowl. Turn dough onto a lightly floured surface. Shape into a ball. Knead for 5 minutes or until smooth. Cover and let stand for 5 minutes.

> Divide dough in half. With greased hands, press dough onto two greased 12-in. pizza pans. Prick dough thoroughly with a fork. Spread crusts with pizza sauce. Top with the Parmesan cheese, sausage, mushrooms, pepperoni and mozzarella cheese. Bake at 425° for 18-20 minutes or until cheese is melted.

YIELD: 2 PIZZAS (8-10 SLICES EACH)

mozzarella pepperoni bread

TERRI TOTI, SAN ANTONIO, TEXAS

My gang enjoys this tempting bread as an appetizer when we have company. We also have it as a quick meal on hectic evenings.

1 loaf (1 pound) French bread

3 tablespoons butter, melted

3 ounces sliced turkey pepperoni

1-1/2 cups (6 ounces) shredded part-skim mozzarella cheese

3 tablespoons minced fresh parsley

> Cut loaf of bread in half widthwise; cut into 1-in. slices, leaving slices attached at bottom. Brush butter on both sides of each slice. Arrange pepperoni between slices; sprinkle with cheese and parsley.

> Place on an ungreased baking sheet. Bake at 350° for 12-15 minutes or until cheese is melted.

YIELD: 24 SLICES

tip Herb butters like those served in restaurants are very easy to make. Simply combine 1 tablespoon of minced fresh herbs with 1/2 cup softened butter or margarine. Spoon the mixture onto a piece of plastic wrap, roll into a log and freeze until ready to use.

TASTE OF HOME TEST KITCHEN
Sopes (pronounced "SOH-peh") is a traditional Mexican dish. You can often find the Mexican ingredients in the ethnic section of larger local supermarkets.

sopes

2 cups masa harina

1 teaspoon salt

1-1/3 cups warm water

1-1/2 cups shredded cooked chicken breast

1 cup salsa, divided

1/4 cup shortening

1 cup refried beans

1 cup shredded lettuce

1/2 cup crumbled queso fresco

> In a small bowl, combine masa harina and salt; stir in water. Knead until mixture forms a ball. Divide dough into 16 portions; shape into balls and cover with plastic wrap.

> Working between two sheets of plastic wrap, press four balls into 3-1/2-in. circles. On an ungreased griddle, cook dough circles over medium-low heat for 1-2 minutes or until bottoms are lightly set. Turn and cook 2 minutes longer. Remove from the heat; quickly pinch edge of circles to form a 1/2-in. rim. Return to the griddle; cook 2 minutes longer or until bottoms are lightly browned. Remove to wire racks; cover. Repeat with remaining dough.

> In a small saucepan, combine chicken and 1/2 cup salsa. Cook over medium-low heat until heated through, stirring occasionally. In a large skillet, melt shortening. Cook sopes over medium-high heat for 2 minutes on each side or until crisp and lightly browned. Remove to paper towels to drain.

> To assemble, layer each sope with refried beans, chicken mixture and remaining salsa. Sprinkle with lettuce and queso fresco. Serve immediately.

YIELD: 16 SERVINGS

> Cut bread in half horizontally; hollow out top and bottom, leaving a 3/4-in. shell. (Discard removed bread or save for another use.)

> In a small bowl, combine the mayonnaise, mustard, pimientos and hot pepper sauce; spread 1/4 cup in the bottom bread shell. Layer with a fourth of the provolone, ham, salami, turkey and mozzarella. Spread with more of the mayonnaise mixture. Repeat layers three times (you may not use up all of the mayonnaise mixture). Replace bread top and wrap tightly with plastic wrap. Chill for at least 3 hours.

> Remove from the refrigerator 30 minutes before serving. Cut into wedges; serve with remaining mayonnaise mixture if desired.

YIELD: 6-8 SERVINGS

spicy summer sub

BARB MCMAHAN, FENTON, MISSOURI
A few years back, I served this sandwich to friends and family who came to help with our garage sale. Everyone was impressed with the preparation and mingling of flavors.

1 round loaf (1-1/2 pounds) rye bread

1 cup mayonnaise

2 tablespoons Dijon mustard

1 jar (2 ounces) diced pimientos, drained

1/4 to 1/2 teaspoon hot pepper sauce

1/2 pound sliced provolone cheese

1/4 pound sliced fully cooked ham

1/4 pound sliced Genoa salami

1/4 pound sliced cooked turkey

1/4 pound sliced mozzarella cheese

guacamole turkey sandwiches

MARCI MCDONALD, AMARILLO, TEXAS
This may sound like a strange combination, but it is without a doubt the best sandwich you'll ever eat!

1 package (3 ounces) cream cheese, softened

1/3 cup prepared guacamole

1/4 cup picante sauce

3 submarine sandwich buns (about 8 inches), split

1-1/2 cups shredded lettuce

1 medium tomato, thinly sliced

9 slices smoked deli turkey

9 bacon strips, cooked and drained

> In a bowl, combine the cream cheese, guacamole and picante sauce; spread over cut side of buns. On bun bottoms, layer half of the lettuce, all of the tomato, turkey and bacon, then remaining lettuce. Replace tops. Cut sandwiches in half; wrap in plastic wrap. Refrigerate until serving.

YIELD: 6 SERVINGS

mediterranean pizza

PAMELA BROOKS, SOUTH BERWICK, MAINE
Tangy marinated artichokes add flavor to both the crust and the topping of this delicious specialty pizza.

2 jars (6-1/2 ounces each) marinated artichoke hearts

1 loaf (1 pound) frozen bread dough, thawed

1 teaspoon dried basil

1 teaspoon dried oregano

1/2 teaspoon dried thyme

2 cups (8 ounces) shredded Monterey Jack cheese, divided

1/4 pound thinly sliced deli ham, julienned

1 cup halved cherry tomatoes

1 cup chopped ripe olives

1/4 cup crumbled feta cheese

> Drain artichokes, reserving marinade. Chop artichokes; set aside. On a floured surface, roll bread dough into a 15-in. circle. Transfer to a greased 14-in. pizza pan; build up edges slightly. Brush the dough lightly with reserved marinade.

> Combine the basil, oregano and thyme; sprinkle over marinade. Sprinkle with 1 cup Monterey Jack cheese, ham, artichokes, tomatoes, olives and feta cheese. Sprinkle with remaining Monterey Jack cheese. Bake at 400° for 20-25 minutes or until crust and cheese are lightly browned.

YIELD: 4-6 SERVINGS

italian subs

DELORES CHRISTNER, SPOONER, WISCONSIN
Olive lovers are sure to rejoice over this stacked sandwich! Stuffed and ripe olives are marinated in white wine vinegar and garlic before using them to flavor these speedy salami, ham and provolone subs.

1/3 cup olive oil

4-1/2 teaspoons white wine vinegar

1 tablespoon dried parsley flakes

2 to 3 garlic cloves, minced

1 can (2-1/4 ounces) sliced ripe olives, drained

1/2 cup chopped stuffed olives

1 loaf (1 pound, 20 inches) French bread, unsliced

24 thin slices hard salami

24 slices provolone cheese

24 slices fully cooked ham

Lettuce leaves, optional

> In a bowl, combine the oil, vinegar, parsley and garlic. Stir in olives. Cover and refrigerate for 8 hours or overnight.

> Cut bread in half lengthwise. Place olive mixture on the bottom of bread. Top with the salami, cheese and ham; add lettuce if desired. Replace top. Cut into 2-in. slices. Insert a toothpick in each slice.

YIELD: 10 SERVINGS

ELAINE SWEET, DALLAS, TEXAS

For a light bite, try this twist on traditional bruschetta. I really like asparagus, so I'm always using it in different recipes.

asparagus bruschetta

3 cups water

1/2 pound fresh asparagus, trimmed and cut into 1/2-inch pieces

2 cups grape tomatoes, halved

1/4 cup minced fresh basil

3 green onions, chopped

3 tablespoons lime juice

1 tablespoon olive oil

3 garlic cloves, minced

1-1/2 teaspoons grated lime peel

1/4 teaspoon salt

1/4 teaspoon pepper

1 French bread baguette (8 ounces), cut into 12 slices and toasted

1/2 cup crumbled blue cheese

> In a large saucepan, bring water to a boil. Add the asparagus; cover and boil for 2-4 minutes. Drain and immediately place asparagus in ice water. Drain and pat dry.

> In a large bowl, combine the asparagus, tomatoes, basil, onions, lime juice, oil, garlic, lime peel, salt and pepper. Using a slotted spoon, spoon asparagus mixture onto bread. Sprinkle with blue cheese.

YIELD: 6 SERVINGS

pork 'n' pear lettuce wraps

CHERYL PERRY, HERTFORD, NORTH CAROLINA
When the weather's mild, I like to prepare the pork and pears on the grill. No matter how you make it, however, this Asian-inspired appetizer is delicious!

2 cups pear nectar

3 tablespoons minced fresh gingerroot

2 tablespoons butter

1/2 teaspoon coriander seeds, crushed

1/2 teaspoon ground cumin

1 tablespoon brown sugar

1/2 teaspoon cayenne pepper

2 Asian pears, peeled, halved and cored

4 garlic cloves, minced

1 teaspoon salt

1 pork tenderloin (3/4 pound)

10 green onions, cut into 1-inch pieces

10 Bibb or Boston lettuce leaves

> In a small saucepan, combine the first five ingredients. Bring to a boil; reduce heat. Simmer until sauce is reduced to 1-1/4 cups; keep warm.

> Combine brown sugar and cayenne; sprinkle over pears. Place on a greased broiler pan. Rub garlic and salt over tenderloin. Place on broiler pan with pears.

> Broil 4-6 in. from the heat for 9 minutes. Turn; broil 7-9 minutes longer or until a meat thermometer reads 160° and pears are lightly browned. Let stand for 5 minutes.

> Cut each pear half into five slices. Cut pork into 10 slices. Place two slices of pear, a slice of pork and onions on each lettuce leaf. Top with sauce; wrap lettuce around filling. Serve immediately.

YIELD: 10 WRAPS (1-1/4 CUPS SAUCE)

tomato rosemary focaccia

DOROTHY SMITH, EL DORADO, ARKANSAS
This quick Italian flat bread is a savory snack and is also good with soup or a salad.

1 tube (13.8 ounces) refrigerated pizza crust

2 tablespoons olive oil

2 garlic cloves, minced

1/4 teaspoon salt

1 tablespoon minced fresh rosemary or 1 teaspoon dried rosemary, crushed, divided

2 to 3 plum tomatoes, thinly sliced

1 small red onion, thinly sliced

> Unroll pizza crust onto a greased baking sheet. Combine the oil, garlic, salt and half of the rosemary; spread over crust. Top with tomatoes and onion; sprinkle with remaining rosemary.

> Bake at 425° for 12-15 minutes or until golden. Cut into rectangles.

YIELD: 6 SERVINGS

> Turn onto a floured surface; knead until smooth and elastic, about 6-8 minutes. Place in a greased bowl, turning once to grease top. Cover and let rise in a warm place until doubled, about 1 hour.

> Punch dough down. Divide into three portions. Cover and let rest for 10 minutes. Shape each portion into an 8-in. circle; place on greased baking sheets. Cover and let rise until doubled, about 30 minutes.

> Using the end of a wooden spoon handle, make several 1/4-in. indentations in each loaf. Brush with remaining oil. Sprinkle with green onions, rosemary, sage and oregano. Bake at 400° for 20-25 minutes or until golden brown. Remove to wire racks. Serve with olive oil for dipping if desired.

YIELD: 3 LOAVES

herbed onion focaccia

MELANIE EDDY, MANHATTAN, KANSAS
This recipe makes three savory flat breads, but don't be surprised to see them all disappear from the table!

1 tablespoon active dry yeast

1 teaspoon sugar

1-1/2 cups warm water (110° to 115°), divided

6 tablespoons olive oil, divided

2 teaspoons salt

4 to 4-1/2 cups all-purpose flour

3 tablespoons finely chopped green onions

1-1/2 teaspoons minced fresh rosemary or 1/2 teaspoon dried rosemary, crushed

1-1/2 teaspoons small fresh sage leaves or 1/2 teaspoon rubbed sage

1-1/2 teaspoons minced fresh oregano plus 1/2 teaspoon dried oregano

Seasoned olive oil or additional olive oil, optional

> In a large mixing bowl, dissolve yeast and sugar in 1/2 cup warm water; let stand for 5 minutes. Add 4 tablespoons oil, salt, 2 cups flour and remaining water. Beat until smooth. Stir enough remaining flour to form a soft dough.

nutty chicken sandwiches

NANCY JOHNSON, LAVERNE, OKLAHOMA
Crushed pineapple gives these chicken salad sandwiches a bit of sweetness, while pecans add a little crunch.

1 cup shredded cooked chicken breast

1 hard-cooked egg, chopped

1/2 cup unsweetened crushed pineapple, drained

1/3 cup mayonnaise

1/2 teaspoon salt

1/8 teaspoon pepper

1/4 cup chopped pecans, toasted

1/2 cup fresh baby spinach

8 slices white bread, crusts removed

> In a small bowl, combine the chicken, egg, pineapple, mayonnaise, salt and pepper. Cover and refrigerate for at least 1 hour.

> Just before serving, stir in pecans. Place spinach on four slices of bread; top with chicken salad and remaining bread. Cut each sandwich into quarters.

YIELD: 16 TEA SANDWICHES

artichoke veggie pizza

TASTE OF HOME TEST KITCHEN
A sun-dried tomato spread is used as the base for this vegetable-laden treat.

1 tube (13.8 ounces) refrigerated pizza crust

1 package (8 ounces) cream cheese, softened

1/2 cup sun-dried tomato spread

1 can (14 ounces) water-packed artichoke hearts, rinsed, drained and finely chopped

1/2 cup chopped sweet onion

1 can (4-1/4 ounces) chopped ripe olives, drained

3/4 cup sliced carrots

3/4 cup chopped green pepper

1-1/2 cups fresh broccoli florets, chopped

1 cup (4 ounces) shredded Italian cheese blend

> Press pizza dough into a greased 15-in. x 10-in. x 1-in. baking pan. Prick dough thoroughly with a fork. Bake at 400° for 13-15 minutes or until golden brown. Cool.

> In a small mixing bowl, beat cream cheese and tomato spread until blended. Stir in the artichokes. Spread over crust. Sprinkle with the onion, olives, carrots, green pepper, broccoli and cheese; press down lightly. Refrigerate for 1 hour. Cut into squares. Refrigerate leftovers.

YIELD: 3 DOZEN

grilled vegetable cheese bread

SUNDRA HAUCK, BOGALUSA, LOUISIANA
Here in the Deep South, tomatoes are really delicious on the Fourth of July. They're super on this bread, which is good any time you fire up the grill.

1 loaf (1 pound) French bread, sliced lengthwise

1/4 cup olive oil

3 large tomatoes, thinly sliced

2 cups thinly sliced zucchini

1 cup (4 ounces) shredded cheddar cheese

1 jar (4 ounces) sliced pimientos, drained

1 can (4-1/4 ounces) chopped ripe olives, drained

2 teaspoons Creole seasoning

1/4 cup grated Parmesan cheese

> Brush cut sides of bread with oil. Layer with tomatoes and zucchini; sprinkle with cheddar cheese, pimientos, olives and Creole seasoning.

> Prepare grill for indirect heat. Place bread on grill rack. Grill, covered, over indirect medium heat for 10-12 minutes or until zucchini is crisp-tender. Sprinkle with Parmesan cheese; grill 2-4 minutes longer or until melted.

YIELD: 8 SERVINGS

Editor's Note: The following spices may be substituted for 1 teaspoon Creole seasoning: 1/4 teaspoon each salt, garlic powder and paprika; and a pinch each of dried thyme, ground cumin and cayenne pepper.

turkey tortilla spirals

PEGGY GRIEME, PINEHURST, NORTH CAROLINA
No one suspects that these addictive pinwheels are light. People are always surprised by how easy they are to make.

3/4 pound thinly sliced deli turkey

6 flour tortillas (8 inches)

1 package (8 ounces) fat-free cream cheese

6 tablespoons finely chopped pecans

1 can (16 ounces) whole-berry cranberry sauce, divided

1/4 cup chopped celery

2 green onions, thinly sliced

> Place turkey on tortillas to within 1/4 in. of edge. Spread cream cheese over turkey; sprinkle with pecans. Spread each with 2 tablespoons cranberry sauce. Roll up jelly-roll style; wrap tightly in plastic wrap. Refrigerate for 1 hour or until firm.

> Just before serving, cut each roll into six pieces. In a small bowl, combine the celery, onions and remaining cranberry sauce. Serve with tortilla spirals.

YIELD: 3 DOZEN

veggie ham crescent wreath

DIXIE LUNDQUIST, CHANDLER, ARIZONA
Impress your guests with the look and flavor of this pretty crescent roll appetizer. The pineapple cream cheese adds a sweet touch.

2 tubes (8 ounces each) refrigerated crescent rolls

1/2 cup spreadable pineapple cream cheese

1/3 cup diced fully cooked ham

1/4 cup finely chopped sweet yellow pepper

1/4 cup finely chopped green pepper

1/2 cup chopped fresh broccoli florets

6 grape tomatoes, quartered

1 tablespoon chopped red onion

> Remove crescent dough from tubes (do not unroll). Cut each roll into eight slices. Arrange in an 11-in. circle on an ungreased 14-in. pizza pan.

> Bake at 375° for 15-20 minutes or until golden brown. Cool for 5 minutes before carefully removing to a serving platter; cool completely.

> Spread cream cheese over wreath; top with ham, peppers, broccoli, tomatoes and onion. Store in the refrigerator.

YIELD: 16 APPETIZERS

CAROLE RESNICK, CLEVELAND, OHIO

Guests may raise their eyebrows when you tell them the ingredients in this special strudel. But after one taste, they'll be raising their hands for the recipe!

pear mushroom strudels

1 cup finely chopped mushrooms

1 small onion, finely chopped

1/2 cup butter, divided

2 small pears, peeled and thinly sliced

3/4 cup shredded Gruyere or Swiss cheese

1/3 cup sliced almonds

1 tablespoon stone-ground mustard

1/2 teaspoon salt

1/4 teaspoon pepper

10 sheets phyllo dough (14 inches x 9 inches)

1/3 cup grated Parmesan cheese

> In a large skillet, cook mushrooms and onion in 2 tablespoons butter until tender. Stir in pears; cook 3 minutes longer. Remove from the heat; stir in the Gruyere, almonds, mustard, salt and pepper. Cool to room temperature.

> Melt remaining butter. Place one sheet of phyllo dough on a work surface; brush evenly with butter. Sprinkle with 1-1/2 teaspoons Parmesan cheese. Layer with four more sheets of phyllo, brushing each sheet with butter and sprinkling with cheese. (Keep remaining phyllo dough covered with plastic wrap and a damp towel to prevent it from drying out.)

> Spread half of the pear mixture in a 2-in.-wide strip along a short side of dough. Roll up jelly-roll style, starting with the pear side; pinch seams to seal. Brush with butter. Transfer to a parchment paper-lined 15-in. x 10-in. x 1-in. baking pan.

> Repeat with remaining phyllo, butter, Parmesan cheese and pear mixture.

> Bake at 375° for 16-20 minutes or until golden brown. Cool for 5 minutes. Cut each strudel into 12 slices.

YIELD: 2 STRUDELS (12 SLICES EACH)

> Spread half of crab filling to within 1 in. of edges. Fold the two short sides over filling. Starting with the long side, roll up jelly-roll style.

> Transfer to a greased 15-in. x 10-in. x 1-in. baking pan. Brush top with butter; score top lightly at 1-in. intervals. Repeat with remaining phyllo, butter and filling.

> Bake at 375° for 20-25 minutes or until golden brown. Let stand for 5 minutes. Cut into slices along scored lines.

YIELD: 2 DOZEN

ham buns

ESTHER SHANK, HARRISONBURG, VIRGINIA
These tasty sandwiches are a great way to use leftover ham. Friends with whom I've shared the recipe tell me that Ham Buns disappear fast at parties and potlucks. Use mini-buns and make ahead for an easy meal or snack.

1/2 cup butter, softened

1 small onion, grated

1 tablespoon poppy seeds

2 teaspoons Worcestershire sauce

2 teaspoons prepared mustard

1-1/4 cups finely chopped fully cooked ham (about 8 ounces)

1 cup (4 ounces) shredded Swiss cheese

6 to 8 hamburger buns, split or 16 to 20 mini buns

> In a bowl, combine the butter, onion, poppy seeds, Worcestershire sauce and mustard. Add ham and cheese; mix well. Divide evenly among the buns.

> Place in a shallow baking pan and cover with foil. Bake at 350° for 15 to 20 minutes or until hot.

YIELD: 6-8 MAIN DISH OR 16-20 APPETIZER SERVINGS

crab 'n' brie strudel slices

JENNIFER PFAFF, INDIANAPOLIS, INDIANA
Mouthwatering Brie, succulent crab and a hint of pear make this delicate pastry a favorite.

1/2 pound fresh crabmeat

6 ounces Brie cheese, rind removed, and cut into 1/4-inch cubes

2-1/2 cups finely chopped peeled ripe pears

1/2 cup thinly sliced green onions

1/2 cup diced fully cooked ham

2 teaspoons lemon juice

1 garlic clove, minced

Dash pepper

14 sheets phyllo dough (14 inches x 9 inches)

3/4 cup butter, melted

> In a large bowl, combine the first eight ingredients; set aside.

> Place one sheet of phyllo dough on a work surface; brush with butter. Repeat with 6 more sheets of phyllo, brushing each layer with butter. (Keep remaining phyllo covered with plastic wrap and a damp towel to prevent it from drying out.)

chicken quesadillas

LINDA MILLER, KLAMATH FALLS, OREGON

Tender homemade tortillas make this savory snack, filled with chicken and melted cheese, extra special.

4 cups all-purpose flour

1-1/2 teaspoons salt

1/2 teaspoon baking powder

1 cup shortening

1-1/4 cups warm water

1 cup each shredded cheddar, part-skim mozzarella and pepper Jack cheese

2 cups diced cooked chicken

1 cup sliced green onions

1 cup sliced ripe olives

1 can (4 ounces) chopped green chilies, drained

Salsa and sour cream

> In a bowl, combine the flour, salt and baking powder. Cut in shortening until crumbly. Add enough warm water, stirring until mixture forms a ball. Let stand for 10 minutes. Divide quesadillas into 28 portions.

> On a lightly floured surface, roll each portion into a 7-in. circle. Cook on a lightly greased griddle for 1-1/2 to 2 minutes on each side, breaking any bubbles with a toothpick if necessary. Keep warm.

> In a bowl, combine the cheeses. For each quesadilla, place a tortilla on the griddle; sprinkle with about 2 tablespoons cheese mixture, 2 tablespoons chicken, 1 tablespoon onions, 1 tablespoon olives and 1 teaspoon chilies. Top with 1 tablespoon cheese mixture and another tortilla. Cook for 30-60 seconds; turn and cook 30 seconds longer or until cheese is melted. Cut into wedges. Serve with the salsa and sour cream.

YIELD: 28 SERVINGS

turkey roll-ups

PAULA ALF, CINCINNATI, OHIO

Whether served whole for lunch or cut into bite-size appetizers, these light wraps are always a hit. We prefer this blend of herbs, but feel free to use any combination you'd like.

1 package (8 ounces) fat-free cream cheese

1/2 cup reduced-fat mayonnaise

1/4 teaspoon dried basil

1/4 teaspoon dried oregano

1/4 teaspoon dill weed

1/4 teaspoon garlic powder

10 flour tortillas (6 inches), warmed

1 medium onion, chopped

10 slices deli turkey breast (1 ounce each)

Shredded lettuce

> In a small mixing bowl, combine the first six ingredients; beat until smooth. Spread over the tortillas. Sprinkle with onion; top with turkey and lettuce. Roll up tightly jelly-roll style; serve immediately.

YIELD: 10 SERVINGS

KELLIE MULLEAVY, LAMBERTVILLE, MICHIGAN

I came up with this recipe as a way to make a sandwich feed a large group at once. The clever braid design always impresses my guests.

reuben braids

6 ounces cooked corned beef brisket, chopped (about 1 cup)

1-1/2 cups (6 ounces) shredded Swiss cheese

3/4 cup sauerkraut, rinsed and well drained

1 small onion, chopped

3 tablespoons Thousand Island salad dressing

1 tablespoon Dijon mustard

1/2 teaspoon dill weed

2 packages (8 ounces each) refrigerated crescent rolls

1 egg white, lightly beaten

1 tablespoon sesame seeds

> In a large bowl, combine the first seven ingredients. Unroll one tube of crescent dough onto an ungreased baking sheet; seal seams and perforations.

> Spread half of corned beef filling down center of rectangle. On each long side, cut 1-in.-wide strips to within 1 in. of filling. Starting at one end, fold alternating strips at an angle across filling; seal ends. Repeat with remaining crescent dough and filling. Brush egg white over braids; sprinkle with sesame seeds.

> Bake at 375° for 25-30 minutes or until golden brown. Cool on wire racks for 5 minutes before cutting into slices. Refrigerate leftovers.

YIELD: 2 LOAVES (8 SERVINGS EACH)

curried chicken
tea sandwiches

ROBIN FUHRMAN, FOND DU LAC, WISCONSIN
At the Victorian-theme bridal shower I hosted, I spread dressed-up chicken salad on heart-shaped slices of bread. Apples and dried cranberries add color and tang.

2 cups cubed cooked chicken

1 medium unpeeled red apple, chopped

3/4 cup dried cranberries

1/2 cup thinly sliced celery

1/4 cup chopped pecans

2 tablespoons thinly sliced green onions

3/4 cup mayonnaise

2 teaspoons lime juice

1/2 to 3/4 teaspoon curry powder

12 slices bread

Lettuce leaves

> In a bowl, combine the first six ingredients. Combine mayonnaise, lime juice and curry powder; add to chicken mixture and stir to coat. Cover and refrigerate until ready to serve.

> Cut each slice of bread with a 3-in. heart-shaped cookie cutter if desired. Top with lettuce and chicken salad.

YIELD: 6 SERVINGS

tree and star
crab sandwiches

KAREN GARDINER, EUTAW, ALABAMA
To cool off during summer—or any season at all—try the finger food that starts with this flavorful crab filling. I regularly serve the spread at Christmas get-togethers. It's a hit every time. For man-size sandwiches, there's no need to use cookie cutters.

3/4 cup mayonnaise

3/4 cup shredded sharp cheddar cheese

1 can (6 ounces) crabmeat, drained, flaked and cartilage removed

2 tablespoons prepared French salad dressing

1/2 teaspoon prepared horseradish

Dash hot pepper sauce

48 bread slices

Fresh dill sprigs

> In a bowl, combine the first six ingredients; set aside. Using 2-1/2-in. cookie cutters, cut stars and Christmas trees out of bread (two stars or trees from each slice). Spread half of the cutouts with crab mixture; top with remaining cutouts. Garnish with dill.

YIELD: 4 DOZEN

> On a baking sheet coated with cooking spray, roll dough into a small rectangle. Let rest for 5-10 minutes.

> In a small bowl, combine the butter and seasonings. Roll out dough into a 14-in. x 10-in. rectangle. Brush with half of the butter mixture. Layer ham, mozzarella cheese, turkey and cheddar cheese lengthwise over half of the dough to within 1/2 in. of edges. Fold dough over and pinch firmly to seal. Brush with remaining butter mixture.

> Bake at 400° for 10-12 minutes or until golden brown. Cut into 1-in. slices. Serve immediately with pizza sauce if desired.

YIELD: 4-6 SERVINGS

baked deli sandwich

SANDRA MCKENZIE, BRAHAM, MINNESOTA
Frozen bread dough, easy assembly and quick baking time make this stuffed sandwich an appetizer I rely on often. This is one of my most-requested recipes. It's easy to double for a crowd or to experiment with different meats and cheeses.

1 loaf (1 pound) frozen bread dough, thawed

2 tablespoons butter, melted

1/4 teaspoon garlic salt

1/4 teaspoon dried basil

1/4 teaspoon dried oregano

1/4 teaspoon pizza seasoning

1/4 pound sliced deli ham

6 thin slices part-skim mozzarella cheese

1/4 pound sliced deli smoked turkey breast

6 thin slices cheddar cheese

Pizza sauce, warmed, optional

party pitas

JANETTE ROOT, ELLENSBURG, WASHINGTON
Whenever the ladies of our church host a bridal shower, these pita sandwiches are on the menu. Not only are they simple and delicious, they look nice on the table.

1 package (8 ounces) cream cheese, softened

1/2 cup mayonnaise

1/2 teaspoon dill weed

1/4 teaspoon garlic salt

8 mini pita breads (4 inches)

16 fresh spinach leaves

3/4 pound shaved fully cooked ham

1/2 pound thinly sliced Monterey Jack cheese

> In a large mixing bowl, beat the cream cheese, mayonnaise, dill and garlic salt until blended.

> Cut each pita in half horizontally; spread 1 tablespoon cream cheese mixture on each cut surface. On eight pita halves, layer spinach, ham and cheese. Top with remaining pita halves. Cut each pita into four wedges; secure with a toothpick.

YIELD: 32 PIECES

pepper-crusted tenderloin crostini

TASTE OF HOME TEST KITCHEN
Caramelized onions add a touch of sweetness to this impressive hors d'oeuvre.

2 large onions, thinly sliced

6 tablespoons butter, softened, divided

2 teaspoons sugar

1 tablespoon olive oil

1 beef tenderloin roast (1-1/2 pounds)

2 to 3 teaspoons coarsely ground pepper

2 garlic cloves, minced

3/4 teaspoon salt

2 teaspoons prepared horseradish

1 French bread baguette (10-1/2 ounces), cut into 30 slices

Minced fresh parsley

> In a large skillet over medium-low heat, cook onions in 3 tablespoons butter for 5 minutes or until tender. Add sugar; cook over low heat for 30-40 minutes longer or until onions are golden brown, stirring frequently.

> Meanwhile, rub oil over tenderloin. Combine the pepper, garlic and salt; rub over beef. In a large skillet, brown beef on all sides. Transfer to a baking sheet. Bake at 425° for 20-25 minutes or until meat reaches desired doneness (for medium-rare, a meat thermometer should read 145°; medium, 160°; well-done, 170°). Let stand for 10 minutes.

> In a small bowl, beat horseradish and remaining butter until blended. Spread over bread slices. Place on a baking sheet. Broil 3-4 in. from heat for 2-3 minutes or until lightly golden brown.

> Thinly slice the beef; place on toasted bread. Top with caramelized onions. Garnish with parsley.

YIELD: 2-1/2 DOZEN

southwestern chicken pizza

ROBIN POUST, STEVENSVILLE, MARYLAND
Our family loves Mexican food and pizza, so I combined the two into this sensation.

1 medium onion, julienned

1 medium green pepper, julienned

1/4 cup water

1 tube (10 ounces) refrigerated pizza crust

1-1/4 cups salsa

2 packages (6 ounces each) ready-to-use Southwestern chicken strips

2 cups (8 ounces) shredded Mexican cheese blend

1/4 teaspoon garlic powder

1/4 teaspoon dried cilantro flakes

> In a microwave-safe bowl, combine the onion, green pepper and water. Cover and microwave on high for 2-4 minutes or until vegetables are crisp-tender; drain well.

> Unroll pizza crust onto a greased baking sheet, stretching gently to form a 14-in. x 10-in. rectangle. Spread with salsa. Top with chicken and onion mixture. Sprinkle with cheese, garlic powder and cilantro. Bake at 400° for 15-20 minutes or until crust is golden and cheese is melted. Cut into squares.

YIELD: 8 SLICES

Editor's Note: This recipe was tested in a 1,100-watt microwave.

game day
faves

pizza fondue

MARGARET SCHISSLER, MILWAUKEE, WISCONSIN
Great for a game-day gathering or any party, this hearty appetizer can be made with Italian sausage instead of ground beef if you prefer. Add a little more pizza sauce if the mixture seems too thick.

1/2 pound ground beef

1 cup chopped fresh mushrooms

1 medium onion, chopped

1 garlic clove, minced

1 tablespoon cornstarch

1-1/2 teaspoons fennel seed

1-1/2 teaspoons dried oregano

1/4 teaspoon garlic powder

2 cans (15 ounces each) pizza sauce

2-1/2 cups (10 ounces) shredded cheddar cheese

1 cup (4 ounces) shredded part-skim mozzarella cheese

2 tablespoons chopped ripe olives

Breadsticks, bagel chips, baked pita chips and/or tortilla chips

> In a large skillet, cook the beef, mushrooms and onion over medium heat until meat is no longer pink. Add garlic; cook 1 minute longer. Drain. Stir in the cornstarch, fennel, oregano and garlic powder until blended. Stir in pizza sauce.

> Bring to a boil; cook and stir for 1-2 minutes or until thickened. Gradually stir in cheeses until melted. Stir in olives. Keep warm.

> Serve with the breadsticks, bagel chips, pita chips and/or tortilla chips.

YIELD: 5-1/2 CUPS

grilled glazed drummies

LAURA MAHAFFEY, ANNAPOLIS, MARYLAND
It's nice to have a wing recipe you can prepare on the grill. My family actually prefers these mild-tasting chicken wings to traditional hot wings.

1 cup ketchup

1/3 cup soy sauce

4 teaspoons honey

3/4 teaspoon ground ginger

1/2 teaspoon garlic powder

3 pounds fresh or frozen chicken drumettes, thawed

> In a small bowl, combine the first five ingredients. Pour 1 cup marinade into a large resealable plastic bag. Add the chicken; seal bag and turn to coat. Refrigerate for at least 4 hours or overnight. Cover and refrigerate remaining marinade for basting.

> Drain chicken and discard marinade. Grill, covered, over medium heat for 15-20 minutes or until juices run clear, turning and basting occasionally with reserved marinade.

YIELD: ABOUT 2 DOZEN

> Meanwhile, using a 1-in. round cookie cutter, cut out 10 shapes from cheese slices. Immediately place on burgers; serve on rolls.

YIELD: 10 SERVINGS

bacon-wrapped meatballs

PAMELA SHANK, PARKERSBURG, WEST VIRGINIA
My hearty appetizers are a hit at whatever kind of party I make them for. The appealing aroma while baking is irresistible.

2 eggs, lightly beaten

2 tablespoons milk

3/4 cup shredded Parmesan cheese

1/4 cup seasoned bread crumbs

1/2 teaspoon salt

1/4 teaspoon pepper

1 pound lean ground beef (90% lean)

24 bacon strips, cut in half widthwise

> In a large bowl, combine the eggs, milk, cheese, bread crumbs, salt and pepper. Crumble beef over mixture and mix well. Shape into 1-in. balls.

> In a large skillet, cook bacon over medium heat until partially cooked but not crisp. Remove to paper towels to drain. Wrap a piece of bacon around each meatball; secure with a wooden toothpick.

> Place meatballs on a greased rack in a shallow baking pan. Bake at 375° for 8 minutes. Turn; bake 3-5 minutes longer or until meat is no longer pink and bacon is crisp.

YIELD: 4 DOZEN

party time
mini cheeseburgers

TASTE OF HOME TEST KITCHEN
Kids of all ages love the taste of these moist and mouthwatering mini burgers. Juiced up with pickle relish and topped with cheese slices, these "sliders" will disappear before halftime.

1 egg, lightly beaten

2 tablespoons dill pickle relish

2 tablespoons ketchup

2 teaspoons Worcestershire sauce

2 teaspoons prepared mustard

1/4 cup quick-cooking oats

1/4 teaspoon pepper

1/8 teaspoon garlic powder

1 pound ground beef

3 slices process American cheese

10 dinner rolls, split

> In a large bowl, combine the first eight ingredients. Crumble beef over mixture and mix well. Shape into 10 patties. Broil 3-4 in. from the heat for 4-6 minutes on each side or until a meat thermometer reads 160° and juices run clear.

KATHY ROGERS, HUDSON, OHIO

Welcome your gang with this south-of-the-border specialty! Hearty enough to serve as a meal, these flavorful and filling treats draw raves whenever I serve them.

mini chimichangas

1 pound ground beef

1 medium onion, chopped

1 envelope taco seasoning

3/4 cup water

3 cups (12 ounces) shredded Monterey Jack cheese

1 cup (8 ounces) sour cream

1 can (4 ounces) chopped green chilies, drained

1 package (1 pound) egg roll wrappers (14 count)

1 egg white, lightly beaten

Oil for deep-fat frying

Salsa and additional sour cream

> In a large skillet, cook beef and onion over medium heat until meat is no longer pink; drain. Stir in taco seasoning and water. Bring to a boil. Reduce heat; simmer, uncovered, for 5 minutes, stirring occasionally. Remove from the heat; cool slightly.

> In a large bowl, combine the cheese, sour cream and chilies. Stir in beef mixture. Place an egg roll wrapper on work surface with one point facing you. Place 1/3 cup filling in center. Fold bottom third of wrapper over filling; fold in sides.

> Brush top point with egg white; roll up to seal. Repeat with remaining wrappers and filling. (Keep remaining egg roll wrappers covered with waxed paper to avoid drying out.)

> In a large saucepan, heat 1 in. of oil to 375°. Fry chimichangas for 1-1/2 minutes on each side or until golden brown. Drain on paper towels. Serve warm with salsa and sour cream.

YIELD: 14 SERVINGS

tip

When shredding a block of cheese, place the base of the box grater inside a rolled-down gallon-size plastic bag. When you've finished grating the entire block, just pull out the grater, unroll the bag, seal it and store the freshly grated cheese in the refrigerator. There's no mess.

tex-mex dip

TERRI NEWTON, MARSHALL, TEXAS
Perfect for a party, this dip is a real crowd-pleaser. The flavors of the ingredients blend very well, and it makes a large platter of dip.

1 can (16 ounces) refried beans

1/4 cup picante sauce

1-1/2 cups prepared guacamole

1/2 cup sour cream

1/2 cup mayonnaise

4-1/2 teaspoons taco seasoning

1 cup (4 ounces) shredded cheddar cheese

1 can (2-1/4 ounces) sliced ripe olives, drained

Chopped green onion, shredded lettuce and chopped tomatoes

Tortilla chips

> In a small bowl, combine the beans and picante sauce. Spread onto a serving platter. Spread with guacamole.

> In another small bowl, combine the sour cream, mayonnaise and taco seasoning; spread over guacamole. Sprinkle with cheese, olives, onion, lettuce and tomatoes. Refrigerate until serving. Serve with tortilla chips.

YIELD: 12-14 SERVINGS

sweet-sour sausage bites

MARETTA BULLOCK, MCNEIL, ARKANSAS
As a pastor's wife, I frequently entertain church groups in my home, so I'm always looking for new recipes. These quick and easy appetizers are not only delicious, they're colorful, too. I've made them many times.

1/2 pound smoked sausage, cut into 1/2-inch slices

1 can (20 ounces) pineapple chunks

4 teaspoons cornstarch

1/2 teaspoon salt

1/2 cup maple syrup

1/3 cup water

1/3 cup white vinegar

1 large green pepper, cut into 3/4-inch pieces

1/2 cup maraschino cherries

> In a large skillet, saute the sausage for 3-5 minutes or until lightly browned. Drain on paper towels; set aside. Drain pineapple, reserving juice; set the pineapple aside.

> In a large skillet, combine the cornstarch, salt and reserved pineapple juice until smooth. Stir in the syrup, water and vinegar. Bring to a boil; cook and stir for 2-3 minutes or until thickened. Add the sausage, green pepper, cherries and pineapple. Simmer, uncovered, for 5 minutes or until peppers are crisp-tender. Transfer to a shallow serving dish. Serve with toothpicks.

YIELD: 4 CUPS

> On a lightly floured surface, roll out dough to 1/8-in. thickness. Cut with a football-shaped cookie cutter. Place 2 in. apart on ungreased baking sheets.

> Bake at 350° for 8-10 minutes or until lightly browned. Remove to wire racks to cool.

> In a large bowl, combine confectioners' sugar and enough hot water to achieve spreading consistency; beat until smooth. Place 3 tablespoons glaze in a small bowl; set aside.

> Add cocoa to remaining glaze; stir until smooth. Spread brown glaze over cookies. Pipe white glaze onto cookies to form football laces.

YIELD: 4-1/2 DOZEN

touchdown cookies

SISTER JUDITH LABROZZI, CANTON, OHIO
With some simple, sweet touches, you can transform regular sugar cookies into a special treat for football fans.

1 cup butter, softened

1 cup sugar

2 eggs

1 teaspoon vanilla extract

3 cups all-purpose flour

2 teaspoons cream of tartar

1 teaspoon baking soda

GLAZE:
2 cups confectioners' sugar

4 to 5 tablespoons hot water

3 to 4 teaspoons baking cocoa

> In a large bowl, cream butter and sugar until light and fluffy. Add eggs, one at a time, beating well after each addition. Beat in vanilla. Combine the flour, cream of tartar and baking soda; gradually add to creamed mixture and mix well. Cover and refrigerate for 3 hours or until easy to handle.

three-cheese dunk

MS. BIBS ORR, OCEANSIDE, CALIFORNIA
Here's a versatile dip that can be served with vegetables, crackers and even fruit.

2 cups (16 ounces) 4% cottage cheese, drained

3 tablespoons mayonnaise

1 tablespoon prepared horseradish

1 tablespoon spicy brown mustard

1/4 teaspoon salt

1/8 teaspoon pepper

1 cup (4 ounces) finely shredded cheddar cheese

1/2 cup crumbled blue cheese

3 green onions, finely chopped

Sliced fresh pears or apples, assorted vegetables or crackers

> In a food processor, combine the cottage cheese, mayonnaise, horseradish, mustard, salt and pepper; cover and process until blended.

> Transfer to a small bowl. Fold in the cheddar cheese, blue cheese and onions. Cover and refrigerate for 1 hour or until chilled. Serve with pears, apples, vegetables or crackers.

YIELD: 3 CUPS

LILY-MICHELE ALEXIS, LOUISVILLE, KENTUCKY

When you want a real "meaty" addition to your buffet, reach for these finger-licking-good ribs! Their sweet flavor and fall-off-the-bone tenderness will have guests wanting more.

honey garlic ribs

6 pounds pork baby back ribs, cut into two-rib portions

2 cups water, divided

3/4 cup packed brown sugar

2 tablespoons cornstarch

1 teaspoon garlic powder

1/4 teaspoon ground ginger

1/4 cup soy sauce

1/2 cup honey

> Place ribs bone side down in a large roasting pan; pour 1 cup of water over ribs. Cover tightly and bake at 350° for 1-1/2 hours.

> In a small bowl, combine the brown sugar, cornstarch, garlic powder and ginger. Stir in the soy sauce, honey and remaining water until smooth. Drain fat from roasting pan; pour sauce over ribs.

> Bake, uncovered, for 45 minutes or until meat is tender.

YIELD: 24 SERVINGS

mexican chicken roll-ups

JULIE MCDANIEL, BATESVILLE, INDIANA
Refrigerated crescent rolls make these hearty appetizers easy to assemble. Keep the ingredients on hand for last-minute snacking.

2-1/2 teaspoons cornmeal, divided

2-1/4 cups cubed cooked chicken

1 cup (4 ounces) shredded cheddar cheese

1/2 cup sliced ripe olives

1/2 cup sour cream

1 can (4 ounces) chopped green chilies, drained

1/4 cup chopped onion

2 tubes (8 ounces each) refrigerated crescent rolls

1 egg white

1 tablespoon water

Salsa

> Grease a baking sheet and sprinkle with 1-1/2 teaspoons cornmeal; set aside. In a large bowl, combine the chicken, cheese, olives, sour cream, chilies and onion; set aside.

> Separate crescent dough into eight rectangles; firmly press perforations to seal. Spread 1/2 cup chicken mixture over each rectangle to within 1 in. of edges. Roll up, starting from long side. Place 1 in. apart on prepared pan.

> In a small bowl, beat egg white and water until foamy; brush over roll-ups. Sprinkle with remaining cornmeal. Bake at 375° for 20-25 minutes or until golden brown. Serve warm with salsa. Refrigerate leftovers.

YIELD: 8 SERVINGS

shrimp on rosemary skewers

AMBER JOY NEWPORT, HAMPTON, VIRGINIA
Fresh sprigs of rosemary are the clever skewers for these shrimp kabobs. You can serve this as an hors d'oeuvre or as a main course.

8 fresh rosemary sprigs, about 6 inches long

1/2 cup orange marmalade

1/2 cup flaked coconut, chopped

1/4 teaspoon crushed red pepper flakes

1/4 teaspoon minced fresh rosemary

1-1/2 pounds uncooked large shrimp, peeled and deveined

> Soak rosemary sprigs in water for 30 minutes. In a small bowl, combine the marmalade, coconut, pepper flakes and minced rosemary; set aside 1/4 cup for serving.

> Coat grill rack with cooking spray before starting the grill. Thread shrimp onto rosemary sprigs. Grill for 4 minutes. Turn; baste with some of the remaining marmalade mixture. Grill 3-4 minutes longer or until shrimp turn pink; baste again. Serve with reserved marmalade mixture.

YIELD: 8 SERVINGS

> Divide into six portions. On a lightly floured surface, roll each portion into an 8-in. circle. Cut into eight wedges and place on greased baking sheets.

> Bake at 375° for 17-20 minutes or until edges are lightly browned. Cool on wire racks. Store in an airtight container.

YIELD: 4 DOZEN

coconut chicken bites

LINDA SCHWARZ, BERTRAND, NEBRASKA

These tender nuggets are great for nibbling, thanks to the coconut and seasonings. I've served these several times at parties, and everyone enjoyed them.

2 cups flaked coconut

1 egg

2 tablespoons milk

3/4 pound boneless skinless chicken breasts, cut into 3/4-inch pieces

1/2 cup all-purpose flour

Oil for deep-fat frying

1 teaspoon celery salt

1/2 teaspoon garlic powder

1/2 teaspoon ground cumin

> In a blender or food processor, process coconut until finely chopped. Transfer to a bowl and set aside. In another bowl, combine egg and milk. Toss chicken with flour; dip in egg mixture, then in coconut. Place in a single layer on a baking sheet. Refrigerate for 30 minutes.

> In an electric skillet or deep-fat fryer, heat 2 in. of oil to 375°. Fry chicken, a few pieces at time, for 1-1/2 minutes on each side or until golden brown. Drain on paper towels; place in a bowl. Sprinkle with celery salt, garlic powder and cumin; toss to coat. Serve warm.

YIELD: 3 DOZEN

homemade crisp crackers

TASTE OF HOME TEST KITCHEN

Store-bought crackers have nothing on these cheesy crisps. Make them in advance and keep them handy in an airtight container for anytime snacking.

1-3/4 cups all-purpose flour

1/2 cup cornmeal

1/2 teaspoon baking soda

1/2 teaspoon sugar

1/2 teaspoon salt

1/2 teaspoon garlic powder

1/4 teaspoon Italian seasoning

1/2 cup cold butter, cubed

1-1/2 cups (6 ounces) shredded Colby-Monterey Jack cheese

1/2 cup plus 2 tablespoons cold water

2 tablespoons cider vinegar

> In a large bowl, combine the first seven ingredients; cut in butter until crumbly. Stir in cheese. Gradually add water and vinegar, tossing with a fork until dough forms a ball. Wrap in plastic wrap and refrigerate for 1 hour or until firm.

orange-glazed chicken wings

HOLLY MANN, AMHERST, NEW HAMPSHIRE
I normally don't care for wings, but after I tried this recipe that was shared by a co-worker, it changed my mind about these lovely glazed wings.

15 whole chicken wings (about 3 pounds)

1-1/2 cups soy sauce

1 cup orange juice

1 teaspoon garlic powder

> Cut chicken wings into three sections; discard wing tips. In a large resealable plastic bag, combine the soy sauce, orange juice and garlic powder; add wings. Seal bag and turn to coat; refrigerate overnight.

> Drain and discard marinade. Place chicken wings in a greased foil-lined 15-in. x 10-in. x 1-in. baking pan. Bake at 350° for 1 hour or until juices run clear and glaze is set, turning twice.

YIELD: 2-1/2 DOZEN

Editor's Note: 3 pounds of uncooked chicken wingettes may be substituted for the whole chicken wings. Omit the first step.

cranberry meatballs and sausage

MARYBELL LINTOTT, VERNON, BRITISH COLUMBIA
Years ago, I found a version of this recipe in a cookbook. At first taste, my family judged it a keeper. The tangy, saucy meatballs are requested by our friends whenever I host card night. We also take the yummy bites on camping trips.

1 egg, beaten

1 small onion, finely chopped

3/4 cup dry bread crumbs

1 tablespoon dried parsley flakes

1 tablespoon Worcestershire sauce

1/4 teaspoon salt

1 pound bulk pork sausage

1 can (16 ounces) jellied cranberry sauce

3 tablespoons cider vinegar

2 tablespoons brown sugar

1 tablespoon prepared mustard

1 package (1 pound) miniature smoked sausage links

> In a large bowl, combine the first six ingredients. Crumble bulk sausage over the mixture and mix well. Shape into 1-in. balls. In a large skillet, cook meatballs over medium heat until browned; drain.

> In a large saucepan, combine the cranberry sauce, vinegar, brown sugar and mustard. Cook and stir over medium heat until cranberry sauce is melted. Add the meatballs and sausage links. Bring to a boil. Reduce heat; simmer, uncovered, for 10-15 minutes or until meatballs are no longer pink and sauce is slightly thickened.

YIELD: 14-16 SERVINGS

prosciutto chicken kabobs

ELAINE SWEET, DALLAS, TEXAS
Everyone will think you spent hours preparing these simple, clever grilled wraps, served with a guacamole-like dip. Basil gives the chicken plenty of flavor.

3/4 cup five-cheese Italian salad dressing

1/4 cup lime juice

2 teaspoons white Worcestershire sauce for chicken

1/2 pound boneless skinless chicken breasts, cut into 3-inch x 1/2-inch strips

12 thin slices prosciutto

24 fresh basil leaves

AVOCADO DIP:
2 medium ripe avocados, peeled

1/4 cup minced fresh cilantro

2 green onions, chopped

2 tablespoons lime juice

2 tablespoons mayonnaise

1-1/2 teaspoons prepared horseradish

1 garlic clove, minced

1/4 teaspoon salt

> In a large resealable plastic bag, combine the salad dressing, lime juice and Worcestershire sauce; add chicken. Seal bag and turn to coat; refrigerate for 1 hour.

> Drain and discard marinade. Fold prosciutto slices in half; top each with two basil leaves and a chicken strip. Roll up jelly-roll style, starting with a short side. Thread onto metal or soaked wooden skewers.

> Grill, covered, over medium heat for 5 minutes on each side or until chicken is no longer pink.

> Meanwhile, in a small bowl, mash the avocados. Stir in cilantro, onions, lime juice, mayonnaise, horseradish, garlic and salt. Serve with kabobs.

YIELD: 12 APPETIZERS

flavorful sausage balls

OLIVE LAMB, CUSHING, OKLAHOMA
I whip up a batch of these meatballs in a matter of minutes. They're a great treat on busy nights when you need something fast.

1 pound bulk pork sausage

1 egg, beaten

1/2 cup dry bread crumbs

3/4 cup ketchup

1/4 cup packed brown sugar

2 tablespoons white vinegar

2 tablespoons soy sauce

> In a bowl, combine sausage and egg. Sprinkle with bread crumbs; mix well. Shape into 1-in. balls.

> In a skillet, brown meatballs; drain. Combine remaining ingredients; pour over meatballs. Simmer for 10 minutes or until meat is no longer pink.

YIELD: 2-1/2 DOZEN

JACQUELYNNE STINE, LAS VEGAS, NEVADA
A crisp, golden coating surrounds these butterflied shrimp stuffed with bacon and cream cheese. You'll want to make a meal out of them!

crispy shrimp poppers

20 uncooked medium shrimp, peeled and deveined

4 ounces cream cheese, softened

10 bacon strips

1 cup all-purpose flour

2 eggs, lightly beaten

2 cups panko (Japanese) bread crumbs

Oil for deep-fat frying

> Butterfly the shrimp along the outside curves. Spread about 1 teaspoon cream cheese inside each shrimp. Cut bacon strips in half lengthwise; wrap a piece around each shrimp and secure with toothpicks.

> In three separate shallow bowls, place the flour, eggs and bread crumbs. Coat the shrimp with flour; dip into eggs, then coat with bread crumbs.

> In an electric skillet or deep-fat fryer, heat oil to 375°. Fry shrimp, a few at a time, for 3-4 minutes or until golden brown. Drain on paper towels. Discard toothpicks before serving.

YIELD: 20 APPETIZERS

pigskin sandwiches

SISTER JUDITH LABROZZI, CANTON, OHIO
Guests won't need much coaching to run for sandwiches when they're served on tasty football buns. I baked these fun bites for a theme party.

1 package (1/4 ounce) active dry yeast

1/2 cup sugar, divided

2 cups warm water (110° to 115°), divided

1/2 cup plus 2 tablespoons butter, softened, divided

1-1/2 teaspoons salt

1 egg, lightly beaten

6-1/2 to 7 cups all-purpose flour

Mayonnaise or mustard, optional

Lettuce leaves and sliced tomatoes

18 slices process American cheese

2-1/2 pounds sliced deli ham

4 ounces cream cheese, softened

> In a large bowl, dissolve yeast and 2 teaspoons sugar in 1/4 cup warm water. Let stand for 5 minutes. Add 1/2 cup butter, salt, egg and remaining sugar, water and 4 cups flour. Beat until smooth. Stir in enough remaining flour to form a soft dough.

> Turn onto a floured surface; knead until smooth and elastic, about 6-8 minutes. Place in a greased bowl, turning once to grease top. Cover and let rise in a warm place until doubled, about 1 hour.

> Punch dough down. turn onto a lightly floured surface; divide into 18 pieces. Shape into ovals; place 2 in. apart on greased baking sheets. Cover and let rise until doubled, about 30 minutes.

> Bake at 350° for 18-23 minutes or until golden. Melt remaining butter; brush over buns. Remove from pans to wire racks to cool.

> Split buns. Spread with mayonnaise or mustard if desired. Top with lettuce, tomato, cheese and ham. Replace tops. Place cream cheese in a plastic bag; cut a small hole in the corner of the bag. Pipe football laces on sandwiches.

YIELD: 18 SERVINGS

tumbleweeds

VICTORIA JOHNSON, VENICE, FLORIDA
I like making these crisp and creamy treats because they require only four ingredients. It's hard to stop eating them. They're irresistible.

1 can (12 ounces) salted peanuts

1 can (7 ounces) potato sticks

3 cups butterscotch chips

3 tablespoons peanut butter

> Combine peanuts and potato sticks in a bowl; set aside. In a microwave, heat butterscotch chips and peanut butter at 70% power for 1-2 minutes or until melted, stirring every 30 seconds. Add to peanut mixture; stir to coat evenly.

> Drop by rounded tablespoonfuls onto waxed paper-lined baking sheets. Refrigerate until set, about 5 minutes. Store in an airtight container.

YIELD: ABOUT 4-1/2 DOZEN

> In an electric skillet or deep-fat fryer, heat oil to 375°. Cook potatoes in oil in batches for 2-3 minutes or until deep golden brown, stirring frequently.

> Remove with a slotted spoon; drain on paper towels. Immediately sprinkle with reserved seasoning mixture. Store in an airtight container.

YIELD: 10 CUPS

pretzels with mustard

TASTE OF HOME TEST KITCHEN
The quick sauce for these wonderful pretzels adds an almost-homemade note to appetizer buffets. They also make a great after-school snack along with a cup of hot cider or glass of cold milk.

1/2 cup Dijon mustard

1/3 cup honey

1 tablespoon white wine vinegar

2 teaspoons sugar

Large soft pretzels, warmed

> In a small bowl, whisk the mustard, honey, vinegar and sugar until blended. Serve with soft pretzels.

YIELD: 3/4 CUP

fiery potato chips

SUE MURPHY, GREENWOOD, MICHIGAN
Seasoned with chili powder and cayenne pepper, these paper-thin chips are surefire crowd-pleasers.

4 medium unpeeled potatoes

4 teaspoons salt, divided

4 cups ice water

1 tablespoon chili powder

1 teaspoon garlic salt

1 teaspoon dried parsley flakes

1/4 to 1/2 teaspoon cayenne pepper

Oil for deep-fat frying

> Using a vegetable peeler or metal cheese slicer, cut potatoes into very thin lengthwise strips. Place in a large bowl; add 3 teaspoons salt and ice water. Soak for 30 minutes; drain.

> Place potatoes on paper towels and pat dry. In a small bowl, combine the chili powder, garlic salt, parsley, cayenne and remaining salt; set aside.

MICHELLE GAUER, SPICER, MINNESOTA
If your favorite appetizers are cheesy potato skins and buffalo chicken wings, you'll find this recipe one to cheer about. Loaded with cheese, sour cream and onion, hearty stuffed potatoes get a sassy bite from mild wing sauce.

buffalo chicken-topped potatoes

4 medium potatoes (about 1-1/2 pounds)

3/4 cup shredded cheddar cheese, divided

1/2 cup sour cream

2 tablespoons buffalo wing sauce, divided

1 pound boneless skinless chicken breasts, cubed

1/4 teaspoon salt

1/4 teaspoon chili powder

1 tablespoon canola oil

2 tablespoons white vinegar

2 tablespoons butter

Additional sour cream and chopped green onions

> Scrub and pierce potatoes. Bake at 375° for 1 hour or until tender. When cool enough to handle, cut each potato in half lengthwise. Scoop out the pulp, leaving thin shells.

> In a large bowl, mash the pulp with 1/2 cup cheese, sour cream and 1 tablespoon buffalo wing sauce. Spoon into potato shells. Sprinkle with remaining cheese.

> Place on a baking sheet. Bake 8-12 minutes longer or until heated through. Meanwhile, sprinkle chicken with salt and chili powder.

> In a large skillet, cook chicken in oil over medium heat for 6-8 minutes or until no longer pink. Stir in the vinegar, butter and remaining buffalo wing sauce; cook and stir 2-3 minutes longer.

> Spoon chicken mixture over potatoes. Serve with additional sour cream and onions.

YIELD: 8 SERVINGS

honey-mustard turkey meatballs

BONNIE DURKIN, NESCOPECK, PENNSYLVANIA
I turn to this recipe often during the holidays. It's nice to have a turkey meatball that doesn't taste like you should have used beef. These tangy meatballs can be prepared ahead and frozen, so even drop-in guests can be treated to a hot snack.

1 egg, lightly beaten

3/4 cup crushed butter-flavored crackers

1/2 cup shredded part-skim mozzarella cheese

1/4 cup chopped onion

1/2 teaspoon ground ginger

6 tablespoons Dijon mustard, divided

1 pound ground turkey

1 tablespoon cornstarch

1/4 teaspoon onion powder

1-1/4 cups unsweetened pineapple juice

1/4 cup chopped green pepper

2 tablespoons honey

> In a bowl, combine the egg, cracker crumbs, cheese, onion, ginger and 3 tablespoons mustard. Crumble turkey over mixture and mix well. Shape into 30 (1-in.) balls. Place in a greased 13-in. x 9-in baking dish. Bake, uncovered, at 350° for 20-25 minutes or until juices run clear.

> In a saucepan, combine the cornstarch and onion powder. Stir in the pineapple juice until smooth. Add the pepper and honey. Bring to a boil; cook and stir 2 minutes or until thickened. Reduce heat; stir in remaining mustard until smooth.

> Brush meatballs with about 1/4 cup sauce and bake 10 minutes longer. Serve remaining sauce as a dip for meatballs.

YIELD: 2-1/2 DOZEN

stuffed butterflied shrimp

JOAN ELLIOTT, DEEP RIVER, CONNECTICUT
These flavorful, baked shrimp can be an appetizer or entree. I've handed out this recipe to many friends and family members.

24 uncooked unpeeled large shrimp

1 cup Italian salad dressing

1-1/2 cups seasoned bread crumbs

1 can (6-1/2 ounces) chopped clams, drained and minced

6 tablespoons butter, melted

1-1/2 teaspoons minced fresh parsley

> Peel shrimp, leaving tail section on. Make a deep cut along the top of each shrimp (do not cut all the way through); remove the vein. Place shrimp in a shallow dish; add salad dressing. Set aside for 20 minutes.

> Meanwhile, in a large bowl, combine the bread crumbs, clams, butter and parsley. Drain and discard salad dressing from shrimp. Arrange shrimp in a greased 13-in. x 9-in. baking dish. Open shrimp and press flat; fill each with 1 tablespoon of crumb mixture. Bake, uncovered, at 350° for 20-25 minutes or until shrimp turn pink.

YIELD: 2 DOZEN

hot mustard popcorn

DIANE HIXON, NICEVILLE, FLORIDA
When friends pop over, I like to dish up yummy munchies like this one.

1 teaspoon ground mustard

1/2 teaspoon dried thyme

1/2 teaspoon salt

1/4 teaspoon pepper

Dash cayenne pepper

3 quarts freshly popped popcorn

> Combine the first five ingredients. Place popcorn in a large bowl; add seasonings and toss to coat.

YIELD: 3 QUARTS

buffalo chicken dip

PEGGY FOSTER, FLORENCE, KENTUCKY
Here's a great dip my family loves for football parties and other get-togethers. Everywhere I take it, people ask for the recipe.

1 package (8 ounces) cream cheese, softened

1 can (10 ounces) chunk white chicken, drained

1/2 cup buffalo wing sauce

1/2 cup ranch salad dressing

2 cups (8 ounces) shredded Colby-Monterey Jack cheese

Tortilla chips

> Spread cream cheese into an ungreased shallow 1-qt. baking dish. Layer with chicken, buffalo wing sauce and ranch dressing. Sprinkle with cheese.

> Bake, uncovered, at 350° for 20-25 minutes or until cheese is melted. Serve warm with tortilla chips.

YIELD: ABOUT 2 CUPS

skewered shrimp

JOAN MORRIS, LILLIAN, ALABAMA
A ginger mixture is used as both a marinade and a sauce for these barbecued shrimp. Serve them with toothpicks as an appetizer or stir into pasta for an entree.

3 tablespoons soy sauce

2 tablespoons lemon juice

1 tablespoon chili sauce

1 tablespoon minced fresh gingerroot

1 pound uncooked medium shrimp, peeled and deveined

> In a bowl, combine the soy sauce, lemon juice, chili sauce and ginger; mix well. Pour half into a large resealable plastic bag; add the shrimp. Seal bag and turn to coat; refrigerate for 2 hours. Cover and refrigerate remaining marinade.

> Drain and discard marinade from shrimp. Thread onto metal or soaked wooden skewers. Grill, uncovered, over medium heat for 6-8 minutes or until shrimp turn pink, turning once. Serve with reserved marinade.

YIELD: 4 SERVINGS

sesame chicken bites

KATHY GREEN, LAYTON, NEW JERSEY
So tender and tasty, these chicken bites are greatly enhanced by a honey-mustard dipping sauce. I used to spend several days creating hors d'oeuvres for our holiday open house, and these were among the favorites.

1/2 cup dry bread crumbs

1/4 cup sesame seeds

2 teaspoons minced fresh parsley

1/2 cup mayonnaise

1 teaspoon onion powder

1 teaspoon ground mustard

1/4 teaspoon pepper

1 pound boneless skinless chicken breasts, cut into 1-inch cubes

2 to 4 tablespoons vegetable oil

HONEY-MUSTARD SAUCE:
3/4 cup mayonnaise

4-1/2 teaspoons honey

1-1/2 teaspoons Dijon mustard

> In a large resealable plastic bag, combine the bread crumbs, sesame seeds and parsley; set aside. In a small bowl, combine the mayonnaise, onion powder, mustard and pepper. Coat chicken in mayonnaise mixture, then add to crumb mixture, a few pieces at a time; shake to coat.

> In a large skillet, cook chicken in oil in batches until juices run clear, adding additional oil as needed. In a small bowl, combine the sauce ingredients. Serve with the chicken.

YIELD: 8-10 SERVINGS

ginger meatballs

SYBIL LESON, HOUSTON, TEXAS
These sweet and tangy meatballs have caused many guests to ask, "What is that delicious flavor?" For a crowd, double the recipe and keep them warm in a slow cooker.

1 egg

1/2 cup finely crushed gingersnaps (about 11 cookies)

1 teaspoon salt

1-1/2 pounds ground beef

1 cup ketchup

1/4 cup packed brown sugar

2 tablespoons Dijon mustard

1/2 teaspoon ground ginger

> In a large bowl, combine the egg, cookie crumbs and salt. Crumble beef over mixture and mix well. Shape into 1-in. balls. Place meatballs 1 in. apart in ungreased 15-in. x 10-in. x 1-in. baking pans. Bake, uncovered, at 350° for 15-20 minutes or until no longer pink; drain.

> In a large skillet, combine ketchup, brown sugar, mustard and ginger. Add meatballs. Simmer, uncovered, for 15-20 minutes or until heated through, gently stirring several times.

YIELD: ABOUT 3-1/2 DOZEN

tempura chicken wings

SUSAN WUCKOWITSCH, LENEXA, KANSAS

When I moved to Kansas City from Texas, I brought many of my mom's best-loved recipes, including these saucy, sweet-and-sour wings. This recipe turned a friend of mine, who's not a fan of chicken, into a real wing lover.

15 whole chicken wings (about 3 pounds)

1 cup cornstarch

3 eggs, lightly beaten

Oil for deep-fat frying

1/2 cup sugar

1/2 cup white vinegar

1/2 cup currant jelly

1/4 cup soy sauce

3 tablespoons ketchup

2 tablespoons lemon juice

> Cut chicken wings into three sections; discard wing tip section. Place cornstarch in a large resealable plastic bag; add chicken wings, a few at a time, and shake to coat evenly. Dip wings in eggs.

> In an electric skillet or deep-fat fryer, heat oil to 375°. Fry wings for 8 minutes or until golden brown and juices run clear, turning occasionally. Drain on paper towels.

> In a small saucepan, combine the sugar, vinegar, jelly, soy sauce, ketchup and lemon juice. Bring to a boil. Reduce heat; simmer, uncovered, for 10 minutes.

> Place chicken wings in a greased 15-in. x 10-in. x 1-in. baking pan. Pour half of the sauce over wings. Bake, uncovered, at 350° for 15 minutes. Turn wings; top with remaining sauce. Bake 10-15 minutes longer or until chicken juices run clear and coating is set.

YIELD: 2-1/2 DOZEN

Editor's Note: 3 pounds of uncooked chicken wing sections (wingettes) may be substituted for the whole chicken wings. Omit the first step.

flavored oyster crackers

TASTE OF HOME TEST KITCHEN

These jazzed-up oyster crackers have such great flavor, we bet you'll have trouble not eating them all at once! With Parmesan cheese and seasoning from a soup mix, they're a surefire hit on game day.

2 packages (10 ounces each) oyster crackers

1/2 cup canola oil

1/4 cup grated Parmesan cheese

1 envelope savory herb with garlic soup mix

> Place the crackers in a large bowl. Combine the oil, cheese and soup mix; pour over crackers and toss gently. Transfer to two ungreased 15-in. x 10-in. x 1-in. baking pans.

> Bake at 350° for 5-7 minutes, stirring once. Cool. Store in an airtight container.

YIELD: 12 CUPS

DELORES CONDON, PAYNESVILLE, MINNESOTA

Because I live in an area where there aren't many Chinese restaurants, I developed this Asian-inspired starter. A combination of soy and plum sauces, red wine, garlic and ginger creates a full-bodied marinade that infuses every bite with wonderful flavor.

chinese pork tenderloin

1/4 cup sugar

1/4 cup soy sauce

2 tablespoons plum sauce

2 tablespoons ketchup

1 tablespoon dry red wine or beef broth

1 garlic clove, minced

3/4 teaspoon finely chopped crystallized ginger

2 pork tenderloins (3/4 pound each)

Toasted sesame seeds, Chinese-style mustard and additional plum sauce, optional

> In a small bowl, combine the first seven ingredients. Pour 1/3 cup into a large resealable plastic bag; add the pork. Seal bag and turn to coat; refrigerate for 8 hours or overnight, turning several times. Cover and refrigerate remaining marinade for basting.

> Drain and discard marinade. Place pork on a greased rack in a foil-lined roasting pan.

> Bake, uncovered, at 425° for 20-30 minutes or until a meat thermometer reads 160°, brushing occasionally with reserved marinade.

> Let stand for 5-10 minutes before slicing. Sprinkle with sesame seeds and serve with mustard and additional plum sauce if desired.

YIELD: 10 SERVINGS

> Cook ravioli according to package directions. Drain and pat dry. Place eggs in a shallow bowl. In another shallow bowl, combine the bread crumbs, Parmesan cheese, pepper flakes, pepper and garlic salt. Dip ravioli in the eggs, then bread crumb mixture.

> In an electric skillet or deep-fat fryer, heat oil to 375°. Fry ravioli, a few at a time, for 1-2 minutes on each side or until golden brown. Drain on paper towels.

> Arrange ravioli in an ungreased 15-in. x 10-in. x 1-in. baking pan. Spoon sauces over ravioli; sprinkle with cheddar cheese.

> Bake at 350° for 3-5 minutes or until cheese is melted. Sprinkle with onions and olives. Serve immediately with additional spaghetti sauce if desired.

YIELD: 6-1/2 DOZEN

crowd-pleasing ravioli nachos

ROBERT DOORNBOS, JENISON, MICHIGAN
Lightly breaded and deep-fried, ravioli goes to a new level in this hearty party starter. Children and grown-ups can't get enough of the cheesy, flavorful crowd-pleaser.

1 package (25 ounces) frozen cheese ravioli

1 package (25 ounces) frozen sausage ravioli

3 eggs, lightly beaten

2 cups seasoned bread crumbs

2 tablespoons grated Parmesan cheese

1/4 teaspoon crushed red pepper flakes

1/4 teaspoon pepper

1/8 teaspoon garlic salt

Oil for deep-fat frying

3/4 cup Alfredo sauce

3/4 cup spaghetti sauce

2 cups (8 ounces) shredded cheddar cheese

5 green onions, sliced

1 can (3.8 ounces) sliced ripe olives, drained

Additional spaghetti sauce, optional

chicken appetizers

NORMA SNIDER, CHAMBERSBURG, PENNSYLVANIA
Here's a memorable change of pace for your next appetizer tray. Try these chicken meatballs plain or dipped in mustard.

2-1/2 cups minced cooked chicken breast

3 tablespoons finely chopped onion

3 tablespoons finely chopped celery

2 tablespoons finely chopped carrot

2 tablespoons dry bread crumbs

1 egg white

1/2 teaspoon poultry seasoning

Pinch pepper

> In a bowl, combine all ingredients; mix well. Shape into 3/4-in. balls; place on a baking sheet that has been coated with cooking spray. Bake at 400° for 8-10 minutes or until lightly browned.

YIELD: ABOUT 2-1/2 DOZEN

honey-garlic glazed meatballs

MARION FOSTER, KIRKTON, ONTARIO
My husband and I raise cattle on our farm here in southwestern Ontario, so it's no surprise that we're fond of these juicy meatballs. I know your family will like them, too.

2 eggs

3/4 cup milk

1 cup dry bread crumbs

1/2 cup finely chopped onion

2 teaspoons salt

2 pounds ground beef

4 garlic cloves, minced

1 tablespoon butter

3/4 cup ketchup

1/2 cup honey

3 tablespoons soy sauce

> In a large bowl, combine eggs and milk. Add the bread crumbs, onion and salt. Crumble beef over mixture and mix well. Shape into 1-in. balls. Place in two greased 15-in. x 10-in. x 1-in. baking pans. Bake, uncovered, at 400° for 12-15 minutes or until meat is no longer pink.

> Meanwhile, in a large saucepan, saute garlic in butter until tender. Stir in the ketchup, honey and soy sauce. Bring to a boil. Reduce heat; cover and simmer for 5 minutes. Drain meatballs; add to sauce. Carefully stir to evenly coat. Cook for 5-10 minutes.

YIELD: 5-1/2 DOZEN

chocolate-dipped pretzel rods

KAY WATERS, BENLD, ILLINOIS
Kids of all ages enjoy these fun-to-eat treats. Once the pretzels are wrapped with plastic wrap and ribbons, you can slip them inside a glass jar for a great presentation.

2 packages (14 ounces each) caramels

2 packages (10 ounces each) pretzel rods

3 cups chopped toasted almonds

1 pound white candy coating, coarsely chopped

1 pound dark chocolate candy coating, coarsely chopped

> In a microwave, melt caramels; stir until smooth. Pour into an ungreased 8-in. square pan or a tall glass. Leaving 1 in. of space on the end you are holding; roll or dip pretzels in caramel. Allow excess to drip off. Roll in almonds. Place on waxed paper-lined baking sheets and allow to harden.

> Melt white candy coating at 70% power for 1 minute; stir. Microwave at additional 10- to 20-second intervals, stirring until smooth. Repeat dipping procedure with half of the caramel-coated pretzels. Return to baking sheets to harden. Repeat with dark chocolate coating and remaining pretzels.

> Store in an airtight container, or wrap in plastic wrap and tie with a colorful ribbon for gift-giving.

YIELD: ABOUT 4 DOZEN

JESSICA KLYM, KILLDEER, NORTH DAKOTA

A group of us developed this recipe for the North Dakota State Beef Bash Competition, in 1995. We won the contest, and now my family requests this dip for all our special gatherings!

cowboy beef dip

1 pound ground beef

4 tablespoons chopped onion, divided

3 tablespoons chopped sweet red pepper, divided

2 tablespoons chopped green pepper, divided

1 can (10-3/4 ounces) condensed nacho cheese soup, undiluted

1/2 cup salsa

4 tablespoons sliced ripe olives, divided

4 tablespoons sliced pimiento-stuffed olives, divided

2 tablespoons chopped green chilies

1 teaspoon chopped seeded jalapeno pepper

1/4 teaspoon dried oregano

1/4 teaspoon pepper

1/4 cup shredded cheddar cheese

2 tablespoons sour cream

2 to 3 teaspoons minced fresh parsley

Tortilla chips

> In a large skillet, cook the beef, 3 tablespoons onion, 2 tablespoons red pepper and 1 tablespoon green pepper over medium heat until meat is no longer pink; drain. Stir in the soup, salsa, 3 tablespoons ripe olives, 3 tablespoons pimiento-stuffed olives, chilies, jalapeno, oregano and pepper. Bring to a boil. Reduce heat; simmer, uncovered, for 5 minutes.

> Transfer to a serving dish. Top with the cheese, sour cream and parsley; sprinkle with the remaining onion, peppers and olives. Serve with tortilla chips.

YIELD: 3 CUPS

Editor's Note: When cutting hot peppers, disposable gloves are recommended. Avoid touching your face.

chicken bacon bites

BETTY PIERSON, WELLINGTON, FLORIDA

Ginger and orange marmalade give these rumaki-style snacks wonderful flavor. I marinate the wrapped chicken earlier in the day and broil them when guests arrive.

12 bacon strips, halved

10 ounces boneless skinless chicken breasts, cut into 24 cubes

1 can (8 ounces) sliced water chestnuts, drained

1/2 cup orange marmalade

1/4 cup soy sauce

2 garlic cloves, minced

1 teaspoon grated fresh gingerroot

> Place bacon on a broiler rack. Broil 4 in. from the heat for 1-2 minutes on each side or until partially cooked; cool.

> Wrap a piece of bacon around a chicken cube and water chestnut slice; secure with a toothpick. In a resealable plastic bag, combine the marmalade, soy sauce, garlic and ginger. Add wrapped chicken; carefully turn to coat. Seal and refrigerate for 2 hours.

> Drain and discard marinade. Broil chicken for 3-4 minutes on each side or until juices run clear and bacon is crisp. Serve warm.

YIELD: 2 DOZEN

pizza egg rolls

TASTE OF HOME TEST KITCHEN

We gave traditional pizza a twist by rolling up the usual toppings in egg roll wrappers, then deep-frying them. Yum!

1 package (3-1/2 ounces) sliced pepperoni, chopped

1 cup chopped fresh mushrooms

1 medium green pepper, chopped

1/2 cup grated Parmesan cheese

1/2 teaspoon pizza seasoning or Italian seasoning

14 egg roll wrappers

14 pieces string cheese

Oil for deep-fat frying

1 can (15 ounces) pizza sauce, warmed

> In a small bowl, combine the pepperoni, mushrooms, green pepper, Parmesan cheese and pizza seasoning. Place an egg roll wrapper on a work surface with a point facing you; place a piece of string cheese near the bottom corner. Top with about 2 tablespoons pepperoni mixture.

> Fold bottom corner over filling. Fold sides toward center over filling. Using a pastry brush, wet the top corner with water; roll up tightly to seal. Repeat with remaining wrappers, cheese and filling.

> In an electric skillet or deep-fat fryer, heat oil to 375°. Fry egg rolls, a few at a time, for 1-2 minutes on each side or until golden brown. Drain on paper towels. Serve with pizza sauce.

YIELD: 14 EGG ROLLS

coconut shrimp

TACY HOLLIDAY, GERMANTOWN, MARYLAND
Guests are always impressed when I present these restaurant-quality shrimp. A selection of sauces served alongside adds the perfect touch.

1-1/4 cups all-purpose flour

1/4 teaspoon seafood seasoning

1 egg, beaten

3/4 cup pineapple juice

1 package (14 ounces) flaked coconut

1 pound large shrimp, peeled and deveined

Oil for deep-fat frying

Sweet-and-sour sauce, plum sauce or Dijon mustard, optional

> In a bowl, combine the flour, seasoning, egg and pineapple juice until smooth. Place coconut in a shallow bowl. Dip shrimp into batter, then coat with coconut.

> In an electric skillet or deep-fat fryer, heat oil to 375°. Fry shrimp, a few at a time, for 1-1/2 minutes or until golden brown, turning occasionally. Drain on paper towels. Serve with dipping sauce or mustard if desired.

YIELD: ABOUT 1-1/2 DOZEN

garlic-cheese chicken wings

DONNA PIERCE, LADY LAKE, FLORIDA
I developed this recipe several years ago using chicken breasts, then decided to try it on wings as an appetizer, and it was a hit! If you like garlic, you're sure to enjoy these tender, zesty bites.

2 large whole garlic bulbs

1 tablespoon plus 1/2 cup olive oil, divided

1/2 cup butter, melted

1 teaspoon hot pepper sauce

1-1/2 cups seasoned bread crumbs

3/4 cup grated Parmesan cheese

3/4 cup grated Romano cheese

1/2 teaspoon pepper

15 whole chicken wings (about 3 pounds)

> Remove papery outer skin from garlic (do not peel or separate cloves). Cut top off garlic bulbs. Brush with 1 tablespoon oil. Wrap each bulb in heavy-duty foil. Bake at 425° for 30-35 minutes or until softened. Cool for 10-15 minutes.

> Squeeze the softened garlic into a blender or food processor. Add butter, hot pepper sauce and remaining oil; cover and process until smooth. Pour into a shallow bowl. In another shallow bowl, combine the bread crumbs, cheeses and pepper.

> Cut chicken wings into three sections; discard wing tip section. Dip chicken wings into the garlic mixture, then coat with crumb mixture. Place on a greased rack in a 15-in. x 10-in. x 1-in. baking pan; drizzle with any remaining garlic mixture. Bake, uncovered, at 350° for 50-55 minutes or until chicken juices run clear.

YIELD: 2-1/2 DOZEN

Editor's Note: 3 pounds of uncooked chicken wing sections (wingettes) may be substituted for the whole chicken wings. Omit the third step.

pesto chili peanuts

DENNIS DAHLIN, BOLINGBROOK, ILLINOIS
Who'd ever dream of teaming pesto with peanuts? I did, and the result is can't-stop-eating-them munchies that are salty, savory and sure to be in "hot" demand.

1 envelope pesto sauce mix

3 tablespoons olive oil

1 teaspoon chili powder

1/4 teaspoon cayenne pepper

5 cups salted dry roasted peanuts

> In a small bowl, whisk the pesto mix, oil, chili powder and cayenne. Pour into a large resealable plastic bag; add peanuts. Seal bag and shake to coat. Transfer to a greased 13-in. x 9-in. baking pan.

> Bake, uncovered, at 350° for 15-20 minutes, stirring once. Spread on waxed paper to cool. Store in an airtight container.

YIELD: 5 CUPS

enchilada meatballs

MARCIA HARRIS, STEVENSVILLE, MICHIGAN
Before I retired, these tasty little treats were popular during snack time at work. They're a good way to use up leftover corn bread.

2 cups crumbled corn bread

1 can (10 ounces) enchilada sauce, divided

1/2 teaspoon salt

1-1/2 pounds ground beef

1 can (8 ounces) tomato sauce

1/2 cup shredded Mexican cheese blend

> In a large bowl, combine the corn bread, 1/2 cup enchilada sauce and salt. Crumble beef over mixture; mix well. Shape into 1-in. balls.

> Place in a greased 15-in. x 10-in. x 1-in. baking pan. Bake, uncovered, at 350° for 18-22 minutes or until meat is no longer pink.

> Meanwhile, in a small saucepan, heat tomato sauce and remaining enchilada sauce. Drain meatballs; place in a serving dish. Top with sauce and sprinkle with cheese. Serve with toothpicks.

YIELD: ABOUT 4-1/2 DOZEN

tip If you want to substitute other nuts in Pesto Chili Peanuts, go for it! The recipe would also be great with cashews, mixed nuts or almonds. You could also make this recipe to give as gifts for friends and family members during the holidays.

MICHELLE MARTIN, WATERVILLE, OHIO
This flavorful pizza uses marinated chicken and a surprise ingredient, almonds, to pack a tasty punch.

spicy chicken appetizer pizza

1/2 cup rice vinegar

1/4 cup reduced-sodium soy sauce

1 cup chopped green onions, divided

4 garlic cloves, minced

3 teaspoons olive oil, divided

1/2 teaspoon pepper

1/4 teaspoon cayenne pepper

3/4 pound boneless skinless chicken breasts, cut into 1/2-inch pieces

1 tablespoon cornstarch

1 prebaked 12-inch thin pizza crust

1/4 cup shredded Monterey Jack cheese

1/4 cup shredded part-skim mozzarella cheese

2 tablespoons sliced almonds

> In a small bowl, combine the vinegar, soy sauce, 1/2 cup onions, garlic, 1 teaspoon oil, pepper and cayenne. Pour 1/2 cup into a large resealable plastic bag; add chicken. Seal bag and turn to coat; refrigerate for 30 minutes. Cover and refrigerate remaining marinade.

> Drain chicken, discarding marinade. In a large nonstick skillet over medium heat, cook chicken in remaining oil until no longer pink. Combine cornstarch and reserved marinade until blended; stir into skillet. Bring to a boil; cook and stir for 2 minutes or until thickened. Remove from the heat.

> Place the crust on an ungreased baking sheet; top with chicken mixture. Sprinkle with cheeses. Bake at 400° for 12 minutes. Top with almonds and remaining onions. Bake 2-3 minutes longer or until cheese is golden brown.

YIELD: 12 SLICES

seafood appetizer balls

HELEN MCLAIN, QUINLAN, TEXAS

After sampling a similar appetizer at a local restaurant, I went home to create my own. Family and friends like my version even better!

1 can (6 ounces) crabmeat, drained, flaked and cartilage removed

3/4 cup seasoned bread crumbs, divided

1/4 cup finely chopped celery

1/4 cup frozen cooked tiny shrimp, thawed

1 egg, lightly beaten

1 green onion, sliced

1 tablespoon chopped sweet red pepper

1 tablespoon milk

1 teaspoon garlic powder

1/2 teaspoon dried parsley flakes

1/2 teaspoon seafood seasoning

1/2 teaspoon pepper

1 cup crushed butter-flavored crackers (about 25 crackers)

1 egg white, lightly beaten

Oil for deep-fat frying

> In a large mixing bowl, combine the crab, 1/4 cup bread crumbs, celery, shrimp, egg, onion, red pepper, milk, garlic powder, parsley, seafood seasoning and pepper. Shape into 1-in. balls.

> Place the cracker crumbs, egg white and remaining bread crumbs in separate shallow bowls. Roll balls in bread crumbs; dip in egg white, then roll in cracker crumbs.

> In an electric skillet or deep-fat fryer, heat oil to 375°. Fry a few balls at a time for 1-2 minutes on each side or until golden brown. Drain on paper towels. Serve warm.

YIELD: 1-1/2 DOZEN

horseradish cheese spread

CATHY BODELL, FRANKFORT, MICHIGAN

Cheesy, thick and rich, this tasty dip stays put on freshly baked soft pretzels. It's also delicious spread on slices of crusty French bread.

1 package (16 ounces) process cheese (Velveeta), cubed

3/4 cup mayonnaise

1/3 cup prepared horseradish

1/4 cup milk

1/8 teaspoon hot pepper sauce

Baked soft pretzels, optional

> In a heavy saucepan over low heat, combine the cheese, mayonnaise, horseradish, milk and pepper sauce. Cook and stir until cheese is melted and mixture is blended. Serve with pretzels if desired.

YIELD: 2-1/2 CUPS

tip

When planning a tailgate or game-day party, keep the menu nice and simple. Guests are not expecting a seven-course meal at this kind of casual get-together. Three to four homemade dishes should be the maximum. Fill in with purchased items like chips and dip if necessary.

crunchy munchies

blizzard party mix

KELLEY SCOTT, PARMA, OHIO
This yummy combo is sure to be popular. It's perfect for a party, munching at home or giving away as a hostess gift.

2 cups Corn Chex

2 cups miniature pretzels

1 cup dry roasted peanuts

20 caramels, coarsely chopped

1 package (10 to 12 ounces) vanilla or white chips

> In a large bowl, combine the first four ingredients. In a microwave, melt chips; stir until smooth. Pour over cereal mixture and toss to coat.

> Immediately spread onto waxed paper-lined baking sheet; let stand until set, about 20 minutes.

> Break into pieces. Store in an airtight container.

YIELD: 4-1/2 CUPS

iced almonds

SUSAN MARIE TACCONE, ERIE, PENNSYLVANIA
These sugary almonds make a special snack or can be used to dress up a salad or garnish a dessert.

1/4 cup butter

2-1/2 cups whole unblanched almonds

1 cup sugar

1 teaspoon vanilla extract

> In a heavy saucepan, melt butter over medium-high heat. Add almonds and sugar. Cook and stir constantly for 7-8 minutes or until syrup is golden brown. Remove from the heat; stir in vanilla.

> Immediately drop by clusters or separate almonds on a greased baking pan. Cool. Store in an airtight container.

YIELD: 4 CUPS

spiced honey pretzels

MARY LOU MOON, BEAVERTON, OREGON
If your tastes run to sweet and spicy, you'll love these zesty pretzels with a twist. The coating is so tasty, you won't need a dip to enjoy them!

4 cups thin pretzel sticks

3 tablespoons honey

2 teaspoons butter, melted

1 teaspoon onion powder

1 teaspoon chili powder

> Line a 15-in. x 10-in. x 1-in. baking pan with foil; coat the foil with cooking spray. Place pretzels in a large bowl.

> In a small bowl, combine the honey, butter, onion powder and chili powder. Pour over pretzels; toss to coat evenly. Spread into prepared pan.

> Bake at 350° for 8 minutes, stirring once. Cool on a wire rack, stirring gently several times to separate.

YIELD: 8 SERVINGS

> Place vanilla chips and remaining shortening in a microwave-safe bowl. Microwave, uncovered, at 70% power for 1 minute; stir until smooth. Drizzle over popcorn; toss gently to coat as much popcorn as possible. Sprinkle with pecans. Chill until firm before breaking into pieces.

YIELD: 16 CUPS

Editor's Note: This recipe was tested in a 1,100-watt microwave.

snackin' granola

MARLENE MOHR, CINCINNATI, OHIO
Granola's a popular treat with children these days—and this one couldn't be more convenient to prepare. I flavor it with lots of tasty good-for-you ingredients. It's perfect to send in bag lunches or to serve after school. I've also used it when we take family vacations in our car.

2-2/3 cups flaked coconut

1 cup quick-cooking oats

1/4 cup packed brown sugar

1/4 cup raisins or chopped pitted dried plums

1/4 cup chopped dried apricots

2 tablespoons sesame seeds

1/4 cup vegetable oil

1/4 cup honey

1/4 cup semisweet chocolate chips or M&M's

> In a large metal bowl, combine the first six ingredients. In a small saucepan, bring the oil and honey to just a boil. Immediately remove from the heat; pour over coconut mixture, stirring to coat evenly.

> Spread in an ungreased 13-in. x 9-in. baking pan. Bake at 325° for 25 minutes, stirring several times. Transfer to waxed paper to cool. Sprinkle with chocolate chips or M&M's. Store in an airtight container.

YIELD: 7 CUPS

chocolaty popcorn

DIANE HALFERTY, CORPUS CHRISTI, TEXAS
Pack these irresistible nibbles into plastic bags and tie them shut with curling ribbons for a pretty presentation. You could also prepare a batch or two for a bake sale. I guarantee it'll go quickly!

12 cups butter-flavored microwave popcorn

1 package (12 ounces) semisweet chocolate chips

2 teaspoons shortening, divided

1 package (10 to 12 ounces) vanilla or white chips

2 cups coarsely chopped pecans, toasted

> Place the popcorn in a greased 15-in. x 10-in. x 1-in. pan; set aside. Place semisweet chocolate chips and 1 teaspoon shortening in a microwave-safe bowl. Microwave, uncovered, at 70% power for 1 minute; stir until smooth. Drizzle over popcorn.

spiced pecans

TARI AMBLER, SHOREWOOD, ILLINOIS
I usually make at least two batches of these nuts at a time and package in containers to give as hostess gifts.

2 tablespoons sugar

1 teaspoon pumpkin pie spice

1/2 teaspoon salt

1/2 teaspoon ground ginger

2 tablespoons water

2 tablespoons honey

2 teaspoons canola oil

1-1/4 pounds pecan halves (about 5 cups)

> Combine the sugar, pie spice, salt and ginger; set aside. In a Dutch oven, bring the water, honey and oil to a boil. Add pecans; cook and stir until all of the liquid is evaporated, about 1 minute. Immediately sprinkle with reserved sugar mixture; toss to coat.

> Transfer to an ungreased 15-in. x 10-in. x 1-in. baking sheet. Bake at 325° for 15-20 minutes or until browned, stirring twice. Cool on a wire rack. Store in an airtight container.

YIELD: 5 CUPS

nutty cereal crunch

GRACE YASKOVIC, BRANCHVILLE, NEW JERSEY
This is one of my favorite confections to take to large get-togethers. Cinnamon, brown sugar and butter create a lip-smacking coating for cereal and a variety of nuts in this change-of-pace party mix. One handful simply isn't enough!

1 cup butter

1-1/3 cups packed brown sugar

1/2 teaspoon ground cinnamon

6 cups cornflakes

1 cup salted peanuts

1 cup salted cashews

1/2 cup almonds or macadamia nuts

> In a Dutch oven, melt butter; stir in brown sugar and cinnamon until sugar is dissolved. Remove from the heat.

> Combine cornflakes and nuts; add to sugar mixture and stir to coat. Spread onto two greased baking sheets. Cool; break apart. Store in an airtight container.

YIELD: 10 CUPS

honey snack mix

TASTE OF HOME TEST KITCHEN
Little ones can't resist gobbling up the crackers, cereal, raisins and candy in this sweet snack mix.

1 package (10 ounces) honey-flavored bear-shaped graham crackers (about 4 cups)

3 cups Honeycomb cereal

1-1/2 cups Reese's Pieces

1 cup chocolate-covered raisins

> In a large bowl, combine all the ingredients. Store in an airtight container.

YIELD: 9 CUPS

LISA CLAAS, WATERTOWN, WISCONSIN

A batch of this colorful, crunchy mix is perfect for gift-giving or serving at a holiday party. You can use any assortment of candy that you like.

deluxe caramel corn

4 quarts plain popped popcorn

5 cups mini pretzel twists

2 cups packed brown sugar

1 cup butter

1/2 cup dark corn syrup

1/2 teaspoon salt

1/2 teaspoon baking soda

1 cup salted peanuts

2 cups nonchocolate candy (Skittles, gumdrops, etc.)

> Place popcorn and pretzels in a large bowl; set aside. In a large heavy saucepan, combine the brown sugar, butter, corn syrup and salt; cook over medium heat, stirring occasionally, until mixture comes to a rolling boil. Cook and stir until candy thermometer reads 238° (soft-ball stage). Remove from the heat; stir in baking soda. Quickly pour over popcorn and mix thoroughly; stir in peanuts.

> Turn into two greased 13-in. x 9-in. baking pans. Bake at 200° for 20 minutes; stir. Bake 25 minutes longer. Remove from the oven; add candy and mix well. Remove from pans and place on waxed paper to cool. Break into clusters. Store in airtight containers or plastic bags.

YIELD: 6-1/2 QUARTS

Editor's Note: You should test your candy thermometer each time you use it. To do this, simply place the thermometer in a saucepan of boiling water and wait for several minutes. If the thermometer reads 212° in boiling water, it is accurate. If it rises above 212° or does not reach 212°, add or subtract the difference to the temperature called for in the recipe you're making.

harvest snack mix

MARLENE HARGUTH, MAYNARD, MINNESOTA
Candy corn makes this a natural snack for fall gatherings. The sweet and salty flavors are irresistible to many.

2 cups pretzel sticks

1 cup mixed nuts

1/2 cup sunflower kernels

6 tablespoons butter, melted

1/2 teaspoon ground cinnamon

1/8 teaspoon ground cloves

8 cups popped popcorn

1 cup candy corn

1 cup chocolate bridge mix

> In a large bowl, combine the pretzels, nuts and sunflower kernels. Combine the butter, cinnamon and cloves. Drizzle a third of butter mixture over pretzel mixture; toss to coat. Transfer to a greased 15-in. x 10-in. x 1-in. baking pan. Bake at 300° for 15 minutes.

> Place popcorn in a large bowl; drizzle with remaining butter mixture and toss to coat. Stir into pretzel mixture. Bake 15 minutes longer or until heated through. Cool; transfer to a large bowl. Add candy corn and bridge mix; toss to combine.

YIELD: 3 QUARTS

cinnamon granola

LINDA AGRESTA, COLORADO SPRINGS, COLORADO
Although it's meant for breakfast, my family eats this chunky cereal by the handful all day long.

2 cups old-fashioned oats

3/4 cup whole unsalted nuts

2/3 cup flaked coconut

1/2 cup sunflower kernels

1/3 cup sesame seeds

1/3 cup toasted wheat germ

1/4 cup oat bran

2 tablespoons cornmeal

2 tablespoons whole wheat flour

1 tablespoon ground cinnamon

1/2 cup honey

2 tablespoons vegetable oil

2 tablespoons vanilla extract

1/4 teaspoon salt

1 cup golden raisins

> In a large bowl, combine the first 10 ingredients; mix well. In a saucepan, heat honey and oil over medium heat for 4-5 minutes. Remove from the heat; stir in vanilla and salt. Pour over oat mixture and toss to coat.

> Transfer to a greased 15-in. x 10-in. x 1-in. baking pan. Bake at 275° for 45-50 minutes or until golden brown, stirring every 15 minutes. Cool, stirring occasionally. Stir in raisins. Store in an airtight container.

YIELD: 7 CUPS

cereal crunchies

JUANITA CARLSEN, NORTH BEND, OREGON
Folks can't get enough of my irresistible snack mix. A slightly sweet vanilla coating is the perfect match for the blend of mini pretzels, crispy cereal and salted nuts. It's a real crowd-pleaser.

2 cups Multi-Bran Chex

2 cups Corn Chex

2 cups Cheerios

2 cups miniature pretzels

1 cup salted mixed nuts

1/3 cup butter, cubed

1/3 cup packed brown sugar

1/4 cup light corn syrup

2 to 3 teaspoons butter flavoring

1-1/2 teaspoons salt

2 tablespoons vanilla extract

1/4 teaspoon baking soda

> In a large microwave-safe bowl, combine the cereals, pretzels and nuts; set aside. In a large saucepan, combine the butter, brown sugar, corn syrup, butter flavoring and salt. Bring to a boil. Boil, uncovered, for 5 minutes.

> In a small bowl, combine vanilla and baking soda. Remove brown sugar syrup from the heat; stir in vanilla mixture (syrup will foam). Pour over cereal mixture and toss to coat.

> Microwave, uncovered, on high for 2 minutes; stir. Microwave 2-3 minutes longer; stir. Microwave at 50% power for 2-3 minutes, stirring after 2 minutes. Cool for 3 minutes, stirring well several times. Spread onto waxed paper to cool.

YIELD: 8-1/2 CUPS

Editor's Note: This recipe was tested in a 1,100-watt microwave.

striped chocolate popcorn

MARY SCHMITTINGER, COLGATE, WISCONSIN
I'd seen chocolate popcorn in a candy shop and thought I'd try making it. This recipe was a great success.

12 cups popped popcorn

2 cups miniature pretzels

1 cup pecan halves, toasted

1/4 cup butter, melted

4 ounces white candy coating, coarsely chopped

2 ounces milk chocolate candy coating, coarsely chopped

> In a large bowl, combine the popcorn, pretzels and pecans. Drizzle with butter and toss; set aside.

> In a microwave, melt white candy coating at 70% power for 1 minute; stir. Microwave at additional 10- to 20-second intervals, stirring until smooth. Drizzle over popcorn mixture; toss to coat. Spread on foil-lined baking sheets.

> In a microwave, melt milk chocolate coating; stir until smooth. Drizzle over popcorn mixture. Let stand in a cool place until chocolate is set. Store in an airtight container.

YIELD: 17 CUPS

Editor's Note: This recipe was tested in a 1,100-watt microwave.

spiced orange pecans

RUTH PETERSON, JENISON, MICHIGAN

You won't be able to eat just one of these spicy, sugary nibblers. Keep them on hand for unexpected company, or wrap them up for hostess gifts.

2 egg whites, lightly beaten

3 tablespoons orange juice

2 cups pecan halves

1-1/2 cups confectioners' sugar

2 tablespoons cornstarch

2 tablespoons grated orange peel

1 teaspoon ground cinnamon

3/4 teaspoon ground cloves

1/4 teaspoon ground allspice

1/8 teaspoon salt

> In a large bowl, combine egg whites and orange juice. Add pecans and toss to coat; drain. In another large bowl, combine the remaining ingredients. Add pecans and toss to coat.

> Spread in a single layer in a greased 15-in. x 10-in. x 1-in. baking pan. Bake at 250° for 30-35 minutes or until dry and lightly browned. Cool completely. Store in an airtight container.

YIELD: 5 CUPS

cheese ball snack mix

MARY DETWEILER, WEST FARMINGTON, OHIO

Folks love the zippy burst of flavor in every bite of this crunchy treat.

1-1/2 cups salted cashews

1 cup crisp cheese balls snacks

1 cup Corn Chex

1 cup Rice Chex

1 cup miniature pretzels

1 cup chow mein noodles

1/2 cup butter, melted

1 tablespoon soy sauce

1 teaspoon Worcestershire sauce

1/2 teaspoon seasoned salt

1/4 teaspoon chili powder

1/4 teaspoon hot pepper sauce

> In a bowl, combine the cashews, cheese balls, cereals, pretzels and chow mein noodles. In another bowl, combine all the remaining ingredients. Pour over cereal mixture and toss to coat.

> Transfer to an ungreased 15-in. x 10-in. x 1-in. baking pan. Bake at 250° for 1 hour, stirring every 15 minutes.

YIELD: ABOUT 6 CUPS

Editor's Note: This recipe was tested with Planter's Cheeze Balls.

cajun party mix

TWILA BURKHOLDER, MIDDLEBURG, PENNSYLVANIA
*I pack this mix in tins to give to friends and family.
They can't seem to get enough—and it's
so easy to toss together!*

6 cups miniature fish-shaped crackers

6 cups pretzel sticks

3 cups Rice Chex

3 cups Corn Chex

1 can (11-1/2 ounces) mixed nuts

1 cup butter, melted

1 teaspoon garlic powder

1/2 to 1 teaspoon celery salt

1/2 teaspoon cayenne pepper

1/8 teaspoon hot pepper sauce

> In a large roasting pan, combine the first five
  ingredients. Combine the butter, garlic powder,
  celery salt, cayenne and hot pepper sauce; pour
  over cereal mixture and stir to coat.

> Bake, uncovered, at 250° for 35-40 minutes,
  stirring every 15 minutes. Cool completely.
  Store in airtight containers.

YIELD: ABOUT 5 QUARTS

fruity granola

NANCY CHAPMAN, CENTER HARBOR, NEW HAMPSHIRE
*You'll love the chewy sweetness of this honeyed cereal,
fruit and nut mixture. It's great as a snack out of hand or
in a parfait glass, layered with fruit and low-fat yogurt.*

3 cups old-fashioned oats

1/2 cup sliced almonds

1-1/4 cups honey

1/2 cup Grape-Nuts

1 tablespoon butter

1 teaspoon ground cinnamon

2-1/2 cups Wheaties

1/2 cup dried cranberries

1/2 cup raisins

1/2 cup dried banana chips

> In a large bowl, combine oats and almonds;
  spread evenly in a 15-in. x 10-in. x 1-in. baking
  pan coated with cooking spray. Bake at 325° for
  15 minutes.

> In a large bowl, combine the honey, Grape-Nuts,
  butter and cinnamon. Add oat mixture; stir to
  combine. Return mixture to the pan. Bake 15-20
  minutes longer or until golden. Cool on wire rack.

> When cool enough to handle, break granola into
  pieces. Place in a large bowl; stir in the Wheaties,
  cranberries, raisins and banana chips. Store in an
  airtight container in a cool dry place for up to
  2 months.

YIELD: 10 CUPS

tip

Snack mixes and granola make great gifts as
well as treats for your guests. And you don't
have to spend a fortune on containers. Watch
for decorative tins, plates and candy dishes at
bargain prices at stores and rummage sales. Keep them on hand
when you need last-minute gifts.

NANCY SCHLINGER, MIDDLEPORT, NEW YORK
While taking a long car trip, we all grazed on these munchies and didn't even need to stop for dinner. It was a lifesaver while traveling the open road.

motoring munchies

1 package (18 ounces) granola without raisins

1 can (17 ounces) mixed nuts

1 package (15 ounces) raisins

1 package (14 ounces) milk chocolate M&M's

1 package (14 ounces) peanut M&M's

1 package (12-1/4 ounces) Honey-Nut Cheerios

1 package (8.9 ounces) Cheerios

> In a large bowl, combine all ingredients. Store in covered containers or large resealable plastic bags.

YIELD: 4-1/2 QUARTS

critter crunch

WILMA MILLER, PORT ANGELES, WASHINGTON
Young kids will enjoy this fun treat that features a variety of wild animals.

1/4 cup butter

3 tablespoons brown sugar

1 teaspoon ground cinnamon

1-1/2 cups Crispix

1-1/2 cups Cherrios

1-1/2 cups animal crackers

1-1/2 cups honey-flavored bear-shaped graham crackers

1 cup bite-size Shredded Wheat

1 cup miniature pretzels

> In a saucepan or microwave-safe bowl, heat the butter, brown sugar and cinnamon until butter is melted; mix well. In a large bowl, combine the remaining ingredients. Add butter mixture and toss to coat.

> Place in a greased 15-in. x 10-in. x 1-in. baking pan. Bake, uncovered, at 300° for 30 minutes, stirring every 10 minutes. Store in an airtight container.

YIELD: ABOUT 8 CUPS

vanilla popcorn

CAROLYN RONEY, SCIPIO CENTER, NEW YORK
We enjoy traveling, and this recipe makes the perfect driving snack. It's easy, too, because it can be ready in about 10 minutes.

3 quarts popped popcorn

1 cup sugar

1/2 cup butter

1/4 cup light corn syrup

1/4 teaspoon baking soda

1/2 teaspoon vanilla extract

> Place popcorn in a large bowl; set aside. In a saucepan, combine the sugar, butter and corn syrup. Bring to a boil over medium heat; boil and stir until mixture is golden, about 2 minutes.

> Remove from the heat; stir in baking soda and vanilla. Pour over popcorn and toss to coat. Cool slightly; break apart while warm. Store in an airtight container.

YIELD: 3 QUARTS

white chocolate party mix

ROSE WENTZEL, ST. LOUIS, MISSOURI
I get rave reviews every time I prepare this tasty, crispy combination of cereal, popcorn, pretzels, nuts and candies. Coated in white chocolate, this mix is great for meetings, parties and gift-giving.

16 cups popped popcorn

3 cups Frosted Cheerios

1-1/2 cups pecan halves

1 package (14 ounces) milk chocolate M&M's

1 package (10 ounces) fat-free pretzel sticks

1 package English toffee bits (10 ounces) or almond brickle bits (7-1/2 ounces)

2 packages (10 to 12 ounces each) vanilla or white chips

2 tablespoons vegetable oil

> In a large bowl, combine the first six ingredients. In a microwave or heavy saucepan, melt chips and oil; stir until smooth. Pour over popcorn mixture and toss to coat. Immediately spread onto two baking sheets; let stand until dry, about 2 hours. Store in airtight containers.

YIELD: 9-1/2 QUARTS

italian nut medley

KAREN RIORDAN, FERN CREEK, KENTUCKY
Italian salad dressing mix is my secret ingredient—it adds just the right zip to plain mixed nuts.

2 tablespoons butter

4 cups mixed nuts

1 tablespoon soy sauce

1 envelope Italian salad dressing mix

> In a skillet, melt the butter over medium heat. Add nuts; cook and stir constantly for 2 minutes. Stir in soy sauce. Sprinkle with salad dressing mix; stir to coat. Immediately transfer to a greased baking pan and spread in a single layer. Cool. Store in an airtight container.

YIELD: 4 CUPS

spicy nuts

LAURENE NICKEL, NIAGARA ON THE LAKE, ONTARIO
Cayenne pepper gives the nuts a bit of a kick and a nice flavor contrast to the coriander, cinnamon and cloves. My son-in-law can't get enough of these.

1 tablespoon vegetable oil

2 cups cashews or whole unblanched almonds

1/2 to 1 teaspoon cayenne pepper

1/2 teaspoon ground coriander

1/4 teaspoon salt

Dash each ground cinnamon and cloves

> In a heavy skillet, heat oil over medium heat; add nuts. Cook and stir for 3-5 minutes or until lightly browned; drain. Add the seasonings; stir to coat. Cool completely.

> To serve warm, place in a baking pan. Heat at 300° for 5 minutes.

YIELD: 2 CUPS

colorful snowballs

KRISTI SMITH, ASHLAND, WISCONSIN
Add a little festive fun to holiday parties with these pretty popcorn balls dotted with red and green M&M's. They're also perfect for bake sales.

1 quart popped popcorn

2 cups crisp rice cereal

20 large marshmallows

1/4 cup butter, cubed

1 cup red and green milk chocolate M&M's

> In a large greased bowl, combine popcorn and cereal. In a large saucepan over low heat, combine marshmallows and butter. Cook and stir until marshmallows are melted and mixture is smooth. Pour over popcorn mixture. Add M&M's; stir until combined.

> When cool enough to handle, shape 1/3 cupfuls into balls with lightly buttered hands. Place on waxed paper-lined baking sheets. Cool.

YIELD: 16 POPCORN BALLS

chocolate wheat cereal snacks

TRACY GOLDER, BLOOMSBURG, PENNSYLVANIA
This crunchy treat is great for any gathering or even a late-night snack. The chocolate-peanut butter combination satisfies any sweet tooth.

6 cups frosted bite-size Shredded Wheat

1 cup milk chocolate chips

1/4 cup creamy peanut butter

1 cup confectioners' sugar

> Place cereal in a large bowl; set aside. In a microwave, melt chocolate chips and peanut butter; stir until smooth. Pour over cereal and stir gently to coat. Let stand for 10 minutes.

> Sprinkle with confectioners' sugar and toss to coat. Cool completely. Store in an airtight container.

YIELD: 6 CUPS

TERRY MALY, OLATHE, KANSAS

Originally, these crunchy nuts were used to top a salad, but I adjusted the recipe so they could stand on their own as a snack. Cayenne pepper gives them a little kick, making the nuts a fun party starter.

cinnamon 'n' spice pecans

1/3 cup butter, melted

2 teaspoons ground cinnamon

3/4 teaspoon salt

1/2 teaspoon cayenne pepper

1 pound pecan halves

> In a bowl, combine the butter, cinnamon, salt and cayenne. Stir in pecans until evenly coated. Transfer to an ungreased 15-in. x 10-in. x 1-in. baking pan. Bake at 350° for 15-18 minutes or until pecans are toasted, stirring every 5 minutes.

YIELD: 4 CUPS

sweet minglers

MARY OBEILIN, SELINSGROVE, PENNSYLVANIA
This four-ingredient idea is perfect for a late-night treat or a pick-me-up any time of the day. I sometimes take a batch to work, and it's always eaten up quickly. It's a slightly different cereal treat because of the chocolate and peanut butter.

1 cup (6 ounces) semisweet chocolate chips

1/4 cup creamy peanut butter

6 cups Corn or Rice Chex

1 cup confectioners' sugar

> In a large microwave-safe bowl, melt chocolate chips on high for 1 minute. Stir; microwave 30 seconds longer or until the chips are melted. Stir in peanut butter. Gently stir in cereal until well coated; set aside.

> Place confectioners' sugar in a 2-gallon plastic storage bag. Add cereal mixture and shake until well coated. Store in an airtight container in the refrigerator.

YIELD: ABOUT 6 CUPS

beary good snack mix

DORIS WEDIGE, ELKHORN, WISCONSIN
Here's a cute and crunchy nibbler for kids' parties! My family also loves to take this tasty mix on hikes for a boost of energy.

1 package (10 ounces) honey bear-shaped crackers (about 4 cups)

1 package (7 ounces) dried banana chips (about 2 cups)

2 cups M&M's

1 cup salted peanuts

1 cup dried cranberries

> In a large bowl, combine all the ingredients. Store in an airtight container.

YIELD: 10 CUPS

peanut butter chocolate pretzels

MARCIA PORCH, WINTER PARK, FLORIDA
The pretzels are easy for any age to make but pretty enough to share with friends. You can add color sprinkles to customize them for any occasion.

2 cups (12 ounces) semisweet chocolate chips

4 teaspoons vegetable oil, divided

35 to 40 large thin pretzel twists

1/2 cup peanut butter chips

> In a microwave or heavy saucepan, melt chocolate chips and 3 teaspoons oil until smooth. Dip pretzels; shake off excess. Place on waxed paper-lined baking sheets to set.

> Melt the peanut butter chips and remaining oil; transfer to a small resealable bag. Cut a small hole in the corner of bag; drizzle over half of the pretzels. Let dry. Store in an airtight container.

YIELD: ABOUT 3 DOZEN

sweet bites

wonton kisses

DARLENE BRENDEN, SALEM, OREGON

These wrapped bundles, each filled with a sweet chocolate candy kiss, are sure to delight guests at your next party.

24 milk chocolate kisses

24 wonton wrappers

Oil for frying

Confectioners' sugar

> Place a chocolate kiss in the center of a wonton wrapper. (Keep remaining wrappers covered with a damp paper towel until ready to use.) Moisten edges with water; fold opposite corners together over candy kiss and press to seal. Repeat.

> In an electric skillet, heat 1 in. of oil to 375°. Fry wontons for 2-1/2 minutes or until golden brown, turning once. Drain on paper towels. Dust with confectioners' sugar.

YIELD: 2 DOZEN

 tip To dress up the Wonton Kisses for any event, you can dust them with baking cocoa or even colored sugars. You can also try any flavor of kisses that suit your fancy! The kisses also make unique additions to cookie platters or for desserts after a casual meal.

apricot crescents

TAMYRA VEST, SCOTTSBURG, VIRGINIA

When I was in college, my roommate's mother sent these flaky horns in a holiday care package. I've been making them ever since. When I mail them to my parents, I put an equal number in two tins labeled "his" and "hers" so there's no squabbling over who gets more.

1 cup cold butter

2 cups all-purpose flour

1 egg yolk

1/2 cup sour cream

1/2 cup apricot preserves

1/2 cup flaked coconut

1/4 cup finely chopped pecans

Sugar

> In a bowl, cut butter into flour until the mixture resembles coarse crumbs. Beat egg yolk and sour cream; add to crumb mixture and mix well. Cover and refrigerate for several hours or overnight.

> Divide dough into fourths. On a sugared surface, roll each portion into a 10-in. circle. Turn dough over to sugar top side. Combine preserves, coconut and pecans; spread over circles. Cut each circle into 12 wedges and roll each wedge into a crescent shape, starting at the wide end. Sprinkle with sugar.

> Place points down 1 in. apart on ungreased baking sheets. Bake at 350° for 15-17 minutes or until set and very lightly browned. Immediately remove to wire racks to cool.

YIELD: 4 DOZEN

CHARLENE CRUMP, MONTGOMERY, ALABAMA

Whenever I serve these bite-size cakes, they get rave reviews...and I get requests for the recipe. They're wonderful at a ladies' luncheon or as an addition to a cookie platter.

lemon tea cakes

1-1/2 cups butter, softened

1 package (8 ounces) cream cheese, softened

2-1/4 cups sugar

6 eggs

3 tablespoons lemon juice

2 teaspoons lemon extract

1 teaspoon vanilla extract

1-1/2 teaspoons grated lemon peel

3 cups all-purpose flour

GLAZE:
5-1/4 cups confectioners' sugar

1/2 cup plus 3 tablespoons 2% milk

3-1/2 teaspoons lemon extract

> In a large bowl, cream the butter, cream cheese and sugar until light and fluffy. Add eggs, one at a time, beating well after each addition. Beat in the lemon juice, extracts and lemon peel. Add flour; beat just until moistened.

> Fill greased miniature muffin cups two-thirds full. Bake at 325° for 10-15 minutes or until a toothpick inserted near the center comes out clean. Cool for 5 minutes before removing from pans to wire racks to cool completely.

> In a small bowl, combine the glaze ingredients. Dip the tops of the cakes into glaze; place on waxed paper to dry.

YIELD: 8-1/2 DOZEN

spicy ginger scones

REBECCA GUFFEY, APEX, NORTH CAROLINA

This recipe was created for Thanksgiving weekend. The candied ginger gives these scones a special zing!

2 cups biscuit/baking mix

2 tablespoons sugar

1 teaspoon ground cinnamon

1/4 teaspoon ground ginger

1/4 teaspoon ground nutmeg

2/3 cup half-and-half cream

1/2 cup golden raisins

2 tablespoons chopped crystallized ginger

Additional half-and-half cream and sugar

> In a large bowl, combine the biscuit mix, sugar, cinnamon, ginger and nutmeg. Stir in cream just until moistened. Stir in raisins and ginger.

> Turn onto a floured surface; knead 10 times. Transfer dough to a greased baking sheet. Pat into a 9-in. circle. Cut into eight wedges, but do not separate. Brush tops lightly with additional cream; sprinkle with additional sugar.

> Bake at 425° for 12-15 minutes or until golden brown. Serve warm.

YIELD: 8 SCONES

sweet berry bruschetta

PATRICIA NIEH, PORTOLA VALLEY, CALIFORNIA

I've made this recipe by toasting the bread on a grill at cookouts. No matter how I serve it, however, I never seem to have any leftovers.

10 slices French bread (1/2 inch thick)

5 teaspoons sugar, divided

6 ounces fat-free cream cheese

1/2 teaspoon almond extract

3/4 cup fresh blackberries

3/4 cup fresh raspberries

1/4 cup slivered almonds, toasted

2 teaspoons confectioners' sugar

> Place bread on an ungreased baking sheet; lightly coat with cooking spray. Sprinkle with 2 teaspoons sugar. Broil 3-4 in. from the heat for 1-2 minutes or until lightly browned.

> In a small bowl, combine the cream cheese, almond extract and remaining sugar. Spread over toasted bread. Top with berries and almonds; dust with confectioners' sugar.

YIELD: 10 PIECES

brownie tarts

SHARON WILKINS, GRANDE POINTE, ONTARIO
I often take these chocolate goodies to potluck dinners for our country dance club.

1/2 cup butter, softened

1 package (3 ounces) cream cheese, softened

1 cup all-purpose flour

FILLING:
1/2 cup semisweet chocolate chips

2 tablespoons butter

1/2 cup sugar

1 egg, beaten

1 teaspoon vanilla extract

1/2 cup chopped pecans, optional

Maraschino cherry halves, optional

> In a mixing bowl, cream the butter and cream cheese. Add flour; mix well. Cover and refrigerate for 1 hour.

> Shape into 1-in. balls. Place in ungreased miniature muffin cups; press into the bottom and up the sides to form a shell.

> For filling, melt chocolate chips and butter in a small saucepan. Remove from the heat; stir in sugar, egg and vanilla. Add the pecans if desired. Spoon into shells.

> Bake at 325° for 30-35 minutes or until toothpick inserted near the center of the brownies comes out clean. Cool for 10 minutes before removing from pans to wire racks. Garnish brownies with cherries if desired.

YIELD: 2 DOZEN

fluffy fruit dip

SUE PENCE, ALEXANDRIA, VIRGINIA
We've been making this sweet dip in my family for many generations. Serve it throughout the year with whatever fresh fruits are in season.

1/2 cup sugar

2 tablespoons all-purpose flour

1 cup unsweetened pineapple juice

1 tablespoon butter

1 egg, lightly beaten

1 cup heavy whipping cream, whipped

Assorted fresh fruit

> In a small saucepan, combine sugar and flour. Gradually whisk in pineapple juice. Add butter. Cook and stir until butter is melted and mixture comes to a boil. Cook and stir for 1-2 minutes or until thickened.

> Remove from the heat. Stir a small amount of hot mixture into egg; return all to the pan, stirring constantly. Bring to a gentle boil; cook and stir for 1 minute. Remove from the heat. Cool to room temperature, stirring several times.

> Fold in whipped cream. Cover and refrigerate for at least 1 hour. Serve with fruit.

YIELD: ABOUT 2-1/2 CUPS

puff pastry pillows

ROBERT RYAN, NEWTON, IOWA

My family and co-workers love these pretty, sweet treats. By using prepared puff pastry you have a fun dessert without much fuss.

1 package (17.3 ounces) frozen puff pastry, thawed

1 egg

1/4 cup milk

1 to 2 tablespoons coarse or granulated sugar

FILLING:

1/4 cup all-purpose flour

1 cup milk

1 cup butter, softened

1 cup sugar

1 teaspoon vanilla extract

1/2 teaspoon almond extract

1/4 teaspoon salt

> Carefully open each puff pastry sheet. Cut each sheet of pastry at creases, forming 3 strips. Cut each strip widthwise into 7 pieces.

> Combine egg and milk; lightly brush egg mixture over pastry. Sprinkle with sugar. Place on lightly greased baking sheets. Bake at 400° for 10-12 minutes or until golden brown. Remove to wire racks to cool. Split into top and bottom halves.

> In a saucepan, combine the flour and milk until smooth. Bring to a boil over medium heat; cook and stir for 1 minute or until thickened. Cool.

> Transfer to a mixing bowl; beat in the butter, sugar, vanilla, almond extract and salt until light and fluffy, about 10 minutes. Spread 1 tablespoonful on bottom half of each pastry; replace tops. Store in refrigerator.

YIELD: ABOUT 3-1/2 DOZEN

baklava tartlets

ASHLEY EAGON, KETTERING, OHIO

Want a quick treat that's delicious and easy? These tartlets do the trick. You can serve them right away, but they're better after chilling for about an hour in the refrigerator. A little sprig of mint will add just a touch of color.

2 cups finely chopped walnuts

3/4 cup honey

1/2 cup butter, melted

1 teaspoon ground cinnamon

1 teaspoon lemon juice

1/4 teaspoon ground cloves

3 packages (1.9 ounces each) frozen miniature phyllo tart shells

> In a small bowl, combine the first six ingredients; spoon 2 teaspoonfuls into each tart shell. Refrigerate until serving.

YIELD: 45 TARTLETS

TOPPING:

1 package (8 ounces) fat-free cream cheese

1/4 cup packed brown sugar

1/2 teaspoon ground cinnamon

1/2 teaspoon vanilla extract

3 medium Granny Smith apples, thinly sliced

1/4 cup fat-free caramel ice cream topping

1/4 cup chopped unsalted dry roasted peanuts

> In a large bowl, cream butter and sugars until light and fluffy. Beat in the egg, oil, corn syrup and vanilla. Combine the flours, baking powder, salt and cinnamon; gradually add to creamed mixture and mix well.

> Press dough onto a 14-in. pizza pan coated with cooking spray. Bake at 350° for 12-15 minutes or until lightly browned. Cool on a wire rack.

> In a small bowl, beat the cream cheese, brown sugar, cinnamon and vanilla until smooth. Spread over crust. Arrange apples over the top. Drizzle with caramel topping; sprinkle with peanuts. Serve immediately.

YIELD: 12 SLICES

caramel apple pizza

TARI AMBLER, SHOREWOOD, ILLINOIS
Here's a fun take on a classic treat. Folks love the flavor and never guess it's light!

1/4 cup butter, softened

1/4 cup sugar

1/4 cup packed brown sugar

1 egg

2 tablespoons canola oil

1 tablespoon light corn syrup

1 teaspoon vanilla extract

1 cup whole wheat pastry flour

3/4 cup all-purpose flour

1/2 teaspoon baking powder

1/4 teaspoon salt

1/4 teaspoon ground cinnamon

ice cream snowballs

SISTER JUDITH LABROZZI, CANTON, OHIO
There's no better way to enjoy this festive ice cream specialty than in the warm atmosphere of a get-together with friends and family.

1/2 gallon vanilla ice cream, softened

1 package (10 ounces) flaked coconut

Fresh mint, optional

> Scoop ice cream into 12 balls. Place on a baking sheet and freeze until solid. Roll in coconut. Garnish with mint if desired.

YIELD: 12 SERVINGS

ginger chocolate temptation

ELISE LALOR, ISSAQUAH, WASHINGTON
Chocolate-covered candied ginger is one of my favorite treats, so I knew this recipe was for me! Every bite of this creamy custard is rich, smooth and decadent.

2 cups heavy whipping cream

1 vanilla bean, split lengthwise

8 ounces bittersweet chocolate. chopped

6 egg yolks, lightly beaten

1/4 cup minced crystallized ginger, divided

Heavy whipping cream, whipped, optional

> In small heavy saucepan, combine cream and vanilla bean. Bring to a boil. Reduce heat; simmer, uncovered, for 5 minutes. Remove the vanilla bean and scrape the inside of the bean to remove the seeds; add seeds to the pan. Discard vanilla bean.

> Stir in chocolate until melted. Stir 1/2 cup chocolate mixture into egg yolks; return all to the pan. Cook and stir until mixture reaches 160° and coats the back of a metal spoon. Remove from the heat. Stir in 2 tablespoons ginger.

> Pour into 12 demitasse or espresso cups. Refrigerate for at least 1 hour. Just before serving, garnish with whipped cream and remaining ginger if desired.

YIELD: 12 SERVINGS

mint dip with brownies

CAROL KLEIN, FRANKLIN SQUARE, NEW YORK
My sister shared this simple recipe with me many years ago. The cool, refreshing dip also tastes terrific with fresh strawberries.

1 package fudge brownie mix (8-inch square pan size)

3/4 cup sour cream

2 tablespoons brown sugar

2 tablespoons green creme de menthe

> Prepare and bake brownies according to package directions. Cool on a wire rack. Meanwhile, in a small bowl, combine the sour cream, brown sugar and creme de menthe; cover and refrigerate until serving.

> Cut brownies into 1-in. diamonds. Serve with dip.

YIELD: 1 DOZEN (3/4 CUP DIP)

tip

You may find that lining your baking pan with aluminum foil makes cutting brownies easier. Once baked, simply lift the brownies right out of the pan! Cleaning the pan is a snap, too. And to easily cut the brownies, try using a pizza cutter.

CONNIE BARZ, SAN ANTONIO, TEXAS
These bite-size muffins are perfect for casual get-togethers. At church functions, the muffins disappear in no time.

peanut butter mini muffins

1-3/4 cups all-purpose flour

2/3 cup packed brown sugar

2-1/2 teaspoons baking powder

1/4 teaspoon salt

1 egg

3/4 cup 2% milk

2/3 cup chunky peanut butter

1/4 cup canola oil

1-1/2 teaspoons vanilla extract

2/3 cup miniature semisweet chocolate chips

> In a large bowl, combine the flour, brown sugar, baking powder and salt. In another bowl, combine the egg, milk, peanut butter, oil and vanilla. Stir into dry ingredients just until moistened. Fold in chocolate chips.

> Fill greased or paper-lined miniature muffin cups two-thirds full. Bake at 350° for 15-17 minutes or until a toothpick inserted near the center comes out clean. Cool for 5 minutes before removing from pans to wire racks. Serve warm.

YIELD: 4 DOZEN

Editor's Note: Reduced-fat or generic brands of peanut butter are not recommended for this recipe.

> For glaze, in a small saucepan, combine the sugar, cornstarch, pineapple juice, water and lemon juice until smooth. Bring to a boil; cook and stir for 2 minutes or until thickened. Transfer to a small bowl; refrigerate until cooled but not set.

> In a small bowl, beat cream cheese and confectioners' sugar until smooth; fold in whipped topping. Spread over tops of cookies. Arrange fruit on top; drizzle with glaze. Refrigerate for 1 hour or until chilled.

YIELD: 1 DOZEN

caramel corn chocolate bars

JEAN ROCZNIAK, ROCHESTER, MINNESOTA
A handful of ingredients is all you need to whip up these wonderful bars. They're perfect for just about any occasion you might host.

5 cups caramel corn

1 cup chopped pecans

1 package (10-1/2 ounces) miniature marshmallows, divided

1/4 cup butter, cubed

1/2 cup semisweet chocolate chips

> In a large bowl, combine caramel corn, pecans and 1 cup marshmallows. In a small heavy saucepan, melt butter over low heat. Add chips and remaining marshmallows; cook and stir until smooth.

> Pour over caramel corn mixture; toss to coat. With buttered hands, press into a greased 13-in. x 9-in. pan. Cool. Cut with a serrated knife.

YIELD: 2 DOZEN

sugar cookie fruit pizzas

MARGE HODEL, ROANOKE, ILLINOIS
Purchased sugar cookies make a sweet crust for these colorful fruit pizzas. Make them throughout the year with a variety of fresh and canned fruits.

1/2 cup sugar

1 tablespoon cornstarch

1/2 cup unsweetened pineapple juice

1/4 cup water

2 tablespoons lemon juice

4 ounces cream cheese, softened

1/4 cup confectioners' sugar

1-3/4 cups whipped topping

12 sugar cookies (3 inches)

1 cup fresh blueberries

1 cup chopped peeled kiwifruit

1/2 cup chopped fresh strawberries

tip When to chop? If the word "chopped" comes before the ingredient when listed in a recipe, then chop the ingredient before measuring (1 cup chopped nuts). If the word "chopped" comes after the ingredient, then chop after measuring (1 cup nuts, chopped).

chocolate cannoli

TASTE OF HOME TEST KITCHEN
Here's a version of a famous Italian dessert that features a creamy filling dotted with chocolate chunks. The chopped pistachios are an attractive touch.

1 egg

1/4 cup sugar

1/4 cup butter, melted

1/2 teaspoon vanilla extract

1/4 teaspoon grated lemon peel

1/8 teaspoon almond extract

1/2 cup all-purpose flour

1/4 teaspoon baking powder

FILLING:
3/4 cup sugar

3 tablespoons cornstarch

1 cup milk

1-1/8 teaspoons vanilla extract

1 drop cinnamon oil, optional

1-3/4 cups ricotta cheese

1 milk chocolate candy bar with almonds (4-1/4 ounces), chopped

1/2 cup chopped pistachios

> In a large bowl, beat the egg, sugar, butter, vanilla, lemon peel and almond extract until blended. Combine flour and baking powder; stir into egg mixture and mix well.

> Bake in a preheated pizzelle iron according to manufacturer's directions until golden brown. Remove cookies and immediately shape into tubes. Place on wire racks to cool.

> In a small saucepan, combine sugar and cornstarch. Stir in milk until smooth. Bring to a boil; cook and stir for 2 minutes or until thickened. Stir in vanilla and cinnamon oil if desired. Cool completely.

> In a large bowl, beat ricotta cheese until smooth. Gradually beat in custard mixture. Fold in chocolate. Spoon or pipe into shells. Dip each side in pistachios. Serve immediately. Refrigerate leftovers.

YIELD: 12 FILLED PIZZELLES

peanut butter cheese ball

TESSIE HUGHES, MARION, VIRGINIA
I've made this change-of-pace cheese ball for many occasions, and it's always well received.

1 package (8 ounces) cream cheese, softened

1-1/2 cups peanut butter

1/2 cup confectioners' sugar

1 teaspoon vanilla extract

3/4 cup chopped peanuts

Apple slices

> In a small bowl, beat cream cheese until fluffy. Add the peanut butter, confectioners' sugar and vanilla; beat until smooth.

> Shape into a ball; roll in peanuts. Wrap in plastic wrap. Refrigerate until serving. Serve with apples.

YIELD: 2-1/2 CUPS

apple cartwheels

MIRIAM MILLER, THORP, WISCONSIN
When you need to entertain a group of children, whip up these stuffed apple rings. The yummy filling is an irresistible combination of creamy peanut butter, sweet honey, miniature chocolate chips and raisins.

1/4 cup peanut butter

1-1/2 teaspoons honey

1/2 cup miniature semisweet chocolate chips

2 tablespoons raisins

4 medium unpeeled Red Delicious apples, cored

> In a small bowl, combine peanut butter and honey; fold in chocolate chips and raisins.

> Fill centers of apples with peanut butter mixture; refrigerate for at least 1 hour. Cut apples into 1/4-in. rings.

YIELD: ABOUT 2 DOZEN

tip

Instead of filling the cored apples in Apple Cartwheels, slice them and use the stuffing as a dip (no need to refrigerate before enjoying). To help prevent apples from browning, toss with a little citrus soda or lemon juice. You can also try the recipe with almond butter or chocolate-hazelnut spread.

miniature almond tarts

KAREN VAN DEN BERGE, HOLLAND, MICHIGAN
My family requests these adorable little tarts at the holidays. I always enjoy making them since the almond paste in the filling reflects our Dutch heritage, plus they're popular at special gatherings.

1 cup butter, softened

2 packages (3 ounces each) cream cheese, softened

2 cups all-purpose flour

FILLING:
6 ounces almond paste, crumbled

2 eggs, beaten

1/2 cup sugar

FROSTING:
1-1/2 cups confectioners' sugar

3 tablespoons butter, softened

4 to 5 teaspoons milk

Maraschino cherry halves (about 48)

> In a mixing bowl, cream the butter and cream cheese. Add flour; mix well. Cover and refrigerate for 1 hour.

> Shape into 1-in. balls. Place in ungreased miniature muffin cups; press into the bottom and up the sides to form a shell.

> For filling, combine the almond paste, eggs and sugar in a mixing bowl. Beat on low speed until blended. Fill each shell with about 1-1/2 teaspoons filling.

> Bake at 325° for 25-30 minutes or until edges are golden brown. Cool for 10 minutes before removing to wire racks to cool completely.

> For frosting, combine the confectioners' sugar, butter and enough milk to achieve desired consistency. Pipe or spread over tarts. Top each with a cherry half.

YIELD: ABOUT 4 DOZEN

> In a small heavy saucepan over low heat, melt white chocolate with 1/4 cup cream, orange juice, extract and peel. Stir until chocolate is melted. Remove from the heat; stir in walnuts. Cool for 10-12 minutes.

> Using a small spoon, fill paper or foil candy cups about two-thirds full with cooled chocolate mixture. Chill for 30 minutes.

> Meanwhile, in a small saucepan, combine coffee granules and remaining cream. Cook and stir over low heat until coffee is dissolved. Add semisweet chocolate; cook and stir until chocolate is melted. Spoon about 1/2 teaspoon over each cup. Store in an airtight container at room temperature.

YIELD: ABOUT 4 DOZEN

strawberry cookie tarts

TASTE OF HOME TEST KITCHEN
For an even more festive touch on the Fourth of July, top half of the cookies with strawberries or raspberries and the other half with blueberries.

1/2 cup vanilla or white chips, melted and slightly cooled

1 package (3 ounces) cream cheese, softened

1/2 cup whipped topping

1/4 cup confectioners' sugar

1 teaspoon lemon juice

1/2 teaspoon vanilla extract

12 sugar cookies (about 2-1/2 inches)

4 to 5 fresh strawberries, sliced

> In a small mixing bowl, beat the melted chips, cream cheese, whipped topping, sugar, lemon juice and vanilla until smooth. Spread about 1 heaping tablespoon onto each cookie. Top with sliced strawberries. Refrigerate until serving.

YIELD: 1 DOZEN

orange cappuccino creams

LUCILE CLINE, WICHITA, KANSAS
As hostess gifts, cookie tray additions or potluck contributions, these mocha-orange morsels are sure to be a sweet success.

12 ounces white baking chocolate, chopped

6 tablespoons heavy whipping cream, divided

1-1/2 teaspoons orange juice

1/2 teaspoon orange extract

1-1/2 teaspoons finely grated orange peel

1/4 cup finely chopped walnuts

2 teaspoons instant coffee granules

4 ounces semisweet chocolate, chopped

JUDY BOND, DUNCAN, BRITISH COLUMBIA

A summertime favorite, these cherry delights freeze nicely and make a wonderful treat for unexpected guests.

stuffed cherries dipped in chocolate

1-1/2 pounds fresh dark sweet cherries with stems

1 package (8 ounces) cream cheese, softened

2 tablespoons ground hazelnuts

2 tablespoons maple syrup

2 cups white baking chips

12 teaspoons shortening, divided

1-1/2 cups milk chocolate chips

1-1/2 cups semisweet chocolate chips

> Pit cherries through the sides, leaving stems intact. In a small bowl, beat cream cheese until smooth. Stir in hazelnuts and syrup. Pipe into cherries.

> In a small microwave-safe bowl, melt vanilla chips and 5 teaspoons shortening at 70% power.

Microwave at additional 10- to 20-second intervals, stirring until smooth. In another bowl, repeat with milk chocolate chips and 3-1/2 teaspoons shortening. Repeat with semisweet chips and remaining shortening.

> Holding stems, dip a third of the stuffed cherries into melted white chocolate; allow excess to drip off. Place on waxed paper; let stand until set. Repeat with remaining cherries and milk chocolate and semisweet chocolate. Dip the white-coated cherries a second time to completely cover; let stand until set.

> Reheat remaining melted chocolate if necessary. Drizzle white chocolate over cherries dipped in milk or semisweet chocolate. Drizzle milk or semisweet chocolate over white chocolate-dipped cherries. Store in an airtight container in the refrigerator.

YIELD: 5 DOZEN

Editor's Note: This recipe was tested in a 1,100-watt microwave.

MAYBRIE, TASTE OF HOME ONLINE COMMUNITY

With a coconut filling, the flavor of these fudgy bites is reminiscent of a favorite candy bar. What a great way to sweeten up an appetizer buffet.

coconut-almond fudge cups

1 package (18-1/4 ounces) chocolate fudge cake mix

1/2 cup butter, melted

1 egg

FILLING:

1/4 cup sugar

1/4 cup evaporated milk

7 large marshmallows

1 cup flaked coconut

TOPPING:

3/4 cup semisweet chocolate chips

1/4 cup evaporated milk

2 tablespoons butter

1/2 cup sliced almonds

> In a large bowl, beat the cake mix, butter and egg until well blended. Shape into 1-in. balls; place in foil-lined miniature muffin cups. Bake at 350° for 8 minutes.

> Using the end of a wooden spoon handle, make a 1/2-in.-deep indentation in the center of each cup. Bake 2-3 minutes longer or until cake springs back when lightly touched. Remove from pans to wire racks to cool.

> For filling, in a microwave-safe bowl, heat sugar and milk on high for 2 minutes, stirring frequently. Add marshmallows; stir until melted. Stir in coconut. Spoon into cooled cups.

> For topping, in another microwave-safe bowl, combine the chocolate chips, milk and butter. Microwave in 10- to 20-second intervals until melted; stir until smooth. Stir in almonds. Spread over filling. Store in the refrigerator.

YIELD: 4 DOZEN

Editor's Note: This recipe was tested in a 1,100-watt microwave.

chocolate peanut clusters

PAM POSEY, WATERLOO, SOUTH CAROLINA

I turn to my slow cooker to prepare these convenient chocolate treats. Making them couldn't be any easier!

1 jar (16 ounces) salted dry roasted peanuts

1 jar (16 ounces) unsalted dry roasted peanuts

1 package (11-1/2 ounces) milk chocolate chips

1 package (10 ounces) peanut butter chips

3 packages (10 to 12 ounces each) white baking chips

2 packages (11-1/2 ounces each) 60% cacao bittersweet chocolate baking chips

> In a 5-qt. slow cooker, combine peanuts. Layer with the remaining ingredients in order given (do not stir). Cover and cook on low for 2 to 2-1/2 hours or until chips are melted.

> Stir to combine. Drop by tablespoonfuls onto waxed paper. Let stand until set. Store in an airtight container at room temperature.

YIELD: 4 POUNDS

almond bars

CHERYL NEWENDORP, PELLA, IOWA
These no-fuss squares make a delicious addition to dessert trays.

1 cup butter, softened

1 cup almond paste

2-1/4 cups sugar, divided

2 eggs

1 teaspoon almond extract

2 cups all-purpose flour

1/2 cup slivered almonds

> In a large bowl, cream the butter, almond paste and 2 cups sugar until light and fluffy. Beat in eggs and extract. Gradually add flour just until moistened.

> Spread into a greased 13-in. x 9-in. baking dish. Sprinkle with remaining sugar; top with almonds.

> Bake at 350° for 30-35 minutes or until a toothpick inserted near the center comes out clean. Cool on a wire rack. Cut into squares. Store in the refrigerator.

YIELD: 4-1/2 DOZEN

citrus mini cakes

LINDA TERRELL, PALATKA, FLORIDA
These moist, bite-size muffins are melt-in-your-mouth good and really dress up a buffet table.

1 package (18-1/4 ounces) yellow cake mix

1-1/4 cups water

3 eggs

1/3 cup canola oil

3-1/2 cups confectioners' sugar

1/2 cup orange juice

1/4 cup lemon juice

Toasted chopped almonds

> In a large bowl, combine the cake mix, water, eggs and oil; beat on low speed for 30 seconds. Beat on medium for 2 minutes.

> Fill well-greased miniature muffin cups two-thirds full. Bake at 350° for 10-12 minutes or until a toothpick inserted near the center comes out clean.

> Meanwhile, in a large bowl, combine the confectioners' sugar and juices until smooth. Cool cakes for 2 minutes; remove from pans. Immediately dip cakes into glaze, coating well. Place top down on wire racks; sprinkle with almonds.

YIELD: ABOUT 6 DOZEN

peachy bruschetta

TASTE OF HOME TEST KITCHEN
Here's a tasty twist on the traditional variety of bruschetta, and it can be served as a colorful appetizer or dessert.

1 French bread baguette (1 pound)

2 tablespoons olive oil

1-1/2 cups chopped fresh strawberries

3/4 cup chopped peeled fresh peaches

1-1/2 teaspoons minced fresh mint

1/2 cup Mascarpone cheese

> Cut baguette into 32 slices, about 1/2 in. thick; place on ungreased baking sheets. Brush with oil. Broil 6-8 in. from the heat for 1-2 minutes or until lightly toasted.

> In a small bowl, combine the strawberries, peaches and mint. Spread each slice of bread with cheese; top with fruit mixture. Broil for 1-2 minutes or until cheese is slightly melted. Serve immediately.

YIELD: 32 APPETIZERS

tip Puff pastry is a light, flaky pastry made from dozens of layers of dough that "puffs" when baked. When thawing puff pastry for recipes like Miniature Napoleons, only remove the number of sheets you need and wrap unused sheets in plastic wrap or foil and return them to the freezer. The sheets will thaw at room temperature in about 30 minutes or in the refrigerator in about four hours.

miniature napoleons

TASTE OF HOME TEST KITCHEN

It can be a challenge to come up with an elegant sweet that works well for a cocktail party. These impressive, bite-size desserts are easy to enjoy while mingling.

6 tablespoons sugar

2 tablespoons cornstarch

1/4 teaspoon salt

1 cup 2% milk

1 egg yolk, lightly beaten

2 tablespoons butter, divided

1/2 teaspoon vanilla extract

1 sheet frozen puff pastry, thawed

1/2 cup heavy whipping cream

2 ounces semisweet chocolate, chopped

> In a small saucepan, combine the sugar, cornstarch and salt. Add milk; stir until smooth. Cook and stir over medium heat until mixture comes to a boil. Stir a small amount into egg yolk; return all to the pan. Bring to a gentle boil, stirring constantly; cook 2 minutes longer.

> Remove from the heat; stir in 1 tablespoon butter and vanilla. Pour into a small bowl; cool to room temperature. Cover surface of custard with waxed paper. Refrigerate, without stirring, for 2-3 hours or until chilled.

> Unfold puff pastry; place on an ungreased baking sheet. Prick dough thoroughly with a fork. Bake according to package directions. Remove to a wire rack to cool.

> In a small bowl, beat cream until stiff peaks form. Fold into custard. Use a fork to split pastry in half horizontally. Spread filling over the bottom half; replace top. Cover and freeze for 4 hours or until firm.

> Cut into 1-1/2-in. x 1-in. rectangles. In a microwave, melt chocolate and remaining butter; stir until smooth. Drizzle over pastries. Freeze until serving.

YIELD: 4-1/2 DOZEN

special stuffed strawberries

MARCIA ORLANDO, BOYERTOWN, PENNSYLVANIA

These morsels can be made ahead of time...and they look really delightful on a tray. I sometimes sprinkle the piped filling with finely chopped pistachio nuts.

24 large fresh strawberries

1/2 cup spreadable strawberry cream cheese

3 tablespoons sour cream

> Remove stems from the strawberries. Place point side up on a cutting board. Cut a deep X in the top of each berry. Carefully spread berries apart.

> In a small bowl, beat cream cheese and sour cream until smooth. Pipe or spoon filling into each berry. Refrigerate until serving.

YIELD: 2 DOZEN

> Remove from the heat. Add maple flavoring and remaining butter (do not stir). Cool to 110° without stirring, about 1 hour. With a portable mixer, beat on low speed for 1-2 minutes or until fudge begins to thicken. With a clean dry wooden spoon, stir in walnuts until fudge begins to lose its gloss, about 5 minutes.

> Spread into prepared pan. Refrigerate until firm, about 30 minutes. Using foil, lift fudge out of pan. Discard foil; cut fudge into 1-in. squares. Store in an airtight container in the refrigerator.

YIELD: 1-1/4 POUNDS

Editor's Note: We recommend that you test your candy thermometer before each use by bringing water to a boil; the thermometer should read 212°. Adjust your recipe temperature up or down based on your test.

maple ginger fudge

STEVE WESTPHAL, MILWAUKEE, WISCONSIN
I combine two fall favorites—maple and ginger—in this sweet, smooth fudge. One piece just isn't enough!

2 teaspoons plus 2 tablespoons butter, divided

2 cups sugar

2/3 cup heavy whipping cream

2 tablespoons light corn syrup

1/4 teaspoon ground ginger

1/2 teaspoon maple flavoring

1/2 cup chopped walnuts

> Line a 9-in. x 5-in. loaf pan with foil and grease the foil with 1 teaspoon butter; set aside. Butter the sides of a small heavy saucepan with 1 teaspoon butter; add the sugar, cream, corn syrup and ginger. Bring to a boil over medium heat, stirring constantly. Reduce heat; cook until a candy thermometer reads 238° (soft-ball stage), stirring occasionally.

peanut butter chocolate meltaways

DARCIE VEZZI, MACDONALD, PENNSYLVANIA
People are amazed how easy it is to make these impressive chocolaty cup candies.

1 package (10 to 13 ounces) white baking chips

1 cup (6 ounces) semisweet chocolate chips

1 cup creamy peanut butter

2 tablespoons shortening

> In a microwave-safe bowl, combine all of the ingredients. Cover and microwave on high for 1-1/2 minutes; stir. Microwave, uncovered, on high 30 seconds longer; stir until smooth.

> Pour into miniature muffin liners. Place on a baking sheet; refrigerate until set. Store in the refrigerator.

YIELD: ABOUT 4 DOZEN

espresso panna cotta

NICOLE CLAYTON, PRESCOTT, ARIZONA
Martini glasses make an elegant impression for such a luscious treat. Best of all, guests can easily mingle while carrying the panna cotta.

1 envelope unflavored gelatin

1 cup milk

3 cups heavy whipping cream

1/2 cup sugar

2 tablespoons instant espresso powder or instant coffee granules

1/8 teaspoon salt

Dark and white chocolate curls

> In a small saucepan, sprinkle gelatin over milk; let stand for 1 minute. Heat over low heat, stirring until gelatin is completely dissolved. Stir in the cream, sugar, espresso powder and salt. Cook and stir until sugar is dissolved. Remove from the heat.

> Pour into six dessert dishes. Cover and refrigerate for 1 hour, stirring every 20 minutes.

> Refrigerate for at least 5 hours longer or until set. Just before serving, garnish with chocolate curls.

YIELD: 6 SERVINGS

french vanilla cream puffs

LEAN HAINES, LAWRENCEVILLE, GEORGIA
French vanilla filling dotted with mini chocolate chips is sandwiched in puffy pastry for this sugary surprise. You could substitute white chocolate or chocolate pudding for the vanilla if you like.

1 cup water

1/2 cup butter

1 cup all-purpose flour

1/4 teaspoon salt

4 eggs

FILLING:
1-1/2 cups cold milk

1 package (3.4 ounces) instant French vanilla pudding mix

1 cup whipped topping

1 package (12 ounces) miniature semisweet chocolate chips

Confectioners' sugar

> In a saucepan, bring water and butter to a boil. Add flour and salt all at once; stir until a smooth ball forms. Remove from the heat; let stand for 5 minutes. Add eggs, one at a time, beating well after each addition. Beat until mixture is smooth and shiny.

> Drop by rounded teaspoonfuls 2 in. apart onto greased baking sheets. Bake at 400° for 20-25 minutes or until golden brown. Remove puffs to wire racks. Immediately cut a slit in each for steam to escape. Cool. Split puffs and remove soft dough.

> For filling, in a mixing bowl, whisk milk and pudding mix for 2 minutes. Refrigerate for 5 minutes. Fold in the whipped topping and chips. Fill cream puffs just before serving; replace tops. Dust with confectioners' sugar.

YIELD: ABOUT 2-1/2 DOZEN

BEVERLY COYDE, GASPORT, NEW YORK

These cute little mini-muffins are packed with banana flavor, chocolate chips and topped off with creamy frosting. They make a great, fast snack when the kids come home from school or a nice dessert option on appetizer buffets.

banana-chip mini cupcakes

1 package (14 ounces) banana quick bread and muffin mix

3/4 cup water

1/3 cup sour cream

1 egg

1 cup miniature semisweet chocolate chips, divided

1 tablespoon shortening

> In a large bowl, combine the muffin mix, water, sour cream and egg; stir just until moistened. Fold in 1/2 cup chocolate chips.

> Fill greased or paper-lined miniature muffin cups two-thirds full. Bake at 375° for 12-15 minutes or until a toothpick inserted near the center comes out clean. Cool for 5 minutes before removing from pans to wire racks to cool completely.

> For frosting, in a small microwave-safe bowl, melt shortening and remaining chocolate chips; stir until smooth. Frost cupcakes.

YIELD: 3-1/2 DOZEN

triple chocolate bundles

TASTE OF HOME TEST KITCHEN
No one will be able to resist three kinds of chocolate wrapped up in a fuss-free flaky dough. These are also delicious topped with a drizzle of melted chocolate.

3 tablespoons semisweet chocolate chips

3 tablespoons vanilla or white chips

3 tablespoons milk chocolate chips

1 tube (8 ounces) refrigerated crescent rolls

Confectioners' sugar, optional

> In a small bowl, combine the first three ingredients. Separate crescent dough into eight triangles. Place triangles on a work surface with the short edge toward you. For each bundle, place 1 tablespoon of chips in the center of each triangle. Bring top point over chips and tuck underneath dough. Fold side points over top, pressing to seal.

> Place on an ungreased baking sheet. Bake at 375° for 10-12 minutes or until golden brown. Cool on a wire rack until serving. Sprinkle with sugar if desired.

YIELD: 8 BUNDLES

cheese-filled shortbread tartlets

CATHY WALERIUS, MOUND, MINNESOTA
These bite-size goodies are a nice treat to add to a get-together. You can store cooled, baked tart shells in an airtight container at room temperature overnight or in the freezer for a few weeks.

1 package (8 ounces) cream cheese, softened

1 cup sweetened condensed milk

1/3 cup lemon juice

1 teaspoon vanilla extract

1 cup butter, softened

1-1/2 cups all-purpose flour

1/2 cup confectioners' sugar

1 tablespoon cornstarch

Fresh raspberries and mint leaves for garnish

> In a small mixing bowl, beat cream cheese until smooth. Gradually beat in the milk, lemon juice and vanilla. Cover and refrigerate for 8 hours or overnight.

> In another mixing bowl, beat the butter, flour, confectioners' sugar and cornstarch until smooth. Roll into 1-in. balls. Place in greased miniature muffin cups; press onto the bottom and up the sides. Prick with a fork.

> Bake at 325° for 20-25 minutes or until golden brown. Immediately run a knife around each tart to loosen. Cool in pans on wire racks.

> Pipe or spoon 1 tablespoon of the cheese filling into each tart shell. Cover and refrigerate until set. Just before serving, garnish as desired.

YIELD: 3 DOZEN

PATRICIA SHINN, FRUITLAND PARK, FLORIDA
I found this gem on a slip of paper in a cookbook I got at a yard sale. These unique morsels get great flavor from browned butter.

coconut peaks

1/4 cup butter

3 cups flaked coconut

2 cups confectioners' sugar

1/4 cup half-and-half cream

1 cup (6 ounces) semisweet chocolate chips

2 teaspoons shortening

> Line a baking sheet with waxed paper; set aside. In a large saucepan, cook butter over medium-low heat until golden brown, about 5 minutes. Remove from the heat; stir in the coconut, sugar and cream.

> Drop by rounded teaspoonfuls onto prepared baking sheet. Refrigerate until easy to handle, about 25 minutes.

> Roll mixture into balls, then shape each into a cone. Return to baking sheet; refrigerate for 15 minutes.

> Meanwhile, in a microwave, melt chocolate chips and shortening; stir until smooth. Dip bottoms of cones into chocolate; allow excess to drip off. Return to waxed paper to harden. Store in an airtight container in the refrigerator.

YIELD: ABOUT 3 DOZEN

chocolate pizza

NORMA OOSTING, HOLLAND, MICHIGAN
Here's a chocolate treat that goes over big with kids of all ages.

8 ounces white baking chocolate, divided

1-1/3 cups semisweet chocolate chips

1/2 cup crisp rice cereal

1/2 cup miniature marshmallows

1/2 cup salted peanuts

1/2 cup flaked coconut

1 cup red and/or candied cherries

> In a microwave-safe bowl, melt six squares of white chocolate with the chocolate chips. Stir until smooth. Stir in the cereal, marshmallows and peanuts.

> Spread into a 10-in. circle on a greased pizza pan or foil-covered cardboard cake circle.

> Sprinkle with coconut and top with cherries. Melt remaining white chocolate; drizzle over pizza. Refrigerate until set.

YIELD: 12-16 SLICES

lemon cream-stuffed grapes

JANIS PLOURDE, SMOOTH ROCK FALLS, ONTARIO
This is a refreshing snack on a hot summer day. The sweet grapes are simple, plus they offer a light change from heartier party foods.

4 ounces cream cheese, softened

3 tablespoons confectioners' sugar

1-1/2 teaspoons lemon juice

1/2 teaspoon grated lemon peel

1 pound seedless globe grapes, rinsed and patted dry

> In a small bowl, beat the cream cheese, confectioners' sugar, lemon juice and peel until blended. Cover and refrigerate for 1 hour.

> Cut a deep X in the top of each grape to within 1/4 in. of bottom. Carefully spread each grape apart. Transfer cream cheese mixture to a heavy-duty resealable plastic bag; cut a small hole in a corner of the bag. Pipe the filling into grapes. Refrigerate until serving.

YIELD: 3 DOZEN

FILLING:

3 tablespoons butter, melted

1/2 cup chopped pecans

1/4 cup sugar

1/2 teaspoon ground allspice

ICING:

2 cups confectioners' sugar

1 tablespoon lemon juice

1 to 2 tablespoons milk

> In a large bowl, combine 2 cups flour, sugar, yeast and salt. In a small saucepan, heat milk and butter to 120°- 130°. Add to dry ingredients; beat just until moistened. Add the bananas, egg and vanilla; beat until smooth. Stir in enough remaining flour to form a soft dough (dough will be sticky).

> Turn onto a floured surface; knead until smooth and elastic, about 6-8 minutes. Place in a greased bowl, turning once to grease top. Cover and let rise in a warm place until doubled, about 1 hour.

> Punch dough down. Turn onto a lightly floured surface; divide in half. Roll each portion into a 16-in. x 6-in. rectangle. Brush with butter to within 1/2 in. of edges. Combine the pecans, sugar and allspice; sprinkle over dough to within 1/2 in. of edges.

> Roll up jelly-roll style, starting with a long side; pinch seam to seal. Cut each into 16 slices. Place cut side up on greased baking sheets. Cover and let rise in a warm place until doubled, about 30 minutes.

> Bake at 400° for 12-15 minutes or until golden brown. Remove from pans to wire racks. Combine icing ingredients; drizzle over rolls. Serve warm.

YIELD: 32 ROLLS

banana-pecan sweet rolls

DOROTHY PRITCHETT, WILLS POINT, TEXAS
Banana adds fun flavor to my sweet bites. I've been known to serve these mouthwatering rolls for dessert, too!

4-3/4 to 5 cups all-purpose flour

1/4 cup sugar

2 packages (1/4 ounce each) active dry yeast

1 teaspoon salt

1 cup milk

1/4 cup butter, cubed

1 cup mashed ripe bananas (about 3 medium)

1 egg

1 teaspoon vanilla extract

party pecan pies

JUDY THERIOT, PIERRE PART, LOUISIANA
Though they're small, these pleasing "pies" are packed with flavor and sized right for a buffet. What's more, they can be stored in the freezer to make party or gift preparations that much easier.

1 cup butter, softened

1 package (8 ounces) cream cheese, softened

2 cups all-purpose flour

FILLING:
2 cups chopped pecans

1-1/2 cups packed brown sugar

2 eggs, beaten

2 tablespoons butter, melted

2 teaspoons vanilla extract

> In a mixing bowl, beat butter and cream cheese. Gradually add flour and mix well. Cover and refrigerate for 1 hour.

> Press tablespoonfuls of dough into the bottom and up the sides of ungreased miniature muffin cups to form shells; set aside. Combine filling ingredients in a mixing bowl; mix well. Spoon about 1 heaping teaspoon into each shell.

> Bake at 325° for 25-30 minutes or until crust is brown and filling is set. Cool for 10 minutes before removing from pans to wire racks.

YIELD: ABOUT 4 DOZEN

special hot chocolate treats

IOLA EGLE, BELLA VISTA, ARKANSAS
Dropping a whipped cream-filled chocolate cup into hot chocolate makes for an extra-special beverage. I make the chocolate cups ahead, chill them, then fill just before serving.

HOT CHOCOLATE MIX:
8 cups nonfat dry milk powder

1 package (15 ounces) instant chocolate drink mix

1-1/2 cups powdered nondairy creamer

1-1/4 cups confectioners' sugar

3 tablespoons instant coffee granules

1/4 teaspoon ground cinnamon

1 envelope unsweetened orange or raspberry soft drink mix

CHOCOLATE CUPS:
1/2 cup semisweet chocolate chips

1 teaspoon shortening

Whipped cream in a can

> In a large bowl, combine the first seven ingredients. Store in an airtight container for up to 6 months.

> For chocolate cups, in a microwave, melt chips and shortening; stir until smooth. With a small pastry brush or 1/2 teaspoon measure, spread chocolate mixture on the inside of 1-in. foil or paper candy cups.

> Place on a baking sheet. Refrigerate for 45 minutes or until firm. Just before serving, remove foil or paper cups and add whipped cream.

YIELD: 11 CUPS HOT CHOCOLATE MIX AND 16 CHOCOLATE CUPS

> **To prepare hot chocolate:** For each serving, combine 1/3 cup mix and 1 cup boiling water; stir to dissolve. Place one filled chocolate cup in each mug; stir until melted.

sugared raisin pear diamonds

JEANNE ALLEN, RYE, COLORADO
With their tender, golden crust and tempting pear and raisin filling, these fabulous bars stand out on any buffet table. Substitute apples for the pears, and you'll still get yummy results!

2-1/2 cups plus 4-1/2 teaspoons all-purpose flour, divided

1/4 cup plus 6 tablespoons sugar, divided

1/2 teaspoon salt

3/4 cup cold butter

1/2 teaspoon grated lemon peel

1/2 cup half-and-half cream

6 cups diced peeled ripe pears (about 7)

6 tablespoons golden raisins

1/4 cup lemon juice

1/8 to 1/4 teaspoon ground cinnamon

1 egg, lightly beaten

Additional sugar

> In a bowl, combine 2-1/2 cups flour, 1/4 cup sugar and salt. Cut in butter and lemon peel until the mixture resembles coarse crumbs. Gradually add cream, tossing with a fork until dough forms a ball.

> Divide in half. Roll out one portion of dough onto lightly floured waxed paper or pastry cloth into a 16-in. x 11-1/2-in. rectangle. Transfer to an ungreased 15-in. x 10-in. x 1-in. baking pan.

> Bake at 350° for 10-15 minutes or until lightly browned. Cool on a wire rack. Increase oven temperature to 400°.

> In a bowl, combine the pears, raisins, lemon juice, cinnamon and remaining flour and sugar. Spread over crust. Roll out remaining dough into a 16-in. x 12-in. rectangle; place over filling. Trim and seal edges. Brush top with the egg; sprinkle with the additional sugar.

> Bake for 30-34 minutes or until golden brown. Cool on a wire rack. Cut into diamond-shaped bars.

YIELD: ABOUT 2 DOZEN

tiny shortbread tarts

KIM VAN RHEENEN, MENDOTA, ILLINOIS
To save time when making these bite-size treats, bake the crusts the day before. Then just cool and store in an airtight container.

1 cup butter, softened

1/2 cup confectioners' sugar

2 cups all-purpose flour

1 can (21 ounces) raspberry, cherry or strawberry pie filling

> In a large bowl, cream butter and confectioners' sugar until light and fluffy. Gradually add flour and mix well.

> Shape into 1-in. balls; press onto the bottom and up the sides of greased miniature muffin cups.

> Bake at 300° for 17-22 minutes or until set. Cool for 15 minutes before carefully removing from pan to a wire rack to cool completely. Spoon 1 teaspoon of pie filling into each tart.

YIELD: ABOUT 3 DOZEN

berry nut tarts

LENA EHLERT, VANCOUVER, BRITISH COLUMBIA
Cranberries are delicious in this spin on individual pecan pies. Folks have a hard time eating just one!

1/2 cup butter, softened

1 package (3 ounces) cream cheese, softened

1 cup all-purpose flour

FILLING:
1-1/2 cups packed brown sugar

2 tablespoons butter, melted

2 eggs, lightly beaten

2 teaspoons vanilla extract

2/3 cup finely chopped cranberries

1/3 cup chopped pecans

> In a small mixing bowl, beat the butter and cream cheese; add flour and mix well. Cover and refrigerate for 1 hour or until easy to handle.

> Cut dough into 12 portions. Press onto the bottom and all the way up the sides of greased muffin cups. In a bowl, combine the brown sugar, butter, eggs and vanilla. Stir in the cranberries and pecans. Spoon into prepared crusts.

> Bake at 350° for 25-30 minutes or until edges are golden brown. Cool for 5 minutes before removing from pan to a wire rack to cool completely. Store in the refrigerator.

YIELD: ABOUT 1 DOZEN

marshmallow treat pops

LINDA DYCHES, ROUND ROCK, TEXAS
My son took these to his first bake sale at school and was the hit of the class. I wrapped the pops in clear plastic wrap, tied them with decorative ribbon and stuck the sticks into a piece of Styrofoam for an attractive display.

3 tablespoons butter

4 cups miniature marshmallows

6 cups crisp rice cereal

24 Popsicle sticks

9 ounces milk chocolate candy coating, coarsely chopped

Decorating sprinkles

9 ounces white candy coating

> In a large saucepan, combine butter and marshmallows. Cook and stir over low heat until melted and smooth. Place the cereal in a large bowl; add the marshmallow mixture and stir until combined. Shape into 2-in. balls; gently insert a Popsicle stick into the center of each ball.

> In a microwave-safe bowl, melt milk chocolate candy coating; stir until smooth. Dip half of the treats in chocolate, allowing excess to drip off. Decorate with sprinkles. Repeat with the white candy coating and remaining treats and decorating sprinkles. Place on waxed paper until set.

YIELD: 2 DOZEN

best
beverages

cherry brandy old-fashioned

TASTE OF HOME TEST KITCHEN
This old-fashioned recipe features brandy instead of whiskey. The addition of maraschino cherry juice makes it a little sweeter.

1 maraschino cherry

1 teaspoon bitters

1/2 teaspoon chopped crystallized ginger

1/3 cup ice cubes

1/3 cup ginger ale, chilled

1-1/2 ounces brandy

1/2 to 1 ounce maraschino cherry juice

Maraschino cherry with a stem, optional

> In a rocks glass, muddle the cherry, bitters and ginger. Add ice. Pour in the ginger ale, brandy and cherry juice. Garnish with a cherry if desired.

YIELD: 1 SERVING

champagne punch

AMY SHORT, LESAGE, WEST VIRGINIA
A blend of four fruit juices pairs well with bubbly Champagne in this party-pleasing punch. A strawberry garnish can add a festive touch.

4 cups orange juice

1 cup ruby red grapefruit juice

1/2 cup lemon juice

1/2 cup lime juice

2 bottles (750 milliliters each) Champagne, chilled

> In a 3-qt. pitcher, combine the juices. Refrigerate until chilled. Just before serving, stir in Champagne. Serve in Champagne glasses.

YIELD: 16 SERVINGS (3 QUARTS)

creamy hot white chocolate

KAREN RIORDAN, FERN CREEK, KENTUCKY
We enjoy this hot beverage all year long but especially around the holidays. It's a tasty change of pace from traditional hot chocolate.

6 cups half-and-half cream, divided

1-1/3 cups white baking chips

2 cinnamon sticks (3 inches)

1/4 teaspoon ground cinnamon

Dash ground nutmeg

3 teaspoons vanilla extract

> In a large saucepan, combine 1/2 cup cream, chips, cinnamon sticks, cinnamon and nutmeg. Cook and stir over low heat until chips are melted. Stir in remaining cream; heat through. Discard cinnamon sticks. Stir in vanilla.

YIELD: 8 SERVINGS

frothy orange-pineapple cooler

DEIDRE FALLAVOLLITA, VIENNA, VIRGINIA
My kids think they've gone to Heaven when I say "yes" to seconds of this smoothie. I never hesitate because it's a wholesome and nutritious recipe.

2 cups unsweetened pineapple juice

1 cup (8 ounces) vanilla yogurt

1 can (6 ounces) frozen orange juice concentrate, thawed

2 small ripe bananas, cut into chunks

1/2 cup frozen unsweetened strawberries

1 drop coconut extract, optional

> In a blender, combine all ingredients; cover and process on high until smooth. Pour into chilled glasses; serve immediately.

YIELD: 6 SERVINGS

cinnamon mocha coffee

TASTE OF HOME TEST KITCHEN
The aroma of cinnamon and cocoa makes this coffee hard to resist. Serve at winter get-togethers, brunches or as a dessert.

1/3 cup ground coffee (not instant coffee granules)

3/4 teaspoon ground cinnamon

1 cup 2% milk

2 to 3 tablespoons sugar

2 tablespoons baking cocoa

1 teaspoon vanilla extract

4 cinnamon sticks, optional

Whipped cream, optional

> In a coffeemaker basket, combine the coffee and ground cinnamon. Prepare 4 cups brewed coffee according to manufacturer's directions.

> Meanwhile, combine the milk, sugar, cocoa and vanilla in a saucepan. Cook over medium-low heat for 5-7 minutes or until small bubbles appear on the sides of the pan, stirring occasionally (do not boil). Pour hot milk mixture into four coffee cups, then add cinnamon-flavored coffee. Garnish with cinnamon sticks and whipped cream if desired.

YIELD: 4 SERVINGS

CLARA COULSTON MINNEY, WASHINGTON COURT HOUSE, OHIO
With Kahlua, Irish cream liqueur and chocolate sandwich cookies, this martini is almost like a dessert. It's an after-dinner drink that's easy to fix.

coffee & cream martini

2 tablespoons coarse sugar

1 teaspoon finely ground coffee

Ice cubes

1-1/2 ounces vodka

1-1/2 ounces Kahlua

1-1/2 ounces Irish cream liqueur

Chocolate syrup, optional

> Sprinkle sugar and coffee on a plate. Moisten the rim of a martini glass with water; hold glass upside down and dip rim into sugar mixture.

> Fill a mixing glass or tumbler three-fourths full with ice. Add the vodka, Kahlua and liqueur; stir until condensation forms on outside of glass.

> Drizzle chocolate syrup on the inside of prepared martini glass if desired. Strain vodka mixture into glass; serve immediately.

YIELD: 1 SERVING

BONNIE HAWKINS, ELKHORN, WISCONSIN

Put some zing in your next brunch buffet with this homemade tomato juice. Fresh basil and hot pepper sauce accent the garden-fresh tomato flavor. You can put it in containers and freeze it, if you wish.

basil tomato juice

8 pounds ripe tomatoes, quartered

2 celery ribs, chopped

1 medium onion, chopped

1/4 cup finely chopped fresh basil

1/4 cup lemon juice

2 tablespoons sugar

1 tablespoon Worcestershire sauce

1 teaspoon salt

3/4 teaspoon hot pepper sauce

> In a stockpot, combine the tomatoes, celery and onion. Bring to a boil. Reduce heat; simmer, uncovered, for 45 minutes or until tender, stirring occasionally.

> Cool slightly; put tomato mixture through a sieve or food mill. Return to the pan. Stir in the remaining ingredients. Bring to a boil. Remove from the heat; cool. Transfer to a pitcher; cover and refrigerate until chilled.

YIELD: ABOUT 2-1/2 QUARTS

green tea frappes

TASTE OF HOME TEST KITCHEN
This delicious frappe captures the flavor of green tea with a hint of sweetness. You'll love the refreshing treat at get-togethers.

3 individual green tea bags

1 cup boiling water

1-1/2 cups ice cubes

3/4 cup fat-free sweetened condensed milk

1/2 cup fat-free milk

> Place tea bags in a small bowl; add boiling water. Let stand for 15 minutes or until lukewarm.

> Discard tea bags. Pour tea into a blender; add the remaining ingredients. Cover and process for 30-45 seconds or until smooth. Pour into chilled glasses; serve immediately.

YIELD: 4 SERVINGS

creamy strawberry breeze

AMY CRUSON, DODGE CITY, KANSAS
Here's a pretty pink smoothie that makes an attractive addition to any daytime gathering. For a festive touch, garnish with a strawberry and a dollop of whipped topping. Yum!

2 cups whole strawberries

2 cups apple juice

3 cups whipped topping

> Place half of the strawberries and apple juice in a blender; cover and process until smooth. Add half of the whipped topping; cover and process until blended. Pour into glasses. Repeat.

YIELD: 4 SERVINGS

frosty chocolate malted shakes

DORA DEAN, HOLLYWOOD, FLORIDA
I played around with our favorite milk shake recipe to come up with this lighter version. I serve it all the time, and no one misses the extra fat or calories.

6 cups low-fat vanilla frozen yogurt

3-1/2 cups fat-free milk

1/4 cup sugar-free instant chocolate drink mix

1/4 cup malted milk powder

1-1/2 teaspoons vanilla extract

> In batches, process all ingredients in a blender until smooth. Pour into tall glasses.

YIELD: 10 SERVINGS

berry yogurt shakes

JACQUIE ADAMS, COLQUITLAM, BRITISH COLUMBIA
We have a few raspberry bushes in our backyard. If my grandchildren don't get the berries first, I use them in recipes like this one. Of course, the kids love the mellow flavor of these shakes. So either way, they win!

2 cups (16 ounces) lemon yogurt

1-1/2 cups fat-free milk

1 cup unsweetened raspberries

Sugar substitute equivalent to 2 tablespoons sugar

> Place all ingredients in a blender; cover and process until smooth. Pour into chilled glasses; serve immediately.

YIELD: 4 SERVINGS

sangria

TASTE OF HOME TEST KITCHEN
Filled with frozen fruit, this fresh blend is a snap to put together and keep cold. And what a thirst-quenching, elegant beverage for summer parties! Serve over ice if desired.

1 bottle (750 milliliters) red Zinfandel or other dry red wine

2 cups diet lemon-lime soda

1/2 cup orange juice

4-1/2 teaspoons sugar

1 cup each frozen unsweetened blueberries, raspberries and sliced peaches

Ice cubes, optional

> In a pitcher, stir the wine, soda, orange juice and sugar until sugar is dissolved. Add the frozen fruit. Serve over ice if desired.

YIELD: 9 SERVINGS

frozen fruit slush

DEBRA CORNELIUS, GRANT, NEBRASKA
This yummy fruit-filled slush sports a tangy citrus flavor. It's especially refreshing on a warm day, but I make it year-round as an after-school snack.

2 cans (8 ounces each) crushed pineapple, drained

1 can (11 ounces) mandarin oranges, drained

5 large ripe bananas, sliced

2 cups sliced fresh strawberries

2 cups water

1 can (12 ounces) frozen lemonade concentrate, thawed

1 can (12 ounces) frozen orange juice concentrate, thawed

1 cup diet lemon-lime soda

> In a blender, place half of the pineapple, oranges, bananas and strawberries; cover and process until smooth. Pour into a large bowl. Repeat. Stir in the remaining ingredients. Pour or spoon 1/2 cup into each of 24 glasses or plastic cups. Cover and freeze for at least 2 hours.

> Remove from the freezer 15 minutes before serving. May be frozen for up to 1 month.

YIELD: 24 SERVINGS

frosty mocha drink

LAUREN NANCE, SAN DIEGO, CALIFORNIA
I like to make this chilly chocolate-flavored coffee drink when friends stop by for a visit. I always double the recipe, however, because I know they'll come back for seconds. For a richer and creamier version, replace the milk with half-and-half cream.

1 cup milk

3 tablespoons instant chocolate drink mix

2 tablespoons instant coffee granules

2 tablespoons honey

1 teaspoon vanilla extract

14 to 16 ice cubes

> In a blender, combine all ingredients; cover and process until smooth. Pour into chilled glasses; serve immediately.

YIELD: 4 SERVINGS

spiced tea

JANICE CONNELLEY, SPRING CREEK, NEVADA
Simply by simmering together spices, tea and fruit juices, I've created a concoction that gives extra zip to party plans. For an extra touch, I put cinnamon stick stirrers in the cups before serving.

3 quarts water, divided

4 tea bags

18 whole cloves

2 cinnamon sticks (3-1/2 inches)

1 can (12 ounces) frozen orange juice concentrate, thawed

1 can (12 ounces) frozen lemonade concentrate, thawed

1 cup sugar

> In a large kettle or Dutch oven over medium heat, bring 1 qt. of water to a boil. Remove from the heat; add tea bags. Cover and steep for 5 minutes. Remove tea bags.

> Place cloves and cinnamon sticks in a double thickness of cheesecloth; bring up corners of cloth and tie with a string (or, if desired, place loose spices in pan and strain tea before serving).

> Place the cheesecloth bag in pan; add the concentrates, sugar, tea and remaining water; bring to a boil. Boil, uncovered, for 6 minutes. Serve hot.

YIELD: 3-1/2 QUARTS

tip Blenders can be hard to clean...unless you try this quick cleaning method. Fill the blender halfway with hot water, add a drop of dishwashing liquid, cover it and blend on high for 10-15 seconds. Then rinse it with hot water and air-dry.

> In a large bowl, combine lime juice and sugar substitute. Cover and refrigerate. Just before serving, stir carbonated water into lime juice mixture.

> For each serving, place 1 tablespoon cherry juice in a glass. Add crushed ice and about 1 cup of lime juice mixture. Garnish with a maraschino cherry and a lime slice.

YIELD: 8 SERVINGS

Editor's Note: This recipe was tested with Splenda no-calorie sweetener.

dill bloody marys

JAY FERKOVICH, GREEN BAY, WISCONSIN
With a nice level of pepper, and just enough dill from the pickle, these Bloody Marys are sure to be crowd pleasing. To make "Contrary Marys," simply leave out the vodka.

1-1/2 cups Clamato juice, chilled

2 tablespoons dill pickle juice

1 tablespoon Worcestershire sauce

1/4 teaspoon celery salt

1/8 to 1/4 teaspoon pepper

1/8 teaspoon hot pepper sauce

1/4 cup vodka, optional

Ice cubes

2 celery ribs

2 pepperoni-flavored meat snack sticks

2 dill pickle spears

2 pitted ripe olives

> In a small pitcher, combine the first six ingredients. Stir in vodka if desired. Pour into two glasses filled with ice; garnish with celery, snack sticks, pickles and olives.

YIELD: 2 SERVINGS

bottoms-up cherry limeade

AWYNNE THURSTENSON, SILOAM SPRINGS, ARKANSAS
My guests enjoy this refreshing cherry-topped drink. It's just right on a hot southern summer evening. And it's pretty, too.

3/4 cup lime juice

Sugar substitute equivalent to 1 cup sugar

2 liters lime carbonated water, chilled

1/2 cup maraschino cherry juice

Crushed ice

8 maraschino cherries with stems

8 lime slices

KIRSTEN GUNDERSON, OTTAWA, ONTARIO

This smoothie is great any time of the day. I especially like to serve it when my kids are in a finicky mood. It's a fun, nutritious treat.

blended fruit chiller

3 cups (24 ounces) fat-free plain yogurt

1 cup unsweetened pineapple juice, chilled

1 cup fresh or frozen unsweetened strawberries

1 medium ripe banana, sliced

1/2 cup fresh or canned unsweetened pineapple chunks

3 tablespoons honey

1 teaspoon vanilla extract

> Place half of each ingredient in a blender; cover and process until blended. Repeat. Pour into chilled glasses; serve immediately.

YIELD: 6 SERVINGS

iced cranberry-mint tea

TASTE OF HOME TEST KITCHEN
Raise a toast to friends, family and sunshine with this cranberry cooler. Fresh mint and a hint of lemon add refreshing fruity flavor.

4 cups water

2/3 cup loosely packed fresh mint leaves

2 tablespoons sugar

8 lemon herbal tea bags

3-1/2 cups reduced-calorie reduced-sugar cranberry juice

1 tablespoon lemon juice

Ice cubes

Lemon slices, optional

> In a large saucepan, bring the water, mint and sugar to a boil. Remove from the heat; add tea bags. Cover and steep for 15 minutes.

> Discard tea bags. Cover and let stand 45 minutes longer. Strain and discard mint leaves. Stir the cranberry and lemon juices into tea. Serve over ice with lemon slices if desired.

YIELD: 8 SERVINGS (2 QUARTS)

fruit slush

DARLENE WHITE, HOBSON, MONTANA
I like to mix up this sweet slush using juices, berries and soft drink mix. Then I store it in the freezer for unexpected company. Simply pour a little citrus soda over scoops of the colorful mixture for frosty and fantastic beverages.

1 can (46 ounces) pineapple juice

8 cups water

1 can (12 ounces) frozen lemonade concentrate, thawed

1 can (12 ounces) frozen orange juice concentrate, thawed

4 cups sugar

2 cups fresh or frozen unsweetened raspberries

2 envelopes unsweetened cherry soft drink mix or other red flavor of your choice

ADDITIONAL INGREDIENT:
Grapefruit or citrus soda

> In a 6-qt. container, combine the first seven ingredients. Cover and freeze for 12 hours, stirring every 2 hours. May be frozen for up to 3 months.

> **For each serving:** Place 1/2 cup fruit slush in a glass. Add 1/2 cup soda.

YIELD: ABOUT 5 QUARTS

cappuccino punch

ROSE REICH, NAMPA, IDAHO
When I tried this punch at a friend's wedding shower, I had to have the recipe. Guests will eagerly gather around the punch bowl when you ladle out this frothy mocha ice cream drink.

1/2 cup sugar

1/4 cup instant coffee granules

1 cup boiling water

8 cups milk

1 quart vanilla ice cream, softened

1 quart chocolate ice cream, softened

> In a small bowl, combine the sugar and coffee; stir in boiling water until dissolved. Cover and refrigerate until chilled.

> Just before serving, pour coffee mixture into a 1-gal. punch bowl. Stir in milk. Add scoops of ice cream; stir until melted.

YIELD: ABOUT 1 GALLON

herb garden tea

MARY HARRISON, HAMILTON, OHIO
This aromatic tea is the perfect drink for a warm-weather luncheon. The mint gives it great taste.

1/4 cup finely chopped lemon balm

1/4 cup finely chopped fresh mint

1/4 cup lemon juice

1/4 cup orange juice

1/4 cup honey

2 liters ginger ale

> In a small bowl, combine the first five ingredients; let stand for 1 hour. Strain; discard herbs.

> Pour tea into a 2-1/2-qt. pitcher. Stir in ginger ale just before serving. Serve in chilled glasses.

YIELD: 9 SERVINGS

refreshing lemon-lime drink

LISA CASTILLO, BOURBONNAIS, ILLINOIS
Here is a lighter version of the margarita—without the alcohol. Bursting with a tantalizing blend of lemon and lime, this sipper is perfect for get-togethers on hot summer days or on a buffet of Mexican favorites.

1 can (12 ounces) frozen limeade concentrate, thawed

2/3 cup thawed lemonade concentrate

1 teaspoon orange extract

1-1/2 cups water

6 cups chilled diet lemon-lime soda

Ice cubes

1 medium lemon, sliced

1 medium lime, sliced

> In a large container, combine the limeade and lemonade concentrates and orange extract. Stir in water.

> Just before serving, stir in lemon-lime soda. Serve over ice. Garnish with lemon and lime slices.

YIELD: 3 QUARTS (12 SERVINGS, 1 CUP PER SERVING)

POLLY COUMOS, MOGADORE, OHIO

Around our house, we often make these yummy shakes. For a healthier version, we substitute fat-free milk and ice cubes for the ice cream. They are fast and nutritious!

tropical pineapple smoothies

1 cup fat-free milk

1 can (8 ounces) unsweetened crushed pineapple

1/2 cup unsweetened pineapple juice

3 tablespoons sugar

1/2 teaspoon vanilla extract

1/4 teaspoon coconut extract

6 ice cubes

> In a blender, place the first six ingredients; cover and process until smooth. Add ice cubes; cover and process until smooth. Pour into chilled glasses; serve immediately.

YIELD: 3 SERVINGS

eggnog shakes

DALE HARTMAN, COVENTRY, RHODE ISLAND
I like to serve this alternative to the traditional favorite. Although made with fat-free ingredients, the easy-to-fix recipe retains the thick, creamy consistency of the classic beverage.

1-1/2 cups fat-free sugar-free vanilla ice cream

1/2 cup fat-free milk

1 tablespoon fat-free whipped topping

Sugar substitute equivalent to 1/2 teaspoon sugar

1/8 teaspoon rum extract

1/8 teaspoon brandy extract or vanilla extract

Dash ground nutmeg

> In a blender, combine the first six ingredients; cover and process until smooth. Pour into chilled glasses; sprinkle with nutmeg.

YIELD: 1-1/2 CUPS

Editor's Note: This recipe was tested with Splenda sugar blend.

vanilla-almond coffee

TINA CHRISTENSEN, ADDISON, ILLINOIS
This recipe is perfect for any coffee lover. Instead of buying flavored coffees, I make my own using extracts for baking. You can try decaffeinated coffee, too.

1 pound ground coffee

2 tablespoons almond extract

2 tablespoons vanilla extract

> Place coffee in a large jar with tight-fitting lid. Add extracts. Cover and shake well. Store in the refrigerator. Prepare coffee as usual.

YIELD: 1 POUND

pomegranate martini

TASTE OF HOME TEST KITCHEN
Ring in the holidays with this crimson creation that sparkles with festive cheer. It's a smooth delight that's sure to be the talk of your get-togethers.

Ice cubes

2 ounces pomegranate juice

1 ounce vodka

1/2 ounce triple sec

1/2 ounce club soda

1/2 teaspoon lemon juice

GARNISH:
Pomegranate seeds, optional

> Fill a shaker three-fourths full with ice. Add the pomegranate juice, vodka, triple sec, club soda and lemon juice. Cover and shake for 10-15 seconds or until condensation forms on outside of shaker. Strain into a chilled cocktail glass. Garnish as desired.

YIELD: 1 SERVING

passion fruit hurricanes

TASTE OF HOME TEST KITCHEN
Here's a fun take on the famous Hurricane drink that's so popular in New Orleans.

2 cups passion fruit juice

1 cup plus 2 tablespoons sugar

3/4 cup lime juice

3/4 cup light rum

3/4 cup dark rum

3 tablespoons grenadine syrup

6 to 8 cups ice cubes

Orange slices and maraschino cherries

> In a pitcher, combine the fruit juice, sugar, lime juice, rum and grenadine; stir until sugar is dissolved. Pour into hurricane or highball glasses filled with ice. Garnish with orange slices and cherries.

YIELD: 6 SERVINGS

creamy lime coolers

ARLYNE MURPHY, SOMERS, NEW YORK
My rich, frothy quencher is refreshing any time of year, but its fresh, tropical taste really beats the heat on hot sunny days.

1 cup unsweetened pineapple juice, chilled

1 tablespoon lime juice

2 tablespoons confectioners' sugar

1/4 teaspoon grated lime peel

1 cup vanilla ice cream, softened

> In a blender, combine the pineapple juice, lime juice, confectioners' sugar, and lime peel; cover and process until blended. Add ice cream; cover and process until smooth. Pour into chilled glasses.

YIELD: 2 SERVINGS

orange tea

SALLY MUELLER, LOVELAND, COLORADO
My children always liked a hot cup of this after walking home from school. The tea is tasty, and it warms you up.

7 cup water

1 can (12 ounces) frozen orange juice concentrate

1/2 cup sugar

2 tablespoons lemon juice

5 teaspoons instant tea

1 teaspoon whole cloves

> In a large saucepan, combine water, orange juice concentrate, sugar, lemon juice and tea. Tie the cloves in a small cheesecloth bag; add to saucepan. Simmer, uncovered, for 15-20 minutes. Remove spice bag. Serve hot. Store leftovers in glass container in refrigerator.

YIELD: 8 SERVINGS (2 QUARTS)

lemon quencher

CLARA COULSTON, WASHINGTON COURT HOUSE, OHIO
Tart and light, this citrus beverage is sweetened with just a touch of honey. It makes a lovely summer cooler any time of day.

5 cups water, divided

10 fresh mint leaves

1 cup lemon juice

2/3 cup honey

2 teaspoons grated lemon peel

Ice cubes

Mint sprigs and lemon peel strips, optional

> In a blender, combine 1 cup water and mint leaves; cover and process for 1 minute. Strain mixture into a pitcher, discarding mint. Add the lemon juice, honey, lemon peel and remaining water; stir until blended. Cover and refrigerate for at least 2 hours.

> Serve in chilled glasses over ice. Garnish with mint sprigs and lemon peel if desired.

YIELD: 8 SERVINGS

sparkling peach bellinis

TASTE OF HOME TEST KITCHEN
We developed this elegant brunch sipper so folks can savor a subtle peach flavor at warm-weather events.

3 medium peaches, halved

1 tablespoon honey

1 can (11.3 ounces) peach nectar, chilled

2 bottles (750 milliliters each) Champagne or sparkling grape juice, chilled

> Line a baking sheet with a large piece of heavy-duty foil (about 18 in. x 12 in.). Place peach halves, cut sides up, on foil; drizzle with honey. Fold foil over peaches and seal.

> Bake at 375° for 25-30 minutes or until tender. Cool completely; remove and discard peels. In a food processor, process peaches until smooth.

> Transfer peach puree to a pitcher. Add the nectar and 1 bottle of Champagne or juice; stir until combined. Pour into 12 champagne flutes or wine glasses; top with remaining Champagne or juice. Serve immediately.

YIELD: 12 SERVINGS

valentine cookie bouquet

MARLENE GATES, SUN CITY, ARIZONA
This cookie bouquet was a blue-ribbon winner at a local fair. It makes a great Valentine centerpiece at a party and is a tasty gift for a loved one.

1 cup butter, softened

1 cup sugar

1/4 cup milk

1 egg

1 teaspoon vanilla extract

2-3/4 cups all-purpose flour

1/2 cup baking cocoa

3/4 teaspoon baking powder

1/4 teaspoon baking soda

24 long wooden skewers

FROSTING:
1/2 cup butter, softened

2 cups confectioners' sugar

2 to 3 tablespoons maraschino cherry juice

> In a large bowl, cream butter and sugar until light and fluffy. Beat in the milk, egg and vanilla. Combine the flour, cocoa, baking powder and baking soda; add to creamed mixture and mix well. Cover and refrigerate for 1 hour or until easy to handle.

> On a lightly floured surface, roll out half of the dough to 1/8-in. thickness. Cut out with a floured 3-in. heart-shaped cookie cutter. Place 1 in. apart on ungreased baking sheets.

> Place skewers on top of each cookie with one end of each skewer about 1 in. from top of each heart. Gently press into the dough. Place a little extra dough over each skewer; press into the cookie to secure.

> Bake at 350° for 8-10 minutes or until firm. Let stand for 2 minutes before removing to wire racks to cool.

> Roll out remaining dough on a lightly floured surface. Cut out with a floured 3-in. heart-shaped cookie cutter. Cut out centers with a 1-in. heart-shaped cookie cutter.

> Bake at 350° for 8-10 minutes or until firm. Let stand for 2 minutes before removing to wire racks to cool.

> In a small bowl, combine butter, confectioners' sugar and enough cherry juice to achieve spreading consistency. Gently spread frosting over cookies with skewers; top with cookies with cutout centers.

YIELD: 2 DOZEN

tip You can use the recipe for Valentine Cookie Bouquet throughout the year. Try cutting out flower shapes in spring, shamrocks for St. Patty's Day, Christmas trees for the holidays or eggs for Easter. Then adjust the frosting using food coloring instead of cherry juice to match the season.

TASTE OF HOME TEST KITCHEN
Refrigerated dough makes short work of this cute and crusty, heart-shaped surprise. Topped with pepperoni, three kinds of cheese, olives, onions and sauce, this yummy appetizer will steal the show at any Valentine's Day party.

be-my-valentine pizza

1 tube (13.8 ounces) refrigerated pizza crust

1/4 cup shredded Italian cheese blend

1/4 cup shredded part-skim mozzarella cheese

2 slices provolone cheese, cut in half

1/4 cup pizza sauce

18 slices pepperoni

1/4 cup chopped onion

1/4 cup sliced ripe olives

> Unroll pizza dough onto a greased baking sheet; flatten dough. With kitchen scissors, cut into a 10-in. heart. (Use dough trimmings to make breadsticks if desired.) Bake at 425° for 8 minutes.

> Combine the Italian and mozzarella cheeses; set aside. Arrange provolone cheese over crust to within 1/2 in. of edges.

> Spread with the pizza sauce. Layer with the pepperoni, onion, olives and cheese mixture. Bake 8-10 minutes longer or until crust is golden brown and cheese is melted.

YIELD: 2 SERVINGS

st. patrick's day popcorn

KAREN WEBER, SALEM, MISSOURI
Everyone's eyes will be smilin' when they see this candy corn with an Irish twist.

4 quarts popped popcorn

1 cup sugar

1/2 cup packed brown sugar

1/2 cup water

1/2 cup light corn syrup

1 teaspoon white vinegar

1/4 teaspoon salt

1/2 cup butter

8 to 10 drops green food coloring

> Place popcorn in a large roasting pan; keep warm in a 250° oven. Meanwhile, in a large heavy saucepan, combine the sugars, water, corn syrup, vinegar and salt. Cook and stir over medium heat until mixture comes to a boil. Cook, stirring occasionally, until a candy thermometer reads 250° (hard-ball stage).

> Remove from the heat; stir in butter until melted. Stir in food coloring. Drizzle over warm popcorn and toss to coat. Cool. Break into pieces. Store in an airtight container.

YIELD: 6 QUARTS

Editor's Note: We recommend that you test your candy thermometer before each use by bringing water to a boil; the thermometer should read 212°. Adjust your recipe temperature up or down based on your test.

irish hot chocolate

TASTE OF HOME TEST KITCHEN
More than a hint of cool mint makes this sipper a special switch from traditional hot chocolate. A dollop of whipped cream with sprinkles of crushed candy lusciously tops each mug.

3-1/2 cups 2% milk

8 ounces white baking chocolate, chopped

1/4 to 1/2 teaspoon peppermint extract

2/3 cup heavy whipping cream

8 spearmint or peppermint candies, crushed

Additional crushed peppermint candies, optional

> In a large saucepan, heat milk over medium heat until steaming. Add chocolate; whisk until smooth. Stir in peppermint extract.

> In a large bowl, beat cream until stiff peaks form. Fold in the crushed candies. Ladle hot chocolate into mugs; dollop with whipped cream. Sprinkle with additional candies if desired.

YIELD: 6 SERVINGS

> Cut second loaf into four equal portions. For ears, shape two portions into 16-in. ropes; fold ropes in half. Arrange ears with open ends touching head. Cut a third portion of dough in half; shape each into a 3-1/2-in. oval for back paws. Cut two 1-in. slits on top edge for toes. Position on each side of the body.

> Divide the fourth portion of dough into three pieces. Shape two pieces into 2-1/2-in. balls for front paws; shape the remaining piece into two 1-in. balls for cheeks and one 1/2-in. ball for nose. Place paws on each side of body; cut two 1-in. slits for toes. Place cheeks and nose on face. Add raisins for eyes and almonds for teeth.

> Brush dough with egg. Cover and let rise in a warm place until doubled, about 30-45 minutes. Bake at 350° for 25-30 minutes or until golden brown. Remove to a wire rack to cool.

> Place bread on a lettuce-lined 16-in. x 13-in. serving tray. Cut a 5-in. x 4-in. oval in center of body. Hollow out bread, leaving a 1/2-in. shell (discard removed bread or save for another use). Line with lettuce and fill with dip.

YIELD: 1 LOAF

easter bunny bread

TASTE OF HOME TEST KITCHEN
With its toothy grin, lovely golden crust and tummy that's perfect for serving dip, this charming rabbit is sure to bring a smile to guests young and old.

2 loaves (1 pound each) frozen bread dough, thawed

2 raisins

2 sliced almonds

1 egg, lightly beaten

Lettuce leaves

Dip of your choice

> Cut a fourth off of one loaf of dough; shape into a pear to form head. For body, flatten remaining portion into a 7-in. x 6-in. oval; place on a greased baking sheet. Place head above body. Make narrow cuts, about 3/4 in. deep, on each side of head for whiskers.

chutney stuffed eggs

MRS. PATRICK DARE, FERGUS, ONTARIO
My aunt shared this recipe with me many years ago. The chutney is a simple and tasty addition to the time-honored appetizers.

12 hard-cooked eggs

6 bacon strips, cooked and finely crumbled

1/4 cup chutney, chopped

3 tablespoons mayonnaise

> Cut eggs in half lengthwise; remove yolks and set whites aside. In a large bowl, mash yolks. Add the bacon, chutney and mayonnaise; mix well.

> Pipe or spoon into the egg whites. Refrigerate until serving.

YIELD: 12 SERVINGS

bunny pineapple smoothies

TASTE OF HOME TEST KITCHEN
*After trying these bunny-topped smoothies, you'll want
to hop back to the buffet for extra servings. Flavored
with orange juice, pineapple sherbet and pina colada
yogurt, they add a tropical taste to Easter gatherings.*

2 cups orange juice

2 pints pineapple sherbet

4 cups (32 ounces) pina colada yogurt

4 medium bananas, quartered

1 cup milk

1 teaspoon vanilla extract

2 cups whipped topping, divided

1 drop red food coloring

> In a blender, combine half of the orange juice,
  sherbet, yogurt, bananas, milk and vanilla; cover
  and process until smooth. Pour into chilled
  glasses. Repeat.

> Place 1-1/2 cups whipped topping in a pastry or
  plastic bag; cut a medium hole in a corner of the
  bag. Pipe a bunny face on each smoothie.

> Tint remaining whipped topping with food
  coloring; place in another bag. Cut a small hole in
  a corner of the bag. Pipe eyes, nose and inside of
  ears on each bunny face. Beginning from the
  nose, gently pull a toothpick through the whipped
  topping toward the edge of the glass to form
  whiskers. Serve immediately.

YIELD: 10 SERVINGS

easter bunny treats

HOLLY JOST, MANITOWOC, WISCONSIN
*These cute treats are easy for our kids to assemble, and
the whole family has fun making them.*

2/3 cup vanilla frosting

30 large marshmallows

Pink gel or paste food coloring

Red and pink heart-shaped decorating sprinkles

60 miniature marshmallows

> Frost the tops of 12 large marshmallows; stack a
  large marshmallow on top of each. Quarter the
  remaining large marshmallows; set aside for ears.
  Tint 1/4 cup frosting pink. Cut a small hole in the
  corner of a pastry or plastic bag; place pink
  frosting in bag.

> Pipe a ribbon between the stacked marshmallows
  for bow tie. With white frosting, attach red hearts
  for eyes and a pink heart for nose. Pipe pink
  whiskers and smile.

> For ears, pipe the center of quartered
  marshmallows pink; attach to head with white
  frosting. With the remaining white frosting,
  attach the miniature marshmallows for legs and
  tail. Let stand until dry.

YIELD: 1 DOZEN

CONSTANCE FENNELL, GRAND JUNCTION, MICHIGAN
Loaded with fresh strawberries and blueberries, this luscious treat is perfect for any Fourth of July or hot-weather get-togethers.

red-white-and-blue berry delight

1/2 cup sugar

2 envelopes unflavored gelatin

4 cups white cranberry-peach juice drink, divided

1 tablespoon lemon juice

2 cups fresh strawberries, halved

2 cups fresh blueberries

CREAM:
1/2 cup heavy whipping cream

1 tablespoon sugar

1/4 teaspoon vanilla extract

> In a large saucepan, combine sugar and gelatin. Add 1 cup cranberry-peach juice; cook and stir over low heat until gelatin is completely dissolved, about 5 minutes. Remove from the heat; stir in lemon juice and remaining cranberry-peach juice.

> Place strawberries in an 8-cup ring mold coated with cooking spray; add 2 cups gelatin mixture. Refrigerate until set but not firm, about 30 minutes. Set aside remaining gelatin mixture.

> Stir blueberries into remaining gelatin mixture; spoon over strawberry layer. Refrigerate overnight. Unmold onto a serving platter.

> In a small bowl, beat cream until it begins to thicken. Add sugar and vanilla; beat until stiff peaks form. Serve with gelatin.

YIELD: 8 SERVINGS

> In a blender, combine the olives, oil, lemon juice, garlic and herbs; cover and process until olives are chopped. Set aside 1/3 cup olive mixture (refrigerate remaining mixture for another use).

> Cut the top third off each baguette; carefully hollow out bottoms, leaving a 1/4-in. shell (discard removed bread or save for another use).

> Spread olive mixture in the bottom of each loaf. Sprinkle with feta cheese. Fold salami slices in half and place over cheese. Top with the spinach, red peppers and artichokes, pressing down as necessary. Replace bread tops. Wrap loaves tightly in foil. Refrigerate for at least 3 hours or overnight.

> Serve cold, or place foil-wrapped loaves on a baking sheet and bake at 350° for 20-25 minutes or until heated through. Cut into slices; secure with a toothpick.

YIELD: 3 DOZEN

antipasto-stuffed baguettes

DIANNE HOLMGREN, PRESCOTT, ARIZONA
These Italian-style sandwiches can be served as an appetizer or even as a light lunch. A homemade olive paste makes every bite delicious.

1 can (2-1/4 ounces) sliced ripe olives, drained

2 tablespoons olive oil

1 teaspoon lemon juice

1 garlic clove, minced

1/8 teaspoon each dried basil, thyme, marjoram and rosemary, crushed

2 French bread baguettes (8 ounces each)

1 package (4 ounces) crumbled feta cheese

1/4 pound thinly sliced Genoa salami

1 cup fresh baby spinach

1 jar (7-1/4 ounces) roasted red peppers, drained and chopped

1 can (14 ounces) water-packed artichoke hearts, rinsed, drained and quartered

watermelon salsa

BETSY HANSON, TIVERTON, RHODE ISLAND
On hot summer days, this sweet salsa with watermelon, pineapple and fresh cilantro is sure to satisfy.

2 cups chopped seedless watermelon

1 can (8 ounces) unsweetened crushed pineapple, drained

1/4 cup chopped sweet onion

1/4 cup minced fresh cilantro

3 tablespoons orange juice

1/8 teaspoon hot pepper sauce

Tortilla chips

> In a large bowl, combine the first six ingredients. Cover and refrigerate for at least 1 hour. Serve with tortilla chips.

YIELD: 3 CUPS

JULIE MOYER, UNION GROVE, WISCONSIN

A rich chocolate frosting makes these brownies really tasty. I always come home with an empty pan when I take these to potlucks.

fudgy patriotic brownies

1 cup butter, cubed

4 ounces unsweetened chocolate, chopped

2 cups sugar

1 teaspoon vanilla extract

4 eggs

1-1/4 cups all-purpose flour

1/2 teaspoon salt

1 cup chopped pecans

FROSTING:

1/4 cup butter, cubed

2 ounces unsweetened chocolate, chopped

3 cups confectioners' sugar

5 to 6 tablespoons milk

1 teaspoon vanilla extract

Red, white and blue decorating icing

> In a microwave-safe bowl, melt butter and chocolate; stir until smooth. Stir in sugar and vanilla. Add eggs, one at a time, stirring well after each addition. Combine flour and salt; stir into chocolate mixture until combined. Stir in pecans.

> Spread into a greased 13-in. x 9-in. baking dish. Bake at 325° for 35-40 minutes or until a toothpick inserted near the center comes out clean. Cool on a wire rack.

> For frosting, in a small heavy saucepan, melt butter and chocolate over low heat; stir until smooth. Remove from the heat. Stir in the confectioners' sugar, milk and vanilla until blended.

> Frost brownies; score into 24 bars. Using a small star-shaped cookie cutter, lightly press a star outline in the center of each brownie. Outline stars with red, white and blue icing.

YIELD: 2 DOZEN

> In a small bowl, combine the water, food coloring and remaining confectioners' sugar. Transfer to a heavy-duty resealable plastic bag; cut a small hole in a corner of bag. Pipe wavy lines downward from pupil, creating the look of bloodshot eyes. Store in an airtight container.

YIELD: 2 DOZEN

boo beverage

TASTE OF HOME TEST KITCHEN
Silly spooks formed with whipped topping garnish glasses of this smooth drink made with sherbet, orange juice and bananas.

2 cups orange juice

2 cups milk

2 pints orange sherbet

4 medium ripe bananas

2 cups whipped topping

18 miniature chocolate chips

> In four batches, process the orange juice, milk, sherbet and bananas in a blender until smooth. Pour into glasses. Cut a hole in the corner of a pastry or plastic bag; fill with whipped topping. Pipe a ghost shape on top of each beverage. Position chocolate chips for eyes.

YIELD: 9 SERVINGS

bloodshot eyeballs

TASTE OF HOME TEST KITCHEN
Little ghouls will find these peanut butter "eyeballs" a scary sensation to nibble!

2 cups confectioners' sugar, divided

1/2 cup creamy peanut butter

3 tablespoons butter, softened

1/2 pound white candy coating, coarsely chopped

24 brown Reese's pieces or milk chocolate M&M's

1 tablespoon water

1/4 to 1/2 teaspoon red food coloring

> In a small bowl, combine 1 cup confectioners' sugar, peanut butter and butter. Shape into 1-in. balls; place on a waxed paper-lined pan. Chill for 30 minutes or until firm.

> In a microwave, melt white candy coating; stir until smooth. Dip balls in coating; allow excess to drip off. Place on waxed paper. Immediately press a Reese's candy onto the top of each eyeball for pupil. Let stand for 30 minutes or until set.

> Place a few pieces of chicken in bag; seal and shake to coat. Dip in eggs, then in crumb mixture. Place on a greased baking sheet. Repeat. Bake at 350° for 15-20 minutes or until juices run clear.

> Cut a small slit into one end of each chicken strip; insert a pepper triangle into each. Serve with barbecue sauce.

YIELD: 15 APPETIZERS

witch's caviar

DARLENE BRENDEN, SALEM, OREGON
I like to serve this dip with triangle-shaped tortillas because they look like pointy witch hats.

2 cans (4-1/4 ounces each) chopped ripe olives, undrained

2 cans (4 ounces each) chopped green chilies, undrained

2 medium tomatoes, seeded and chopped

3 green onions, chopped

2 garlic cloves, minced

1 tablespoon red wine vinegar

1 tablespoon olive oil

1/2 teaspoon pepper

Dash seasoned salt

Tortilla chips

> In a large bowl, combine the first nine ingredients. Cover and refrigerate overnight. Serve with tortilla chips.

YIELD: 4 CUPS

crunchy monster claws

MARY ANN DELL, PHOENIXVILLE, PENNSYLVANIA
Cajun seasoning adds flavor, and a crunchy coating helps keep these chicken fingers moist. They're perfect for any Halloween party.

1 small sweet yellow pepper

2 tablespoons all-purpose flour

2 teaspoons plus 1 tablespoon Cajun seasoning, divided

3 eggs, lightly beaten

1-1/2 cups cornflake crumbs

2 tablespoons chopped green onion

1 pound boneless skinless chicken breasts, cut lengthwise into 3/4-inch strips

Barbecue sauce

> Cut yellow pepper into 15 triangles; set aside. In a large resealable plastic bag, combine flour and 2 teaspoons Cajun seasoning. Place eggs in a shallow bowl. In another shallow bowl, combine the cornflake crumbs, green onion and remaining Cajun seasoning.

HEATHER SNOW, SALT LAKE CITY, UTAH
I came up with this idea for dressing up a veggie tray for our annual Halloween party, and everyone got really "wrapped up" in it.

yummy mummy with veggie dip

1 loaf (1 pound) frozen bread dough, thawed

3 pieces string cheese

2 cups (16 ounces) sour cream

1 envelope fiesta ranch dip mix

1 pitted ripe olive

Assorted crackers and fresh vegetables

> Let dough rise according to package directions. Place dough on a greased baking sheet. For mummy, roll out dough into a 12-in. oval that is narrower at the bottom. For the head, make an indentation about 1 in. from the top. Let rise in a warm place for 20 minutes.

> Bake at 350° for 20-25 minutes or until golden brown. Arrange strips of string cheese over bread; bake 1-2 minutes longer or until cheese is melted. Remove from pan to a wire rack to cool.

> Meanwhile, in a small bowl, combine sour cream and dip mix. Chill until serving.

> Cut mummy in half horizontally. Hollow out bottom half, leaving a 3/4-in. shell. Cut removed bread into cubes; set aside. Place bread bottom on a serving plate. Spoon dip into shell. Replace top. For eyes, cut olive and position on head. Serve with crackers, vegetables and reserved bread.

YIELD: 16 SERVINGS (2 CUPS DIP)

turkey cheese ball

TASTE OF HOME TEST KITCHEN
While the real bird is roasting, you can present your guests with this tasty Thanksgiving turkey.

2 packages (8 ounces each) reduced-fat cream cheese

6 ounces deli smoked turkey, finely chopped

1 cup (4 ounces) shredded cheddar cheese

1 tablespoon finely chopped onion

1 tablespoon Worcestershire sauce

1/2 teaspoon garlic powder

DECORATIONS:
3 packages (3 ounces each) cream cheese, softened

2 tablespoons milk

Brown, orange and yellow paste food coloring

6 large oval crackers

1 large sweet red pepper

1 small yellow summer squash

1 cup pecan halves

Assorted crackers

> In a small bowl, beat the first six ingredients until combined. Shape into a ball; wrap in plastic wrap. Refrigerate for 1 hour or until firm.

> In another small bowl, beat cream cheese and milk until smooth. Divide among four small bowls. With food coloring, tint one bowl brown, one dark orange and one light orange (using yellow and orange); leave one bowl plain.

> Transfer each mixture to a heavy-duty resealable plastic bag; cut a small hole in a corner of each bag.

> For turkey tail feathers, decorate the top halves of large oval crackers with tinted cream cheese.

> Using the red pepper, form the turkey head, neck and wattle. For beak, cut a small triangle from summer squash; attach with cream cheese. Add eyes, using brown and plain cream cheese. Insert pecan halves and decorated crackers into cheese ball. Serve with assorted crackers

YIELD: 1 CHEESE BALL (3 CUPS)

Editor's Note: This recipe was tested with Townhouse Oval Bistro crackers.

hot 'n' spicy cranberry dip

MARIAN PLATT, SEQUIM, WASHINGTON
When I make this appetizer for large holiday events, I double the recipe and use one 16-ounce can of cranberry sauce.

3/4 cup jellied cranberry sauce

1 to 2 tablespoons prepared horseradish

1 tablespoon honey

1-1/2 teaspoons lemon juice

1-1/2 teaspoons Worcestershire sauce

1/8 to 1/4 teaspoon cayenne pepper

1 garlic clove, minced

Miniature hot dogs or smoked sausage links, warmed

Sliced apples or pears

> In a small saucepan, combine the first seven ingredients; bring to a boil, stirring constantly. Reduce heat. Cover and simmer for 5 minutes, stirring occasionally. Serve warm with sausages and/or fruit.

YIELD: 3/4 CUP

zippy cranberry appetizer

MARIE HATTRUP, THE DALLES, OREGON
Tart cranberry flavor blends nicely with mustard and horseradish in this out-of-the-ordinary spread.

1/2 cup sugar

1/2 cup packed brown sugar

1 cup water

1 package (12 ounces) fresh or frozen cranberries

1 to 3 tablespoons prepared horseradish

1 tablespoon Dijon mustard

1 package (8 ounces) cream cheese, softened

Assorted crackers

> In a large saucepan, bring sugars and water to a boil over medium heat. Stir in cranberries; return to a boil. Cook for 10 minutes or until thickened, stirring occasionally. Cool.

> Stir in horseradish and mustard. Transfer to a large bowl; refrigerate until chilled. Just before serving, spread cream cheese over crackers; top with cranberry mixture.

YIELD: 2-1/2 CUPS

squash appetizer cups

LORI BOWES, WATERFORD, MICHIGAN
These cheesy, moist bites always go fast! If I'm in a hurry, I bake the mixture in a greased 9-inch x 13-inch pan and cut into squares.

1-1/2 cups shredded zucchini

1-1/2 cups shredded yellow summer squash

1/2 cup diced onion

1/4 cup shredded Parmesan cheese

1/4 cup shredded Colby cheese

2 tablespoons minced fresh parsley

1-1/2 teaspoons minced fresh marjoram or 1/2 teaspoon dried marjoram

1 garlic clove, minced

1 cup biscuit/baking mix

1/2 teaspoon seasoned salt

Dash pepper

4 eggs, lightly beaten

1/2 cup canola oil

> In a large skillet, saute the zucchini and yellow squash over medium heat until reduced to about 1-1/2 cups, about 10 minutes. Transfer to a small bowl. Add the onion, cheeses, parsley, marjoram and garlic.

> In a large bowl, combine the biscuit mix, seasoned salt and pepper. Stir in eggs and oil just until combined. Fold in squash mixture.

> Fill greased miniature muffin cups three-fourths full. Bake at 350° for 20-25 minutes or until golden brown and a toothpick inserted near the center comes out clean. Cool for 5 minutes before removing from pans to wire racks. Serve warm. Refrigerate leftovers.

YIELD: ABOUT 3 DOZEN

LYNN THOMAS, LAKEWOOD, NEW YORK

All my brothers and sisters like to bring appetizers to our holiday gatherings. This delectable dip came from my brother and is always a favorite.

creamy guacamole spread

2 large ripe avocados, peeled and cubed

1/2 cup mayonnaise

1/4 cup chopped onion

2 teaspoons lemon juice

2 teaspoons Worcestershire sauce

1 teaspoon salt

1 teaspoon hot pepper sauce

Assorted crackers or fresh vegetables

> In a blender, combine the first seven ingredients. Cover and process until blended. Serve with crackers or vegetables.

YIELD: 2 CUPS

 tip
Instantly impress your guests by topping tortilla chips with strategically placed red-pepper strips and zucchini rounds. Top the presentaion with a red-pepper "star" for a little Yuletide flair.

christmas cheese balls

MARGIE CADWELL, EASTMAN, GEORGIA
Christmas at our house just wouldn't be complete without these rich cheese balls. Friends and family ask for them every year.

4 packages (8 ounces each) cream cheese, softened

4 cups (1 pound) shredded cheddar cheese

1 cup chopped pecans

1/4 cup evaporated milk

1 can (4-1/4 ounces) chopped ripe olives, drained

2 garlic cloves, minced

1/2 teaspoon salt

Minced fresh parsley, chopped pecans and paprika

Assorted crackers

> In a small bowl, beat cream cheese and cheddar cheese. Stir in the pecans, milk, olives, garlic and salt. Divide into thirds; roll each into a ball.

> Roll one ball in parsley and one in nuts. Sprinkle one with paprika. Cover and refrigerate. Remove from the refrigerator 15 minutes before serving. Serve with crackers.

YIELD: 3 CHEESE BALLS

santa's snack mix

LORI DANIELS, BEVERLY, WEST VIRGINIA
At Christmas, I love to make homemade gifts such as this crunchy treat.

2 cups Honey-Nut Cheerios

2 cups chow mein noodles

1 cup honey-roasted peanuts

1/2 cup raisins

1/2 cup holiday milk chocolate M&M's

1/2 cup peanut butter chips

1/2 cup vanilla or white chips

> In two wide-mouth quart jars, layer all of the ingredients. Cover jars. Decorate with fabric and ribbon. To serve, pour into a bowl and stir to combine.

YIELD: 7 CUPS

In a small bowl, beat the cream cheese, sour cream, dill and garlic powder until smooth. Spread over wreath; top with broccoli, celery and red pepper. Form a bow garnish with celery leaves.

YIELD: 16 SERVINGS

herbed cheesecake

JULIE TOMLIN, WATKINSVILLE, GEORGIA
Cheesecake isn't just for dessert! This savory version is a favorite that keeps dozens of people happily munching.

3 packages (8 ounces each) cream cheese, softened

2 cups (16 ounces) sour cream, divided

1 can (10-3/4 ounces) condensed cream of celery soup, undiluted

3 eggs

1/2 cup grated Romano cheese

3 garlic cloves, minced

1 tablespoon cornstarch

2 tablespoons minced fresh basil or 2 teaspoons dried basil

1 tablespoon minced fresh thyme or 1 teaspoon dried thyme

1/2 teaspoon Italian seasoning

1/2 teaspoon coarsely ground pepper

Assorted crackers

> In a large bowl, beat the cream cheese, 1 cup sour cream and soup until smooth. Add the eggs, Romano cheese, garlic, cornstarch, basil, thyme, Italian seasoning and pepper; beat until blended.

> Pour into a greased 9-in. springform pan. Place pan on a baking sheet. Bake at 350° for 55-60 minutes or until center is almost set. Cool on a wire rack for 10 minutes. Carefully run a knife around edge of pan to loosen; cool 1 hour longer.

> Refrigerate for at least 4 hours or overnight. Remove sides of pan. Spread remaining sour cream over top. Serve with crackers. Refrigerate leftovers.

YIELD: 24 SERVINGS

appetizer wreath

SHIRLEY PRIVRATSKY, DICKINSON, NORTH DAKOTA
I have lots of fun with this festive wreath. I often place a bowl of stuffed olives in the center.

2 tubes (8 ounces each) refrigerated crescent rolls

1 package (8 ounces) cream cheese, softened

1/2 cup sour cream

1 teaspoon dill weed

1/8 teaspoon garlic powder

1-1/2 cups chopped fresh broccoli florets

1 cup finely chopped celery

1/2 cup finely chopped sweet red pepper

Celery leaves

> Remove the crescent dough from packaging (do not unroll). Cut each tube into eight slices. Arrange in an 11-in. circle on an ungreased 14-in. pizza pan.

> Bake at 375° for 15-20 minutes or until golden brown. Cool for 5 minutes before carefully removing to a serving platter; cool completely.

santa claus cookies

MARY KAUFENBERG, SHAKOPEE, MINNESOTA
I use just six ingredients to create these cute Kris Kringle confections. Store-bought peanut butter sandwich cookies turn jolly with white chocolate, colored sugar, mini chips and red-hots.

12 ounces white baking chocolate, chopped

1 package (1 pound) Nutter Butter sandwich cookies

Red colored sugar

32 vanilla or white chips

64 miniature semisweet chocolate chips

32 red-hot candies

> In a microwave, melt white chocolate at 70% power for 1 minute; stir. Microwave at additional 10- to 20-second intervals, stirring until smooth.

> Dip one end of each cookie into melted chocolate, allowing excess to drip off. Place on wire racks. For Santa's hat, sprinkle red sugar on top part of chocolate. Press one vanilla chip off-center on hat for pom-pom; let stand until set.

> Dip other end of each cookie into melted chocolate for beard, leaving center of cookie uncovered. Place on wire racks. With a dab of melted chocolate, attach semisweet chips for eyes and a red-hot for nose. Place on waxed paper until set.

YIELD: 32 COOKIES

holiday wassail

LUCY MEYRING, WALDEN, COLORADO
This richly colored beverage tastes like Christmastime. Best of all, it comes together without much effort.

4 cups hot brewed tea

1 cup sugar

1 bottle (32 ounces) cranberry juice

1 bottle (32 ounces) apple juice

2 cups orange juice

3/4 cup lemon juice

2 cinnamon sticks (3 inches each)

24 whole cloves, divided

1 orange, sliced

> In a large kettle, combine tea and sugar. Add the juices, cinnamon sticks and 12 of the cloves. Bring to a boil and boil for 2 minutes. Remove from the heat. Serve warm or cool. Garnish punch bowl with orange slices studded with remaining cloves.

YIELD: 12-16 SERVINGS

general index

This handy index lists every recipe by food category and/or major ingredient, so you can easily locate recipes to suit your needs.